Occupiers, Humanitarian Workers, and Polish Displaced Persons in British-Occupied Germany

Occupiers, Humanitarian Workers, and Polish Displaced Persons in British-Occupied Germany

Samantha K. Knapton

BLOOMSBURY ACADEMIC
LONDON • NEW YORK • OXFORD • NEW DELHI • SYDNEY

BLOOMSBURY ACADEMIC
Bloomsbury Publishing Plc
50 Bedford Square, London, WC1B 3DP, UK
1385 Broadway, New York, NY 10018, USA
29 Earlsfort Terrace, Dublin 2, Ireland

BLOOMSBURY, BLOOMSBURY ACADEMIC and the Diana logo are trademarks of
Bloomsbury Publishing Plc

First published in Great Britain 2023
Paperback edition first published 2024

Copyright © Samantha K. Knapton, 2023

Samantha K. Knapton has asserted their right under the Copyright, Designs and
Patents Act, 1988, to be identified as Author of this work.

Cover image: [Germany]: UNRRA/553: One of the many jobs being undertaken by UNRRA
workers who are assisting military authorities in the care and repatriation of displaced
persons of allied nationality in Germany. (© The United Nations)

All rights reserved. No part of this publication may be reproduced or transmitted
in any form or by any means, electronic or mechanical, including photocopying,
recording, or any information storage or retrieval system, without prior
permission in writing from the publishers.

Bloomsbury Publishing Plc does not have any control over, or responsibility for, any
third-party websites referred to or in this book. All internet addresses given in this
book were correct at the time of going to press. The author and publisher regret any
inconvenience caused if addresses have changed or sites have ceased to
exist, but can accept no responsibility for any such changes.

A catalogue record for this book is available from the British Library.

A catalog record for this book is available from the Library of Congress.

ISBN: HB: 978-1-3501-8925-6
PB: 978-1-5266-2928-9
ePDF: 978-1-3501-8926-3
eBook: 978-1-3501-8927-0

Typeset by Deanta Global Publishing Services, Chennai, India

To find out more about our authors and books visit www.bloomsbury.com and
sign up for our newsletters.

For Richard Deswarte:
Mentor, Colleague and Friend

For Artemis

Contents

List of illustrations	x
Acknowledgements	xi
List of abbreviations	xiii
A Note on Translation and Transliteration	xiv

	Introduction	1
	Historical background	2
	Scope and purpose	4
	'In the middle'	7
	Sources	8
1	They say 'the British had the Ruins': Physical destruction, emotional stagnation, and the 'human debris'	11
	The consequences of Potsdam	13
	The DPs: Who, how, and why?	16
	The physical destruction: The British zone in Germany	20
	'Better off' under democracy? Germans' reactions to British occupation	24
	A brief departure from the norm: Establishing international humanitarianism	30
2	'A paradoxical people': Understanding Polish displaced persons	33
	Polishness between the partitions and *Niepodległość*	36
	The 'Quarrels of the Pygmies' and the declaration of war	42
	Occupied Poland: The fourth partition	44
	And you call *this* freedom? The fifth partition	50
3	'Little Poland' in Germany: Life in Polish displaced persons camps	59
	Maczków: 'Little Poland' on the Ems	60
	The physical construction of the imagined community	63
	'Betrayed Ally' or 'Troublesome Nuisance'?: Post-1945 Anglo-Polish relationships in the camps	66
	'Mechanically Pigeonholed': Humanitarian workers and Polish displaced persons	69

4 'Carers' and 'protectors': Encounters between the British military, humanitarian workers, and displaced persons	75
The impetus behind and creation of UNRRA	77
UNRRA was a 'necessary evil': UNRRA, SHAEF and managing the camps	80
The relationship between UNRRA and the military	83
The military government, Lieutenant General Sir Frederick Morgan and attitudes towards Polish displaced persons	87
Forming a bond: UNRRA welfare workers and Polish displaced persons	92
5 'No special obligation . . . We did not take them to Germany': Repatriation and resettlement of Polish displaced persons	99
Repatriation became synonymous with Rehabilitation – but for whom?	101
The duality of being 'screened' by UNRRA and the Polish community	105
The last push: *Operation Carrot* and the beginning of the end for UNRRA	111
Repatriation to resettlement: European Volunteer Worker schemes from *Operation Westward Ho!* to *Operation Black Diamond*	116
6 Idleness bred apathy: Displaced persons left in the camps	125
A new 'Black Book': The London Memorandum	127
A state of limbo in the camps	132
Expanding the possibilities: The IRO and resettlement propaganda	140
A ban on the brain: Elites, intellectuals, and the establishment of schools in Germany	143
Overcoming 'apathy': The development of post-war humanitarianism	148
7 From displaced persons to homeless foreigners: The 'hard core' of DPs left in Germany	155
The end of the IRO	157
The transition of DPs to the German authorities	159

The 'sickness in her midst': Curing the refugee problem in West
    Germany   164
A disappointing caesura: Germany's 'Homeless' Foreigners Law   172

Conclusion   177

Notes   187
Bibliography   225
Index   239

Illustrations

Figures

1.1	Allied Occupation of Germany, 1945	14
2.1	Polen abzeichen (Polish badge) worn by Poles on outer clothing	34
2.2	Poland's border changes between 1939 and 1945	46
3.1	Rhoda Dawson's Polish-language training at Jullouville, France	62
5.1	Percentage of total number of Poles in three western zones of Germany	102
5.2	Poles repatriating from the British zone of occupation, October 1946–January 1947	112
5.3	Timeline of resettlement schemes in Britain	117
7.1	Total number of people under IRO care in Germany (not resettled/repatriated)	158

Tables

6.1	Education of Polish DPs in British Zone of Germany, 1 January 1948	148
7.1	Percentage of National Groups' Arrival Dates in Germany	162
7.2	Number of Times 'Displaced Persons' Mentioned between 25 April 1951 and 25 April 1953	170

Acknowledgements

As always, there are far too many people to thank for their help, guidance, support, advice, encouragement and kindness while writing this book. This research began at Newcastle University, and I am very grateful to Tim Kirk and Felix Schulz, who supervised me throughout my PhD but also continue to provide support and advice as mentors and friends. To my examiners Jessica Reinisch and Daniel Siemens for their insightful questions which helped me reshape the thesis into a book.

As I was still doing my PhD when I took up my first academic post, the book was entirely written while working at the University of East Anglia, and the support from colleagues there has been priceless. I am especially thankful for Jayne Gifford's keen eye for detail and her willingness to read the full manuscript, always providing insightful and probing questions along the way. Becky Taylor for her guidance and willingness to take me under her wing with invaluable advice and much-needed chats. Richard Deswarte for always being ready to listen, debate, and discuss while ensuring I had enough of Adri's wonderful baking to keep me going at the 3 pm slump. I will be forever indebted to Eliza Hartrich, Amanda Dillon, and Helena Carr for their readiness to listen to my work but also provide me with enough cake that I have actually become part cake myself (and I would not have it any other way), alongside Joel Halcomb's magical ability to appear with a freshly brewed pot of coffee just when I needed it most. Between the two universities, I was lucky enough to be surrounded by brilliant colleagues from all walks of life who provided lively lunches, beers, and chips while keeping my academic brain engaged: thanks go particularly to Dannielle Shaw, Stuart Palmer, Chris Jones, Chris Sandal-Wilson, Alberto Murru and Michail Raftakis. Collectively, their friendship and support kept me going.

I am forever grateful to Katarzyna Nowak for her keen insights over the years. Although we have spoken for hours about our shared research, she has also become a dear friend. Katherine Rossy, my fellow UNRRA scholar, frequently provided encouragement but also enriched my understanding of all things UNRRA, which has unquestionably strengthened my work. I am also forever in debt to numerous friends who did not want to talk about my book or research whatsoever, and instead helped me to relax.

During my research I have also benefited from the knowledge and assistance of numerous librarians and archivists from Britain, Germany, and France. Special thanks, however, go to Howard Bailes, who kindly copied and sent Rhoda Dawson's private collection, Gilles Lapers, who provided full access to his personal collection of Maczków materials, and Gary Lawson, who generously shared his grandfather's wartime short story of Wentorf, personal family archive, and memoir of Liselotte Becker with me.

At Bloomsbury, I want to thank Laura Reeves for her unending patience and Rhodri Mogford for his excellent efficiency. Thanks also go to those who anonymously provided comments on the script. Peer reviewers are the backbone of our profession after all, and their comments were greatly appreciated.

I want to thank my mam, dad, and brother for providing me with much-needed support in numerous ways. Lastly, I am grateful to Andy for his willingness to listen to my seemingly endless stream of thoughts, his provision of much-needed coffee and cats, and for just being there in general.

Abbreviations

AK	*Armia Krajowa* (Polish Home Army)
CCDP	Citizens Committee of Displaced Persons
CCG	Control Commission for Germany
CMWS/CMLS	Civil Mixed Watchman's Service/Civil Mixed Liaison Service
COBSRA	Council of British Societies for Relief Services Abroad
DP	displaced person
DPAC	Displaced Persons Assembly Centre
EVW	European Volunteer Worker
FRS	Friends Relief Service
ICRC	International Committee of the Red Cross
IGCR	Intergovernmental Committee on Refugees
IRO	International Refugee Organization
IWM	Imperial War Museum, London
NGO	non-governmental organization
PCIRO	Provisional Committee, International Refugee Organization
POW	prisoner of war
PSL	*Polskie Stronnictwo Ludowe* (Polish Peasant Party)
PU	Polish Union in Germany
SHAEF	Supreme Headquarters Allied Expeditionary Forces
TNA	The National Archives, London
UN	United Nations
UNHCR	United Nations High Commissioner for Refugees
UNRRA	United Nations Relief and Rehabilitation Administration

A Note on Translation and Transliteration

Unless indicated otherwise, all translations are my own. I have attempted to keep the same language used by those who originally wrote the letters, postcards, and memoirs to uphold their style (including factual mistakes, grammar, awkward phrasing, and descriptions).

Introduction

When teaching my first-year history students about migrants and migrations in Europe during the twentieth century, numerous students often express their disbelief that Polish people have a 'history' in Britain that predates 2004 (Poland's entry to the EU). As we begin to unravel the multitude of migrations during the century, they readily start to ask fundamental questions: who defines a border; what are national/ethnic identities; are identities attributed by others; how did so many people end up so far away from 'home'; who helped them get back 'home'; why didn't they all go 'home'?

As these conversations continue, many students realize they know hardly anything about Poland or its relationship with Britain, other than they all know at least one Polish family and assumed they had come to the Britain in 2004. The students, rather unwittingly, start to ask the same questions many historians have approached for the last twenty years over post-war displacement. The multifaceted issues surrounding the uprooting of peoples during wartime, and the consequences it has during peacetime, are only recently being understood in academic circles with very little making it into the mainstream. In the Polish case, it was only in 2019 that the Polish experience of war was depicted on Anglo-speaking TV screens in the BBC drama *World on Fire*. Although well received by audiences, it only lightly touched on Polish experiences, international relationships, and the origins of the breakdown in relations between Britain and Poland focusing on 1939–40. The immediate post-1945 period is left untouched. There is still a long way to go to contextualize the post-war period and show the impact of these years on contemporary society.

In 1945, Britain's official line towards Poland, the creation of international organizations, and the intergovernmental apparatus to reconstruct Germany were all meticulously detailed on paper; the reality on the ground was much different. Consequently, those 'in the middle', namely welfare workers and military officials, had to adapt wartime planning for peacetime purposes and this would prove to have an indelible impact on the (re)construction of the post-war world. Through emphasizing their contribution to the establishment of relationships between countries, peoples, and organizations, a much clearer understanding of post-war humanitarianism will be provided.

Historical background

It would be an understatement to say the post-war landscape in Germany was complex. Alongside the displacement of millions throughout and after the Second World War, this unique period saw the embryonic formation of contemporary international structures to deal with the consequences of war. The unprecedented displacement of people, however, accelerated the need for state-driven international humanitarianism that could also play a vital role in reconstruction, particularly of Germany. As the enemy nation at the heart of Europe, the Allied countries occupied the devastated landscape while also trying to assemble and organize those who had been displaced. Although Poland and Britain were allies before and throughout the war, in the displaced persons (DP) camps within British-occupied Germany the relationship began to sour. Former forced labourers and former Prisoners of War (PWX), alongside those who actively fought alongside the British believed that their wartime experiences, alliances, and records of service would influence how well they were treated in these camps and determine their post-war status. Unfortunately, this was often not the case.

Within British-occupied Germany, the dynamics of who was the enemy altered rapidly as British soldiers and welfare workers held their former enemies in higher regard than their Polish allies. In September 1945, a mere four months after the cessation of hostilities in Europe, the British Allied Liaison Branch circulated a memorandum on Polish displaced persons emphasizing the need for 'understanding':

> Though certain Polish elements are frequently at fault it would appear that all Poles are regarded by many of the British troops as a nuisance. Few attempts have been made to put the psychological aspect of the Polish case to the British soldier, nor is the attitude of the British press helpful. Tactless handling of the situation leads to resentment among the Poles themselves. When this resentment assumes active proportions the British authorities naturally take measures, whether forcible or otherwise, to maintain or restore order. This leads to further discontent and so the vicious circle grows.[1]

British soldiers and relief workers had to be officially and explicitly told that Polish DPs were to be treated as equals, and not readily ascribed the troublesome 'nuisance' label they had hitherto acquired. Military officials quickly neglected their stance, however, as the months dragged on and Polish DPs remained, forming a very visible reminder of how much work was still to be done.

As the Allies made their way through Germany in early 1945, they encountered thousands of people travelling along the roads and through cities. The initial pleasant impression of undisturbed arable land burgeoning with fattened cattle quickly gave way as piles of ragged, discarded clothing were found alongside the roads. As Alan Moorehead, an Allied journalist, witnessed first-hand, 'half the nationalities of Europe were on the move, all moving blindly westward'.[2] The issue of DPs was recognized early on in Allied post-war planning initiatives since the provision of immediate relief was paramount to European recovery. It is likely that the term 'DP' was coined at a Fabian society meeting where the magnitude of the problem was readily understood, a realization one of the Fabian members, Kenneth G Brooks declared would 'cause the heart to sink'.[3]

It has been estimated that up to 60 million Europeans were on the move during and after the Second World War, although the percentage of these defined by the Allies as DPs in the post-war period has been contested in recent years.[4] There are various estimates; however, many agree with the contemporary US Army officer and geographer Malcolm J Proudfoot's assessment that just under 7 million were found in Germany's three western zones by September 1945, with a similar number in the eastern Soviet zone.[5] Of the nearly 2 million Poles spread across Europe, just over 1 million were in the three western zones of Germany: the French, British, and US zones. The largest proportion were in the British zone of occupation, accounting for 510,238 or 79 per cent of its total DP population.[6] The number of camps, and who supervised them, varied greatly: at its peak, the British zone contained more than 443 camps under United Nations Relief and Rehabilitation Administration (UNRRA) care.[7] While many camps contained Poles, a sizeable number were predominantly Polish. Emsland, a rural district of Lower Saxony, ostensibly became known as the 'Polish occupation zone' with the small town of Haren being transformed into Maczków, the unofficial capital of 'Little Poland'.[8] Of the more than 318,000 Poles repatriated from the British zone to Poland between November 1945 and June 1947 very few were accepted onto resettlement schemes elsewhere and only after hesitation. Thousands of others chose to remain in the camps for fear of what awaited them should they return to Poland.[9]

At the same time, the Second World War saw the first instance of a state-driven international humanitarian structure formed to provide basic necessities such as food and shelter, prevent the spread of disease, and ultimately showcase the triumph of democracy. The UNRRA was created in 1943 to provide 'relief and rehabilitation' to DPs, although 'rehabilitation' itself was never defined, leading to numerous practical problems that will be discussed throughout this work.[10] Each of UNRRA's forty-four contributing nations donated 1 per cent of their total national income to the cause, making Britain and the United States UNRRA's largest contributors, contributing 13 and 72 per cent, respectively, and earning them the title 'UNRRA's real parents'.[11] Alongside this new framework, pre-existing and long-established non-governmental organizations (NGOs), such as the International Committee of the Red Cross (ICRC) and the Quaker's Friends Ambulance Service, worked in tandem with UNRRA. The construction of this new framework, of peaceably working alongside one another was, however, an example of one more area meticulously detailed on paper that failed to come to fruition on the ground. In reality, UNRRA became heavily reliant on the Allied military due to chronic understaffing and inadequate personnel, and so the NGOs often operated within their traditional systems rather than within the new framework alongside UNRRA. In the midst of this, welfare workers were employed from across the world, and made up what the Chief of Operations for the UNRRA mission in Germany, Lieutenant General Sir Frederick Morgan, called an 'adventitious assembly of silver-tongued ineffectuals, professional do-gooders, crooks and crackpots'.[12] These people, alongside military personnel assigned as 'protectors' of DPs and welfare workers alike, were the ones 'in the middle' who made an impact on the day-to-day lives within the camps.

Scope and purpose

The immediate post-war period has, over the past two decades, received significant attention.[13] Histories of reconstruction alongside histories of displacement (and resettlement) that make up the post-war refugee story have begun to filter into the mainstream, showing that large-scale population displacement is not a new phenomenon belonging to the twenty-first century.[14] After the official histories of international humanitarian organizations, such as UNRRA and the International Refugee Organization (IRO),[15] very few scholars attempted to approach the subject of post-war reconstruction and/or displacement until the 1980s.[16] Only in the last twenty years have the issues of displacement and individual histories of those displaced come to the fore of academic scholarship. Apart from a now significant gap between the displacement and time of writing, scholars realized they were on the cusp of losing the voices from those displaced in the mid-twentieth century and leading to increased efforts to record oral testimonies for posterity.[17] The result was a sudden upsurge of group or micro histories focusing on a particular ethnicity, nationality, or sometimes even a single DP camp.[18] Additionally, there was a renewed focus on the organizations themselves and attempts to understand how the very idea of international and state-driven humanitarianism was born. This research led to a veritable explosion of works on international humanitarianism and welfare work in the post-war period.[19] Lastly, it has only recently been recognized that the majority of works relating to this period focus heavily on the US zone of occupation with scholars often using information obtained from US sources and applying it to all three western zones.[20] Consequently, works on the British zone in particular, but also the French and Soviet zones, are only just coming to the fore.[21] This work contributes to all of these categories. Using Polish DPs in British-occupied Germany as a focal point, this work analyses the impact of those deemed to be 'in the middle' on post-war constructions of humanitarianism and occupation by combining 'top-down' and 'bottom-up' perspectives, alongside policy formation, and lived experiences. The co-construction of these aid operations emphasizes the significance of individual decisions within these larger networks. A central theme of this work focuses on the individuals ignoring official orders and advice in the DP camps to ensure the best possible result for all was achieved. Throughout this book, the voices of the DPs' 'carers' (welfare workers) and 'protectors' (military officials) will be used as a guide to the various stages of post-war occupation and transition into the Cold War.

At the same time wider questions concerning wartime and post-war understandings of ethnicity, nationality, and larger questions of identity will be addressed using the unique case of Polish DPs. Heavily reliant on their allies, and in particular the British as supposed 'brothers-in-arms', Polish post-war ideals of freedom from tyranny (Nazi and Soviet alike) were dashed at Potsdam in July 1945. Although the 1939 Polish government had found refuge in London during the war, the Allies officially recognized the Polish Provisional Government of National Unity (*Tymczasowy Rząd Jedności Narodowej*, Warsaw) as Poland's ruling power in the post-war world. Coupled with quick and efficient repatriation of Western European nationalities and Soviet DPs throughout the summer of 1945, by September when it was the Polish DPs' turn there was little to entice them back to Poland. The British were unprepared for the staunch resistance they encountered among various nationalities, and in particular the Polish DPs. According to welfare worker Margaret McNeill, the Allies had missed the 'psychological moment' for the quick, efficient, and willing repatriation of Polish nationals; too much had occurred since the war's end, and they were now fearful of returning.[22]

The ideological split between the Soviet-influenced Warsaw government ruling Poland, and the pre-war government exiled in London followed ordinary Polish DPs into the camps of occupied Germany. Nowhere was this split more apparent than in the British zone of Germany where the highest proportion of Polish DPs remained, dislocated from their homeland and attempting to resettle elsewhere but with little opportunity. The implementation of policies from international humanitarian organizations and the military officials ruling the zone were largely ad hoc and based on preconceived notions of what constitutes a 'good' or a 'bad' DP.[23] As Polish DPs struggled to reconcile ideas of place and belonging with their homeland's moving borders, the British military authorities took on a 'superior' role and showed a tendency to treat Poles as 'inferior', akin to the manner they had hitherto been treating colonial counterparts.[24] The construction of nations, the collapse of states, and the legitimacy ascribed to either was thrown into question in the post-war world. Polish identity came under threat from the competing forces of territorial shifts confusing the right of place, from an ideological shift confusing the understanding of Polishness, and from the British refusal to view these shifts as important at all.

This book therefore explores the significance of British attitudes towards Polish DPs in the British zone of occupation in Germany leading up to the enactment of the Homeless Foreigners Law on 21 April 1951 (*Gesetz über die Rechtsstellung heimatloser Ausländer im Bundesgebiet*). The consequences of Poles' treatment at the hands of the British, at all operational levels was an important factor for many in their decision to stay, repatriate or attempt to resettle between 1945 and 1951. Although the US zone also had a large number of Polish DPs, the opportunities afforded to them through resettlement and work schemes, and the support they received from Polish organizations in the United States created different experiences. The derisory attitude of British personnel, the ad hoc implementation of policies, the breaking down of Anglo-Polish relations with the government-in-exile, and the prolongation of Polish DPs' stay in the British zone of Germany all contributed to an increasingly negative, frustrated experience for the Polish DPs in question. Indeed, it would become the bedrock for the 'betrayed ally' rhetoric that became popular among Poles in exile in the post-war years.[25]

During wartime, the Anglo-Polish relationship had been aligned with a mutual hatred of fascism, but in the post-war world there was little reason for

Britain to prioritize its wartime ally over contemporary problems, particularly those concerning the Soviet Union. The Poles in British DP camps in Germany found themselves unable to match the ideal of post-war freedom with the lived reality. At the same time, the British, having stretched their country's capabilities throughout the war, were unable to cope with the increasingly impassioned demands of the Polish DPs in the camps. The breakdown of the Anglo-Polish relationship can be viewed as a marker of wider historical processes developing in the post-war period that also contributed to the reconstruction of Germany.

'In the middle'

Histories of displacement often come in one of two forms. Firstly, and more commonly, understanding displacement has gone hand-in-hand with understanding the formation of institutions governing them. This provides a 'top-down' history focusing on interpreting the drafting and implementation of policies. These histories are important, but they also often cause the displaced to become passive objects in their own history. Secondly, a body of literature is expanding that focuses solely on those on the receiving end of these policies, the 'bottom-up' perspective. These works allow for those on the receiving end of institutional structures and policy implementation to show the lived reality of these actions. Often written as a social history, writers have focused on how displacement was viewed by those who were displaced and what, if anything, the institutions governing them meant. These writings, sometimes histories but also memoirs, autobiographies, and literary works, have added much-needed depth to understanding the human experiences of war. This work seeks to combine the two, providing both a 'top-down' and 'bottom-up' perspective by using those 'in the middle' as interlocutors of policies and experiences. It does this through using the voices of those 'in the middle' to mediate the reactions and comprehension of policies directed towards Polish DPs in British-occupied Germany. Consequently, this research foregrounds the administrative mechanisms, policies and procedures over the 'experience' of individual DPs. The voices of welfare workers, liaison officers, and military officials have been used as a mirror to reflect not only the policies from above but the reactions to the policies from below. These voices offer unique insight into the reactions and subsequent actions of British camp officials, allowing a fresh perspective that has hitherto been neglected.

Sources

Every effort has been made to present the Polish DPs' reception of policies implemented in the British zone. Due to the nature of social sources such as memoirs, diaries, and autobiographies, however, it is difficult to acquire a broad enough scope to accommodate the desire for equal representation. Where possible, the response of Poles to their treatment is discussed, but the record of their experience, echoed in personal reflections, is fragmentary, and the story is often dominated by the perspective of those charged with administering the situation. Polish DPs' experiences have been recovered by reading across the sources that concentrate on the difficulties officials dealt with.

Although the sources emanating from Polish DPs themselves are limited, the ones I have uncovered are highly informative. To counteract the small number of Polish DP voices, the reception of policies in the camps and their effect on Polish DPs can often be found in the diaries, memoirs, and autobiographies of various welfare workers: Rhoda Dawson, Susan Pettiss, Gitta Sereny, Margaret McNeill, Marvin Klemmé, Kathryn Close, Kanty Cooper, Francesca Wilson, and Grigor McClelland's accounts of Polish DPs' reactions to the announcement of the Allies' official recognition of the Polish Provisional Government of National Unity as Poland's legitimate government; to the shifting of Poland's borders westwards as 'new' maps were displayed on camp notice-boards; to UNRRA's implementation of *Operation Carrot*; to the unofficial British announcements of 'forcible repatriation'; to the lifting of the non-fraternization (non-frat) order between the British, Americans, and Germans; and finally to the continuing treatment of Polish DPs as inferior can be used to counterbalance any institutional records.

Welfare workers have recorded the reactions of those who were closest to them in the camps, and due to the Poles' prolonged stay they were often regarded as more than just DPs. The welfare workers' accounts offer a middle ground that is often neglected between the top-down and bottom-up histories; after all, those in middle often find themselves on the positive and negative sides of the upper and lower orders in question. Although one welfare worker's testimony has been used to exhaustion in histories of DP camps between 1945 and 1951, there remain a plethora of other testimonies to analyse and this work strives to give a voice to those who have mainly been neglected hitherto.

Alongside the voices of welfare workers and military officials, archival holdings primarily from Germany, Britain, Poland, and France have been used to provide a layered framework. Beginning with conditions in Germany in 1945, this work uses extensive archival materials to explain choices and decisions of individuals within the context of increasing east-west tensions that were accompanied by accelerated ethnic homogenization of Europe's nation-states in the post-war period. At the heart of this framework, discussions about Polish DPs and their explicit rejection of post-war Poland as their 'homeland' inform how the newly devised humanitarian structures sought to deal with 'recalcitrant' DPs.

This book seeks to enrich not only our understanding of the influence of interactions between multiple international, charitable, and state organizations on a specific DP group but to critically address the relationship between concepts of migration and displacement alongside the construction of state-driven international humanitarian systems and the process of (military) occupation. The Polish DP group in British-occupied Germany found itself in a state of profound confusion and disillusionment in 1945. The juxtaposition of the various agencies and their motives for repatriation, blocking resettlement plans and wholly neglecting integration strategies is told through the 'moral compass' of the camps' middle management. This study thereby emphasizes how the conflicting forces of humanitarianism and militarism during occupation caused a community deeply affected by war to become even more fractured. Using the Polish DP experience as a focal point, it will show how the co-construction of aid operations by humanitarian organizations and military authorities in the immediate post-war era has shaped our understanding of humanitarian relief in the post-war world; more importantly, this complex relationship serves as an example of how the best intentions can sometimes lead to ruin.

1

They say 'the British had the Ruins'

Physical destruction, emotional stagnation, and the 'human debris'

Introduction

As Field Marshal Wilhelm Keitel signed Germany's unconditional surrender to the Allies on 8 May 1945, Germany lay in ruins. Across the country, towns were reduced to rubble, cities were overrun by foreigners brought by force or fleeing advancing Allied armies, and many Germans found themselves homeless, unable to find food and confronted by the total occupation of the Allied forces. The six years of war that had ravaged the European continent had made an indelible mark on the face of Europe, and nowhere was this mark more visible than in the presence of millions of displaced persons (DPs) spread throughout Germany.[1] On both sides of the Atlantic, from Franklin Delano Roosevelt's desk in the White House to Fabian Society gatherings in Oxford, displacement was discussed yet the scale could not have been conceived before the war's end.[2] By May 1945, population displacement was recognized as a foremost concern by the Allies, and if their goal of peace was to be achieved an internationally coordinated relief effort on a scale grander than that at the end of the First World War would be essential. Once formed in 1943, the United Nations Relief and Rehabilitation Administration (UNRRA) declared that 'never before in the history of mankind have men been called upon to solve a relief problem of greater magnitude and complexity than that resulting from the present war'.[3] The scale was only surpassed in the mid-2010s as multitudes of peoples were displaced from their homes during and following war in the Middle East. The international humanitarian organizations' infrastructure to deal with such drastic displacement was born form the immediate post-war period in 1945. Despite over seventy-five years of experience, a focus on individual identities and nationalities still prevents those forcibly displaced from obtaining safe refuge.

At the end of the war in Europe, the composition of the DP population was far more complicated than the Allies had anticipated. Obvious remnants of Nazi victimization liberated from concentration camps existed alongside ex-prisoners of war (POWs), former *Zwangsarbeiter* (forced labourers) and those displaced fleeing the advancing Red Army. Soviet DPs were numerically strong but lacked the official capacity to reject repatriation due to agreements between the Allies at Potsdam and Yalta, which sealed their fate before the war's end.[4] The annexation of the Baltic states by the USSR meant that many Latvian, Lithuanian, and Estonian DPs wishing to return home would be treated as collaborators and war criminals, having fought alongside or in the Wehrmacht. Ukrainian DPs who dreamt of a free Ukraine were reluctant to return to a country dominated by Soviet and Polish occupiers, claiming they would be persecuted upon return.[5] All of these groups were perceived to have had legitimate reasons for refusing repatriation. The legitimacy of Polish DPs, however, to reject the Poland presented to them by the Allies at the end of the war was never fully recognized. It was the commonly held belief among the Allies that Polish DPs were fully repatriable, and little attention was paid to the drastic changes occurring in Poland's political and geographical landscape. In particular, the British viewed Polish DPs' reluctance to repatriate as their taking advantage of the situation for economic gain. The Polish DPs' refusal to accept repatriation readily and willingly became a thorn in the side of not only the British military but also the welfare workers placed in the camps. The difficulties of dealing with the mass of Polish DPs were particularly acute in the British zone due to significant damage to industry, landscape, housing infrastructure, and all other manner of societal necessities caused by Allied bombing. The Poles were an added strain. Consequently, the 'brothers-in-arms' mentality was reduced to empty rhetoric as the British military authorities (and to some extent the welfare workers) were left feeling underappreciated, exhausted, and frustrated, and the Poles were left feeling betrayed.

This chapter offers an insight into the situation in the British zone of Germany at the end of the Second World War as competing DP groups jostled for recognition. Through an overview of the displacement that took place throughout and immediately after the war, it will become clear why so many Polish DPs were found on German soil. This chapter places the influx of British occupation authorities alongside the institutions and their personnel, and their role regarding DPs, German civilians, the administration of Germany, and their working capacity with UNRRA and other international organizations in the wider context of controlling the displaced in Germany's devastated landscape.

Primarily, this chapter shows how Polish DPs were affected by different stages of the British occupation unfolding as it became clear they were more interested in the Germans whose country they were occupying, their own financial position, and Britain's desire to remain an international leader in world affairs than the debris of humanity under their charge for whom Britain had gone to war in the first place.

The consequences of Potsdam

On the advice of the European Advisory Commission, three zones of occupation were initially created in Germany and divided between the United States, Britain, and the USSR (or Soviet Union).[6] The east of Germany, including the northern part of what was previously Prussia, was solely governed by the USSR and became the Soviet zone. The rest of Germany east of the Oder-Neisse Line was annexed and handed over to Poland.[7] The British occupied the industrial Ruhr area and most of North-west Germany, the epicentre of coal and steel production, while the Americans were given the largely rural areas of Bayern, Hesse, and Württemberg-Baden.[8] At the Yalta conference in February 1945, however, the 'Big Three' agreed that France should also be given a zone of occupation. This would be taken from the original zones held by the United States and Britain, with a portion of Berlin: it was said that the Americans had the scenery, the French had the wine, and the British had the ruins.[9] On 5 June 1945 the Allies took control and declared a unilateral agreement on the governance of Germany due to its complete lack of administrative capability and civil administration; this was the official beginning of the total Allied occupation (h).[10]

After redeploying troops that had previously advanced on Berlin, the occupation authorities concentrated on population control, the dismantling of local authorities, and the care of DPs found throughout the cities and in the countryside. At the Potsdam Conference from 17 July to 2 August 1945 the four powers met to discuss the governance of Germany. The consensus was to enforce the 'four D's' which, depending on viewpoint, was often expanded to five D's: denazification, demilitarization, decartelization, democratization, and decentralization.[11] Yet they gave no practicable indication as to how these were to be implemented. It was made clear during the conference that it was to be a united but decentralized Germany, with the aim of giving the German people 'the opportunity to prepare for the eventual reconstruction of their lives on a democratic and peaceful basis'.[12] Controls and measures were put in

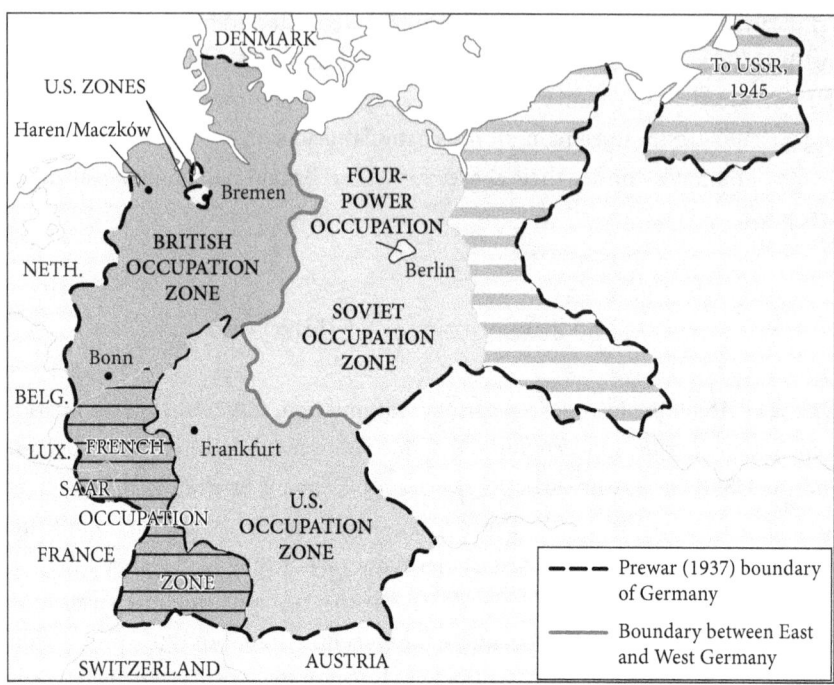

Figure 1.1 Allied Occupation of Germany, 1945. Source: Created by Samantha K. Knapton.

place to severely restrict German intervention. At the same time responsibility for economic control, established by the Allied Control Council, became the direct responsibility of the German authorities. Consequently, any breakdown of control would rest with the Germans themselves. In the British zone the need for German cooperation to avoid total chaos was obvious. This dependence soon became a hindrance, as inchoate purging of German administrative staff at the lower levels left the various sectors in the hands of inexperienced, or worse still, untrustworthy and decidedly pro-Nazi elements.

It was not just the economic policy that hindered relations between the four occupying powers. One of the principal disagreements carried over from Yalta to Potsdam between the Western Allies and the USSR was about the amount of reparation that Germany was to pay, and how and when this would be achieved. After the Potsdam Conference, a very noticeable division between East and West began to surface. On the one hand the West was worried that stripping Germany of its industry would destabilize the economy and bring about conditions ripe for the sowing of communist seeds in the German populace; on the other hand, the USSR was worried that Germany's self-sufficiency, built up through US and

British aid, would pull German industry under the US capitalist umbrella. By the time the conference concluded on 2 August 1945 a deep distrust had developed between East and West, creating conditions in which Cold War tensions would fester and develop with increasing veracity.

Besides putting strict economic controls in place and agreeing on the Allies' governance of Germany, the Potsdam Conference also sealed the fate of Poland. The USSR demanded heavy and immediate reparations, and that they should keep the swathe of Poland that they previously controlled during the war. To compensate, Poland's borders were shifted westwards, displacing an estimated 6 to 8 million Germans. The Potsdam agreement did little to ensure these Germans' safe expulsion, simply stating that the Allies, 'agree that any transfers that take place should be effected in an orderly and humane manner'.[13] Yet little to no enforcement of this stipulation was ever implemented, resulting in a huge loss of life, often through starvation. In a letter to a colleague, a Roman Catholic priest told of the grim reality:

> Already now 300 to 400 people die in Breslau a day, that is 10 000 to 12 000 a month. Now the same methods of extermination are applied to us as we applied to other peoples, only with the one outward appearance of humanity that the Russians and the Poles do not murder senselessly as did our *Waffen SS* and *Gestapo* in the occupied territory to the horror of the whole world. But if one considers the intention, it amounts to the same thing.[14]

This experience in Breslau (modern-day Wrocław) is typical of accounts of the expulsion of ethnic Germans from their homes in the immediate aftermath of the war. The areas to the west of Poland that had been German were soon referred to as the 'Recovered Territories'. This allowed Poles moving hastily out of the now-Soviet part of what had been eastern Poland to feel they had a right to reclaim this land. The 'wild' expulsions that had begun before Potsdam saw little improvement after the conference, as the Allies steadfastly refused to pay to set up an international transfer service that would take care of humanitarian concerns. As R M Douglas asserts, the Allies refused to set up this apparatus because 'they considered the anguish the displaced population would undergo to be a salutary form of re-education, bringing home to the mass of ordinary Germans the personal risks involved in lending support to extremist regimes and wars of aggression'.[15] In short, the Germans were not worth the expense and they had to learn a lesson, regardless of the chaos that would ensue. Consequently, floods of expelled ethnic Germans, or *Vertriebene*, poured into the British zone, adding to the mass of dependants gathering in the devastated region. Britain had officially agreed to accept 1.5 million Germans from the 'Recovered Territories' under *Operation Swallow*; they had not accounted for predominantly receiving what they saw as 'undesirable elements': the elderly, the infirm, pregnant women, and children. The hospitalization and death rates of those being transferred were high as the expellees were packed like cattle into insufficiently heated carts with little food and no medical provisions. The 'human debris' that was being sent to the British zone of occupation was not of much use as they could not help rebuild the devastated landscape or take one of the plentiful positions in industries that badly needed workers. They were yet another addition that would become 'a permanent burden on the British taxpayer'.[16] Britain had expected strong, healthy, male workers, and instead were given society's most feeble and dependent. As they had come from areas now incorporated into Poland, the anger and frustration of the British military government were almost squarely directed at those conducting the expulsions. A deep mistrust had developed as the Foreign Office 'became increasingly convinced that the Poles and Soviets were conspiring to channel all expellees from the "Recovered Territories" in the direction of the British zone, industriously cooking the books along the way'.[17] *Operation Swallow* was meant to be finished in July 1946; however, due to the shambolic way it was handled by all involved, the acute housing shortages in the British zone and the pressure on the German railways, it did not conclude until July 1947. All the while, Polish DPs who had largely been brought to Germany throughout the war as forced labourers were adding to the increasingly desperate situation in the British zone by refusing to return to Poland.

The DPs: Who, how, and why?

The DPs in the western zones of Germany, estimated at 7 million by the end of summer 1945, were by no means a homogenous group. Primarily they were a collection of peoples who had left their homes either under duress or through fear, prompted or forced to join the displaced in post-war Germany largely as one of the tragic consequences of war. The Baltic group, made up of Estonians, Latvians, and Lithuanians, was displaced not by a single cause but rather by a reaction to events throughout the war, often fleeing persecution in many forms. Although all Soviet nationals were to be repatriated regardless of personal wishes under the Yalta agreement, the United States refused to recognize the USSR's annexation of the Baltic states. Instead, these Balts became stateless. According to the Institute for Occupation Issues, the total number of Baltic refugees in Germany at the war's end was about 200,000.[18] Their unrepatriable status meant that 178,904 were still in Europe by 30 September 1945, with 50,572 of these in the British zone. Many Ukrainian DPs refused to be labelled Soviet or Polish citizens and instead, claiming independence, were also not forced to repatriate. Proudfoot does not include Ukrainians as a separate category in his table of 'European Displaced Persons by Claimed Nationality and Location: 30 September 1945'. Yet when discussing UNRRA and military eligibility criteria, he includes 'Ukrainians' as a United Nations category of Displaced Person who were eligible for assistance 'if displaced as a result of war from their countries of origin, citizenship, or previous residence'.[19] The Institute for Occupation Issues recognizes Ukrainian DPs alongside Russian DPs, estimating the total Ukrainian DP population at around 300,000 out of a total of 2 million displaced Russians.[20] Although the Allies were not as sympathetic to the Ukrainian DPs as the Balts, they recognized the need to classify them as their own distinct groups, as return to a Soviet- and Polish-dominated homeland would surely put the majority in a vulnerable position.

Aside from individual populations, the number of unaccompanied children found in Germany amid the rubble was startling. UNRRA had 50,000 children in its care shortly after 8 May 1945, and the number continued to climb.[21] Some had been taken to Germany alongside adults to work in forced labour programmes. The physical and psychological damage was obvious for all to see. But what the Allies had not accounted for was a systematic programme of child removal and 'Germanization', a method designed to weaken Germany's neighbours and replenish the depleted German population. Children deemed fit for 'Germanization' based on their physical appearance and assimilability were placed in approved German households to be raised as Germans. Reports of kidnapped children poured into UNRRA centres and separate child-search teams were created as, according to Mark Wyman, by the 'end of 1946 the UNRRA reported that more than 200,000 queries had been received by Polish welfare agencies searching for lost children'.[22] The reality was that no one knew how many children were really missing as Nicholas Stargardt emphasizes that UNESCO put the figure at around 13 million. Children had been taken from their homes, forced to be labourers, left behind when their parents were taken to concentration camps or perhaps taken there themselves; some 'who had survived the liquidations of ghettos' and other acts of atrocity, as well as German children had been widely dispersed across East-Central Europe.[23] Although the reports of missing children had flooded in, the task of tracing, locating, and homing these children appropriately was a monstrous commission. At the end of UNRRA's work in Germany it had officially processed 14,800 unaccompanied children throughout the three western zones; only 4,400 of these were from the British zone. When the IRO took over in 1947 it was only able to process an additional 189 children before it closed in 1951.[24] The intricacies involved in helping Europe's unaccompanied children were beyond the purview of any international humanitarian organization, yet the flood that descended upon the camps could not be ignored.[25] If the Allies failed the children, they had truly failed humanity.[26] Although the extent of care for unaccompanied children and the tasks of the child-search teams in the British zone are beyond the scope of this project, it is worth noting that many of the children reported kidnapped were taken from the railway and border towns of Poland.

There were many other, smaller categories of DPs in Germany. The Western DPs, largely consisting of French, Belgians, Dutch, Italians, and some Scandinavians were repatriated almost immediately; most of these were ex-POWs (sometimes referred to as PWX) or former forced labourers. One of the primary terms of the Yalta agreement was that Western DPs' repatriation was to be prioritized. Therefore, by 30 September 1945 a mere 7,135 remained in the three western zones of occupation, the majority in the British zone. These numbers were quickly reduced once a transport bottleneck had been cleared.[27]

Soviet DPs constituted one of the largest groups, most being ex-POWs or former forced labourers. In Ulrich Herbert's work on foreign labour in Germany, by August 1944 the combined total of civilian workers and POWs of Soviet nationality in Germany came to 2,758,312.[28] By 30 September 1945, however, a total of 2,034,000 of these had been transferred from the 'SHAEF [Supreme Headquarters Allied Expeditionary Forces] area and the Western zone of Germany and Austria to areas under Soviet Control'.[29] As mentioned, alongside Western DPs, priority was also given to Soviet DPs, even though many were unwilling to return. It was not uncommon for Soviet DPs to present themselves as Poles or Ukrainians, go into hiding, or in the worst cases, commit suicide.[30] As part of the Yalta agreement all Soviet DPs were to be handed over to the Soviet zone in Germany at the earliest possible date, and by 30 September 1945 very few remained in Germany, and even fewer in any of the western zones. The forcible repatriation of these DPs was a point of contention at the Foreign Office; however, it seems that as much thought was given to this policy as to the 'orderly and humane' order for eastern German expellees. It was only after starting the enforced movement of Soviet DPs to the Soviet zone that the morally dubious orders were questioned. Even though SHAEF had originally intended to carry out its agreement to hand over all Soviet nationals to the Soviet authorities, it soon became clear that many had only recently become Soviet citizens through occupation or border changes throughout and immediately after the war. Additionally, when the British and American troops realized that they would have to apply physical force to not just a few but thousands of Soviet nationals, issues of security and personal safety took precedence over Soviet wishes.

Indeed, as John Danylyszlyn argues, the Soviet repatriation policy was 'merely the ugliest manifestation of an all-pervasive Western desire to jettison responsibility for millions of displaced human beings'. Danylyszlyn further argues that despite being initial victims of war, their status quickly shifted to that of an economic and political burden, which could contaminate the already fraught European relations of 1945.[31] If the Soviet DPs were regarded as a burden, however, they were a burden that the Allies could easily rid themselves of. The Poles were a different story. Their DP groups were largely made up of former forced labourers. Again, according to Herbert, by August 1944 Poles accounted for 1,688,080 of the foreign civilian workers and POWs working in the Reich, the majority (66.7 per cent) in agriculture.[32] According to the Institute for Occupation Issues, however, the overall number brought to Germany from Poland throughout the war was closer to 3.5 million (with 700,000 POWs).[33] The hiring of Poles as seasonal labourers in Germany was a practice that had been in place since the end of the nineteenth century, and consequently a large diaspora of Polish seasonal workers had settled in the north-west corner of Germany, that is, the British zone. Many worked in agriculture, but some were miners and were attracted to jobs in the industrial Ruhr area, earning them the title *Ruhrpolen*.[34] The DPs who were present in the British camps at the end of the war, however, were not the same as those from earlier migrations. They had largely been forcibly conscripted to work in Germany as the German war machine grew exponentially. According to Proudfoot, at the end of the war over 1.5 million Poles had been displaced, with 910,000 recorded in the SHAEF areas of Germany, Austria, and Czechoslovakia. Due to the prioritization of Western and Soviet DPs, 816,012 Poles remained in the three western zones alone by 30 September 1945. Those in the camps were largely former forced labourers and ex-concentration camp prisoners; however, many had been members of the *Armia Krajowa* (Home Army or AK) and had been captured and interned after the Warsaw Uprising in 1944.[35] As the Soviets pressed for Poles originally from east of the River Bug to be incorporated into Soviet statistics, the immediate danger of handing those involved in the Warsaw Uprising over to Soviet officials was realized. The Poles presented a curious problem in the US and British zones: they were numerically strong and often fiercely nationalist, but almost entirely dependent on the Allies. The British had pledged allegiance to the Poles and joined the war in retaliation for the German invasion in 1939. Now, six years later, confronted with a mass of Polish DPs in a zone utterly devastated by war, low on supplies and staffed by physically and mentally exhausted military personnel, the Poles' immediate fate was once again in British hands.

The physical destruction: The British zone in Germany

The groups of DPs found in the British zone often mirrored those in the US zone, with some differences in concentration. Although the US zone held the camp with the largest Polish population (Wildflecken), in the British zone an entire town had been turned over to Polish control with the help of the Polish First Armoured Division. Poles were also numerically strong in the British zone both within DP camps and outside them in requisitioned housing, often inhabiting whole streets and creating individual enclaves. The spread of Poles throughout the British zone soon became an additional strain for the British occupation authorities as they became increasingly tangled up in the bureaucratic administration of the German populace and the renewed power systems. Even though the Allies had agreed on the 'four Ds', there was little clarity on how these were to be carried out. In order to understand why the Polish DPs, in their refusal to repatriate and therefore alleviate pressure on the British, became the proverbial straw that broke the camel's back, it is necessary to understand the strains unique to the British zone that created such a fraught atmosphere within which animosity began to flourish.

Denazification: a process deemed to be of such paramount importance that the first expressions of Anglo-American interest in creating a coherent policy appeared as early as 28 April 1944.[36] From this point onwards it became clear that a denazification policy would be needed for immediate implementation once the war was won. How it would be carried out in the zones, however, became a point of contention. The US zone at first carried out denazification with great enthusiasm, purging all those who showed any loyalty to the Third Reich. Whereas the British procedure, later referred to as an *Entnazifizierungswirrwarr*, was just that: a confused and jumbled mess.[37] Although there was an official process for the removal of prominent and loyal Nazis, other necessities such as coal production in the British zone often got in the way of carrying out this process to its full extent. The lacklustre effort to carry out the denazification process in the British zone, however, was both a help and a hindrance. Like many programmes in the immediate post-war years, official policies were not always followed as the restrictive red tape was likely to impede actual advances on the ground towards a more stable and self-sufficient Germany.

The *Fragebogen*, as it was commonly called, became the infamous Anglo-American legacy of the denazification process. It was a questionnaire to determine the perceived level of loyalty to Nazism or the possible level of threat an individual posed towards a future democratic Germany. It was universally hated by both those filling it in and those evaluating it, and soon became a hot topic on both sides of the Atlantic, referred to as the ideological equivalent of tax returns, and it became the subject of numerous critical and satirical songs and stories.[38] The withdrawal of suspected Nazis from their jobs was much wider in the US zone as the Americans cast their net wider. The British believed that true denazification of Germany could only be achieved through long-term re-education of the entire populace, as Nazism was believed to be a consequence of the German character. Therefore, to rid Germany of its inherent Nazi character it was necessary to start at the top. This resulted in a policy focusing predominantly on removing former high-ranking Nazis from positions of power. The British strongly believed that coupling the removal of elites with total reorganization of the German education system would quash the strongest threat to a stable democracy. Once this threat had been removed, the rank and file would follow suit. Moreover, as the British zone was predominantly industrial and the reconstruction of Germany was reliant on its production of coal, steel and other necessities, the removal of those in lower positions of responsibility was avoided as it was perceived as a waste of manpower.[39]

The British zone, which was heavily damaged and severely understaffed, eventually relied on Germans to conduct the denazification process. In consequence, personal vendettas were frequently pursued. The British were forced to bring the denazification process to a close by 1947 as economic concerns became the priority. Indeed, the denazification of industry never truly got underway due to the zone's economic fragility.[40]

Denazification infiltrated all parts of German life, and none more than the German education system. If Nazism was a consequence of the German character, then the education system was the root from which that character grew. Unlike in industry, the British had nothing to gain from retaining former Nazi teachers in schools and universities as they served no economic purpose and created no stability in the economy. It was in education that the denazification process enjoyed the most success, and the British were quick to open new teacher training colleges. By 1946, twenty-eight such colleges had been established. Although the whole denazification process concentrated on Germans, the reality of such a large-scale operation in the British zone meant that Polish DPs were able to build their own education facilities with little interference or restriction, and the British zone became a thriving haven for the Polish DP education system.[41] The primary reason for this lax attitude towards Polish DPs' self-organizing goals in 1945 and 1946 was simply British unwillingness to intervene. It was hoped that by allowing the Polish education facilities to flourish, the German education system might follow suit.[42] Indeed, the rigorous screening process that was to follow in the DP camps paralleled the denazification processes across German society. Although, DP screening also had little chance of success.[43]

As previously argued, the British lack of zeal towards denazification, particularly in the industrial area also had its positive side. Economically, the policy pursued by the British zone was the most conducive to ensuring that a stronger Germany would emerge from the denazification process, which was favoured by all involved. According to Andrew H. Beattie, the western zones of occupation did not just intern 'senior Nazi officials' but a broad range, as the Allies had 'no agreement on what constitutes a senior, mid-ranking or subordinate Nazi leader or official'. Internment was used, however, as a means to prevent the resurgence of Nazi ideas.[44] Yet, the retention of numerous members of the Nazi party, particularly those deemed to have been in subservient positions, has been the source of considerable controversy over the last seventy years as wartime acts have seemingly gone unpunished. The German historian and theologian Lutz Niethammer believed that the goal of the denazification process was not merely the removal of elites, to be replaced with other elites, but also the re-education of the entire German population and the eradication of Nazi thought. He believed the use of German denazification panels was detrimental to the overall goal of the British occupation, describing them as *Mitläuferfabrik* (literally factories that produced followers) which largely targeted the *Nichtwisser* (know-nothings), *Unbeteiligte* (non-participants) and *heimliche Nazigegner* (secret opponents of Nazism). Yet they also enabled the German people to rid themselves of their stained past, '*und mit frischer weißer Weste in die Gesellschaft zurückgeschickt*' (and return to society with fresh, white vests).[45] On the one hand, British denazification policy has come to be viewed as a fiasco by scholars, as it bent the direction of denazification towards the goals of Allied occupation. It predominantly focused on public administration, the police, and education, leaving the industrial and political elites largely untouched. On the other hand, the British denazification policy allowed for the continuation of a rehabilitative theme to be pursued, further inculcating the German people with supposed democratic principles. Coinciding with the attempts to rehabilitate the DPs in camps, the British authorities also attempted to rehabilitate most of the German populace within their zone. While these two types of rehabilitation are no doubt dissimilar in many ways, in the end opting for rehabilitation rather than outright exclusion benefited the Allied (and particularly the Anglo-American) goal of ensuring Germany was left leaning towards democracy and not communism. Ultimately, the denazification policy 'began with a bang' and 'died with a whimper', leaving many concerned about the leniency shown towards the less important Nazis in the zone.[46]

The British military government's denazification policies were carried out with a lacklustre attitude which was symptomatic of its inability to stretch its administrative resources to re-educate and democratize the Germans, while at the same time caring for and persuading Polish DPs in the British zone to repatriate. This was a blessing, however, to those Polish DPs who immediately began the task of constructing an educational system for Polish youth stranded in Germany. Throughout the British zone's attempts to enforce the 'four Ds', there was a constant tug-of-war over the British responsibilities and their level of importance: were they to concentrate on the Germans, or on the very visible and increasingly burdensome Polish DPs. Although decentralization, demilitarization, and decartelization were carried out with little to no attention paid to how these processes would affect DPs in the British zone, the manpower required to transform Germany into an Anglo-American vision of democracy was substantial.

Among the abundance of British-run institutions in Germany, those who were tasked with creating an infrastructure capable of caring for DPs and German citizens alike were faced with a daunting commission. On the back of Churchill's promise of 'food and freedom', the Inter-Allied Committee on Post-War Requirements was set up with Sir Frederick Leith-Ross as chairman.[47] Leith-Ross was given the formidable task of ensuring that food and medical supplies would reach Europe at the end of the war. The impetus behind the creation of this committee eventually led to the creation of UNRRA, and the exclusion of Germans from its remit. In the British zone in May 1945, however, there were numerous organizations vying for control over the Germans, the displaced, POWs and ex-POWs and everyone else in between. After the dissolution of the Supreme Headquarters Allied Expeditionary Forces (SHAEF) in July 1945, the Control Commission for Germany (CCG) British Element, the largest of all occupying powers and a veritable super-bureaucracy, alongside UNRRA's European regional office headed by Leith-Ross and the British Army of the

Rhine headed by Field Marshal Montgomery (or Monty), were charged with overseeing the zone. The sheer complexity of the British occupational apparatus was overwhelming and led to an overlapping of duties between the military, Foreign Office, and UNRRA officials. The plethora of organizational charts detailing the flow of command for the abovementioned organizations is baffling. Adding to the complexity of the British occupation forces was former SHAEF Deputy Chief of Staff Lieutenant General Sir Frederick Morgan, who later became Chief of Operations for the UNRRA mission in Germany. Morgan and Monty had a complex relationship which proved somewhat problematic in an already strained and understaffed zone where disagreements over who should and could take care of all tasks associated with DPs abounded.[48]

Overshadowing the problems of the British occupational apparatus was a clear and decisive change in Britain's global standing. As one of the 'Big Three', Britain expected to take its place among the superpowers in a victorious post-war world. Yet its incumbent financial issues were restrictive on the home front as well as in operations abroad, and nowhere was this more decisively felt than in the British-occupied Germany. For the British, the most urgent priority was security against a resurgence of German aggression and alleviation of the financial burden of providing for their zone in Germany, which had been restricted by industrial impotence. While British planning committees spent an inordinate amount of time discussing the problems of German industrial capacity, basic sustenance soon became the most visible problem in the north-west corner.

'Better off' under democracy? Germans' reactions to British occupation

In January 1945, questions about food distribution and the consequences for public health were beginning to be debated at length in Anglo-American circles. One of the biggest priorities looming over the Allies was to ensure that there could be no repeat of the influenza epidemic that had occurred after the First World War. It was made very plain that medical attention was to be prioritized for those among the occupation forces in Germany and the DPs, with the Germans a secondary thought. Similarly, when asked about the allocation of food supplies, the deputy of the Public Health Branch of SHAEF's G5 Division, Colonel Wilson, responded, 'The question is, how much can you cut the German down and keep him breathing. How much do we dare cut him down'?[49]

Providing adequate foodstuffs became the British zone's principal problem, and the issue continued until the economic fusion of the US and British zones into Bizonia in 1947. In addition to providing enough food for the German inhabitants of the zone, the British military authorities were also responsible for the millions of expellees who had now crowded into the zone, as well as the DPs. Due to the uncertain numbers of Germans arriving week by week from the east as a result of *Operation Swallow*, shipping demand was also increasingly difficult to predict. The occupation plans produced during the war had failed to conceive of such problems, and the shortages soon worsened due to the USSR's unwillingness to allow any free movement of foodstuffs from their own predominantly agricultural zone.[50] During a meeting in 1945 with a delegation from Save Europe Now, Clement Attlee, the British prime minister, blamed the USSR for the shortage of foodstuffs in the British zone as they had disrupted the already-established pattern of supply.[51] The British therefore had to rely on large amounts imported from the US zone, the United States, and Britain itself.

The food shortages aggravated relationships throughout the zone, particularly between the British authorities and German civilians. The British lacked any desire to show the Germans what they were doing to help them rebuild their lives and maintain stability. Barbara Marshall asserted that 'much could have been achieved by the regular flow of information', yet the British government considered 'running the country' its main task, not propaganda. Consequently, rumours spread regarding the outrageously luxurious rations DPs were receiving at the expense of the Germans, and resentment towards the occupiers and jealousy of the DPs grew.[52]

As detailed in SHAEF's *Guide to the Care of Displaced Persons in Germany*, the original ration scales developed for the British zone prioritized DPs over Germans, with foodstuffs to be requisitioned from German sources. The British military government's orders were to 'ensure that the maximum use is made of indigenous resources [and] where indigenous supplies are insufficient to meet the needs of both United Nations displaced persons and the German population, United Nations displaced persons will be given first priority'.[53] The food situation soon reached crisis point, however, with the realization that not enough foodstuffs existed in the heavily industrial British zone to provide for either the DPs or the Germans. Without basic sustenance, it was thought, the very idea of democracy would be in jeopardy. A May 1946 Cabinet Office memorandum lays out the problem of the food shortage in the British zone in twenty points. Detailing the miserable state of affairs and taking into consideration the present situation and the situation if imports were to be reduced, the author concludes:

> If food imports cease, all economic activity in the British Zone will come to a stop. The Germans in the zone will starve rapidly, apart from the farm population. If food imports are reduced by one-half our requirements, the economic life of our zone must be put on a care and maintenance basis. Only those services could be maintained which are essential to do this and to maintain the Forces of Occupation. The Germans in our zone would starve, but more gradually.[54]

The situation was dire: the French, US, and Soviet zones were also suffering from food shortages, but not of this magnitude. There were two dominant fears among the British. The first was that the only groups benefiting from this food shortage were the Nazis and the Communists. The Nazi sympathizers in the British zone had begun their 'whispering campaigns' that denigrated the British declaration of democratic values, whereas the Communists compared life in the British zone to life in the Soviet zone, concluding that 'the food crisis is due to British maladministration', eagerly planting seeds of doubt regarding a democratic Germany. Both were damaging to the whole occupation operation in the British zone, and both condemned the new idea of democracy; as the report conceded, '[if] after a year of the democratic experiment and British administration, starvation is the result, they will be well advised to reject both democracy and the Western way of life'.[55] There was no escaping the political repercussions that would follow German citizens under British control coming close to starvation, and cases of hunger oedema were already being reported across Germany.[56] The second fear was that the supply of foodstuffs to DPs had been calculated based on a certain proportion coming from German sources. Although the majority of calories for the DPs were supplied by imports, 150 calories came from the Germans, and according to Danylyszyn, even though the German contribution was comparatively small it 'was a difficult burden to bear for an increasing German population whose members were being asked to subsist upon the semi-starvation ration of 1,500 calories per day'.[57] If German rations were lowered further to a meagre 1,000 calories per day, issues of nutritional well-being would become a great concern. The cumulative effect on how DPs were perceived, as a result of being the benefactors of the German population's starvation rations, would be disastrous.

The effect accumulated. The British authorities recognized that the existing foodstuffs would not be enough, and that proposals to end imports or reduce them by half would mean almost certain death for many of the zone's inhabitants. Yet, the crisis also made the British reassess who was in their zone and why. The continued presence of many Polish DPs only consolidated the British belief that, in contrast to the other groups in the zone, this was the one group that could be moved out of the zone with relatively few complications. Those who would remain all had, according to the British, legitimate reasons to stay or had only newly arrived in the zone from the 'Recovered Territories'. It soon became a question of where the burden could be lifted most easily, and to the British, the Polish DPs were the obvious answer.

The food situation exacerbated all perceivable weaknesses in the British zone. Had this mass of humanity descended upon a fully functioning economy its resources would undoubtedly have been strained, and the British were being asked to 'accomplish this task in the context of a country which had been rendered semi-derelict by war and then partitioned as the price of defeat'. Adding insult to injury, the German population had been cut off from its food-producing regions as a 'new Poland' was carved from the debris, and there was little hope that these Polish farmers would readily agree to diverting their scarce resources to feed the Germans.[58] Indeed, the 'ruins' of Germany were certainly to be found in the British zone. The lack of food caused decreased productivity in the already insufficiently running industrial plants, and absenteeism soon became common. Rather quickly, the black market became king. This unofficial reliance of many Germans on black-market activities was not part of the new democratic vision that the British occupation authorities wanted to get across to the defeated Germans. The British nutritionist A. P. Meiklejohn believed that if the Germans were not receiving the officially sanctioned rations this was due to 'the inability or unwillingness of the German authorities to control the black market', and not due to food being diverted to other groups.[59] The black market came to be the predominant symbol of DP criminality, with Jacobmeyer stating that 'black market activity was synonymous with DP crime', although he concedes that 'the active complicity of Germans was an indispensable condition for the functioning of the black market'.[60] In an effort to reduce black-market activities, the British relied on disbanding the residual groups of DPs rather than restricting the activities themselves through policing. Once again they focused on the Poles, believing them to be the biggest group of black marketeers; but due to the lack of British manpower and the fact that most of the supplies misappropriated were UNRRA goods, UNRRA was ultimately handed the task of curtailing black-market activities. As will be discussed, many UNRRA welfare workers relied on the black market to supplement the goods for distribution. Consequently, as quickly as policies to reduce trading appeared, they just as quickly faded into obscurity.

In the US zone, as well as among the Germans themselves, Jewish DPs attracted the most attention when involved in the black market. It was generally thought this was due to their 'predisposition' as savvy businessmen or criminals, or a mixture of the two.[61] Whereas in the British zone it was the Polish DPs who attracted the most attention, adding to their 'undesirable' label which would further impede their chances of resettling outside Poland's borders.[62] The Poles frequently drew what Jaroszyńska-Kirchmann believes to be 'disproportionate attention from the German authorities and press'.[63] Unfortunately, although certain Polish elements were thought to be frequently at fault, the German authorities consciously exaggerated publicity about Polish DP criminality in Germany, labelling them a 'social scourge' that would bring ordinary Germans down to their level.[64] Indeed, as Lieutenant General Sir Frederick Morgan, as director of UNRRA operations in Germany, conceded in June 1946, 'while UNRRA is of course indulging in illicit trade of all kinds, it is not doing so to any greater extent than anybody else in Germany and indeed in Europe in General'.[65] By mid-1946, Germany, and the rest of Europe, had become reliant on black-market dealings, but regardless of this admission that it was a widespread and far-reaching practice, the Polish DPs in the British zone retained the 'criminal' label.

The establishment of a democratic Germany was a continuous concern for the Foreign Office. There was a pervading fear that the shortage of foodstuffs would hinder any attempts at democratization, and a belief that 'democracy, as known in the West, could not be built on hunger'.[66] The idea of rationing in Britain to help those in Europe had been proposed as early as October 1945, with Arthur Salter arguing in a House of Commons debate that Britain should 'help the hungry people in Europe from our stocks before increasing rations'.[67] Salter was proposing a continuation rather than a further reduction of rationing in Britain, and thus when bread rationing was introduced in Britain in the summer of 1946 dissatisfaction about feeding those in Europe grew. To many it was inconceivable that further rationing would be brought in for the victors. In an article on 28 June 1946 the *Gloucestershire Echo* summarized the widespread British resentment succinctly:

> The Government has come to a decision which this country never had to take during two world wars, even when the submarine attacks were at their worst and supply ships were being sunk on a big scale. [. . .] It is a decision which will cause grave anxiety and bewilderment, and one which will be accepted with much reluctance. [. . .] Since 1939 the British public has had to put up with manifold inconveniences. This is the worst of all.[68]

The view from the British Homefront was one of increasing exasperation as Britons began to feel their efforts to supply Germans with foodstuffs were in vain, and many did not understand why the victors were introducing bread rationing after the end of the war to help the war's protagonists re-establish their economy. Simultaneously the CCG British Element established from intelligence reports that the Germans were not all that grateful for these sacrifices, and the principal assumption was that they were being punished.[69] Amid these frustrations were the DPs, who were reliant on foreign imports to sustain them for the most part but had been part of the reason to introduce bread rationing in Britain in 1946. According to Reinisch, health officers in Germany were officially instructed to give priority to 'Allied nationals and non-German displaced persons, before considering the requirements of the German population'.[70] By July 1946, however, the situation had become so dire that the ration levels in the British zone's DP camps began to mirror those of the German population. The result was much dissatisfaction and increased antagonism among all groups.

The situation was only alleviated towards the end of 1946 through trade agreements with the US and Soviet zones, as well as a more fruitful harvest in Britain itself. Ultimately, it was only with the introduction of the US European Recovery Program, or Marshall Plan, that the pressure on food supplies in the British zone was finally eased. The Marshall Plan was based on one very definite principle: that economic aid would be provided to Europe as a collective, with no further US loans to individual European countries. Of course, by providing aid as a collective the United States also intended to foster some democratic ideals alongside economic integration. The result was a rather poor set of negotiations throughout 1947 that left the rift between East and West larger than ever as any chance of a pan-European economic recovery programme was lost. By the time the Marshall Plan was officially signed into existence by President Truman in April 1948, the British ability to wield power on an international scale was becoming increasingly restricted and, Britain had become heavily economically dependent on the United States. Additionally, the German attitude towards the British occupation authorities had been severely soured by the shortage of foodstuffs: as Lord Beveridge summarized, it had become 'misery generating hate'.[71]

Throughout the ongoing battle for the British authorities to keep the Germans fed, the DPs in the camps and transit centres were also suffering shortages. UNRRA was meant to assume full control of the DP camps; however, due to having over-promised the number of personnel who would be ready to start work in Germany in 1945, UNRRA reluctantly took on a subordinate role to the military government.[72] UNRRA relied on military intervention for the supply of goods, consequently putting an even greater strain on the British military. As the strain grew to disastrous proportions in Spring 1946, both those in the British zone under military command and those working for UNRRA searched for answers on how to alleviate the problem of too many mouths and not enough food. As indicated earlier, the blame rested on DPs refusing to repatriate, and in particular on the Poles, whose refusal to repatriate was not seen as legitimate.

A brief departure from the norm: Establishing international humanitarianism

The advent of UNRRA in 1943 was heralded as the first truly international effort at humanitarianism. It was believed that once the war ended UNRRA would be able to usher in a new era of post-war international humanitarianism that would become the established norm among the Allied nations, rather than relying on a few select charitable relief agencies and philanthropic individuals and societies. Before the advent of the Second World War, after a major conflict military governance had primarily been used as means of sorting and assessing the damage to a particular place and its people. It was never envisaged that the military would care for injured, homeless, and sick civilians, but only for those classed as POWs. Yet when UNRRA was unable to dispatch teams on the ground at the rate originally promised to General Eisenhower by its first director general, Herbert Lehman, the military had to step in to pick up the slack. Consequently, the provisions made for Europe's DPs were different to those envisaged prior to the war's end. This undoubtedly affected the DP groups in camps in Germany. Although it is accepted among UNRRA scholars that UNRRA's bureaucratic inefficiency was one of the main reasons for the organization's ineptitude, the practical effects of UNRRA's ideals being cut short have not been assessed with regard to specific DP groups. Polish DPs in particular, who were the focus of much scorn from the military authorities, came under extra pressure. Had the organizational apparatus of UNRRA lived up to expectations and the rule of command between military authorities and civilians been adhered to, the experiences of Polish DPs in the British zone could arguably have been different.

UNRRA's ultimate downfall, according to Michael Marrus, was the 'perpetual subordination of UNRRA to the Allied armies'.[73] This theme is repeated throughout contemporary records of UNRRA's welfare workers, administrators, and creators as well as those of later UNRRA scholars. Although

UNRRA was created with the intention of relieving the military authorities of any civilian-related burden, the practicality was far from the reality. UNRRA was subject to an almost constant process of improvisation, as the Europe they had planned for only existed on paper and the situation on the ground was far more complex than predicted. As Jessica Reinisch notes, its constant subordination to the military authorities 'meant a severe limitation of UNRRA's supposedly vast scope and promise, far from the notion of an all-powerful organization dreamt up as an answer to the problems of mass displacement and the limitations of existing piecemeal solutions'.[74] As time passed and the entanglement of bureaucratic red tape was gradually alleviated by Commander Robert Jackson, UNRRA had already passed its point of usefulness, according to the American and British public, and its legacy, among its contemporaries, was left in ruins.

The fanfare that accompanied the opening of UNRRA was to signal a grand alliance between international actors for the benefit of those who were truly in need of humanitarian assistance. Yet from a British point of view, the catalyst for Britain's membership in UNRRA was arguably more the result of a desire to 'keep up appearances' than due to humanitarian motives. Britain's post-war economic situation was far from favourable, and while rationing continued and the average citizen was bombarded with Ministry of Food propaganda posters, Britain had agreed to become UNRRA's second-biggest contributor. Consequently, as early as June 1945 it was agreed in relation to the 'refugees' in the British zone that expenditure should be restricted and reduced if possible.[75] This is not to demean or diminish the humanitarian motives of individuals in the British government who supported UNRRA, such as the Chief Economic Advisor Frederick Leith-Ross. There were many who welcomed the advent of UNRRA with open arms and in some circles this international humanitarian cooperation was seen as long overdue. Britain, however, had become very aware of its own precarious position in international politics, and as a member of the 'Big Three' it had a certain reputation to uphold. UNRRA was the pinnacle of international cooperation, and Britain's co-leading role was an effort to reassert its global power. In practice, Britain's attempt to hold on to its pre-war status as a global superpower was rather futile, as economic instability underwrote the country's retreat from globalism. This reality, however, would not be fully absorbed at Westminster or Whitehall for a very long time.[76] It was becoming clear that the United States was stepping into the spotlight, yet the British were attempting to retain their international prestige as one of the 'Big Three', and with it came total financial culpability for the British zone.

Conclusion

The physical state of post-war Germany undoubtedly hindered any attempts to create a stable and fully functioning environment for its DPs, expellees, and Germans. Among the confusion, the rubble, and the early infrastructure created by the Allies, Polish DPs became one group that made itself immediately distinguishable. After the bulk of the repatriation of Soviet DPs and Westerners had taken place, the British were confronted with a sizeable Polish population jostling for recognition. The military and international organizations were operating as part of an overbearingly bureaucratic machine that overlooked the human element. As tension between the international organizations and the occupying powers grew, the British zone struggled to provide the basic necessities to the myriad of people now under its care. Ultimately, the financial strain on Britain to provide for Polish DPs abroad came to frustrate planners and exasperate those on the ground encouraging repatriation, culminating in the troublesome 'nuisance' label that was so frequently used.

The Allies simply recognized Poles as Poles and not as a collective embodiment of extremely different wartime experiences that came to shape who they were and how they identified themselves. Pre-war Poland was by no means an ethnically homogenous nation: it had been subject to recent territorial shifts and had pursued what the Allies saw as unwarranted policies of territorial aggrandizement against ethnic minorities. By May 1945, according to Czesław Łuczak, a total of 1.9 million citizens of pre-war Poland were in Germany; 1.2 million in the three western zones and 700,000 in the Soviet zone.[77] Yet, this national grouping of 'Poles' in the immediate post-war era according to carefully constructed classifications devised earlier by post-war planners was proving difficult to enforce. The policy of grouping people according to nationality caused havoc in the camps, as some Poles were also Jews, some were Ukrainians, some were Byelorussians, some were of mixed heritage, and some were unsure of their heritage due to their age or loss of their parents or guardians during war. The Poles who found themselves in the British zone of Germany were a product of the Allies' attempts to homogenize a diverse group of people whose identities had become even more confused after further geographical and ideological changes to the Poland they knew. In order to understand why a sizeable number of Polish DPs' rejected the Poland presented to them by the Allies, it is necessary to understand the Poland that was still very much part of their consciousness, identities, and communities before the war, which they had carried with them into peacetime.

2

'A paradoxical people'
Understanding Polish displaced persons

Introduction

If one asks a Pole in Britain, Germany or even the United States about the *Katechizm polskiego dziecka* (Catechism of a Polish child) they can often recite it by heart.[1] Fuelled with religious terminology the *Katechizm* is not a religious verse but rather something that children learn at school.[2] It shows the very real concept of Polishness (*polskość*), a fusion of religiosity and nationalism as it asks children to 'believe in Poland', a land in which they live among their 'own' that was won 'with blood and scars', and for whom they would 'sacrifice' their lives.[3] This combination, termed 'sacral nationalism' by Conor Cruise O'Brien, denotes the intersection of religion and nationalism that becomes heightened when God's will and man's right to a piece of land is disputed, often with bloody consequences. Differing from Emilio Gentile's concept of the sacralization of politics, which focuses on the creation of 'religious dimensions in politics' independent of religious institutions, sacral nationalism focuses on the connection across time and space of a people belonging to 'one moral and spiritual field of force'.[4] In the case of Poland, this is often represented by romantic notions of what and where Poland is, including the common adherence to prominent Polish figures as the very personification of Polishness. In the Polish case, the synthesis of the Polish language, Roman Catholicism, nationalism and disputes over land are almost inseparable, particularly in relation to questions about *who* is Polish. Determining this, and by what criteria, will allow an understanding of where Poland was both physically and ideologically in May 1945, and explain how this affected those in the British zone of occupation.

The end of the war brought with it a surge of Polish nationalism that had been repressed by both Nazis and communists. The Nazis in particular had pursued a methodical policy of repression through terror with the ultimate aim of extinguishing Polishness in every respect.[5] Liberation brought an end to this suppression as feelings of inferiority were erased and an explosion of open displays of Polishness were seen and heard throughout Germany. One Polish DP wrote:

> We have never parted with this flag in the past years of captivity. The enemy put it in the form of red triangles on our chest, in the place where our hearts beat. To humiliate us, the enemy put there only one letter 'P – Pole' – he kept saying it offensively in our face and wanted to disgrace us with this word. But we treated these red triangles as a symbol – the letter 'P' became our pride, and the word 'Pole' was the most beautiful word we could hear in this hated language.[6]

The letter 'P' found on the right lapel of all outer clothing was a stipulation of Germany's *Polenerlasse* (Polish decrees) issued on 8 March 1940. Not wearing this Polish identifier resulted in fines, beatings and sometimes imprisonment. It became the blueprint upon which the Nazis assigned the yellow Star of David for Jews and the Ost symbol for members of the Soviet Union, including Ukrainians. The preceding quote from a former concentration camp prisoner living in a DP camp in Germany captures how some Poles retained a highly charged emotional attachment to their purple and yellow diamonds with the letter 'P' (see Figure 2.1). For them, they were not a symbol of disgrace, but rather of recognition of a Polish purity that cannot be tempered by Nazi aggression.

Figure 2.1 Polen abzeichen (Polish badge) worn by Poles on outer clothing. Source: Imperial War Museum.

Poland had struggled for recognition as an independent state since the fall of the Polish-Lithuanian Commonwealth in 1795. The Second Polish Republic, the era commonly referred to as *Niepodległość* (independence) had only just come to fruition in the interwar years. The British, unwilling and at times unable to comprehend the complexities of Polishness, soon found that the war had only consolidated the Poles' faith in the homeland. The committees that formed in the Polish DP camps early on used the morally just rhetoric of the nineteenth-century Romantic tradition to deepen the resentment among the remaining Polish DPs towards the USSR. Their strong anti-Soviet and anti-communist rhetoric was a product of having enjoyed the brief experience of freedom during the interwar years, making them even more adamant that Poland would never be ruled by outside influences again. Within the camps the development of Polish identity, or Polishness, was defined by cultural ties, language, customs and religion, but also by determination to see Poland revived and free of oppression. The social composition of the camps influenced the DPs' vision of Polishness as Poland's pre-war elite claimed moral and political leadership, often conferring their version of Polishness onto the non-elite. This chapter discusses Polish nationhood in a particular microcosm constructed by a specific section of society that was largely ostracized by the new communist government for political reasons, and which actively continued its pre-war conception of Polishness in the camps.

* * *

In order to understand the construction of Polishness among the Polish DP community in the British zone, and why this led to their outright rejection of the Poland presented to them in 1945 by the Allies, the recent history of Poland, its people, the in- and out-going migrations, the cultural and social development, the turmoil between 1939 and 1945 and the ways in which Polishness survived all have to be understood. The territorial shifts, their inhabitants, the number of Poles found outside Poland's borders at the end of the war and the reasons for their displacement all contribute to the consolidation of Polishness that became an emotive and prominent feature of the Polish DP camps. This chapter does not attempt to give a rigid and specific definition of what it is to be Polish, or of Polish identity. It does not argue that there is one all-encompassing concept of what it means to be Polish, nor are there set criteria by which Poles can be classified. Although it recognizes consistent components of Polish identity that led to the creation of the Polish camp communities in 1945, this chapter argues that Polish identity is, at best, fluid. Borrowing from Benedict Anderson's concept of 'imagined communities' and employing ideas of sacral nationalism, it is argued here that the Polish DP camp community's fluidity was in a constant state of development, collapse, evolution, devolution, clashes, agreements and separations. It was an ongoing process with no harmonious synchronization between all those deemed to be Polish, as issues of class, religion, and traditions were constantly in contention.[7]

For those who could not face returning to a Poland they did not recognize as their home, rejection of repatriation became the key link uniting Polish DPs in the camps.[8] The actors who belonged to the ruling powers were not all oppressive, yet they all helped to shape the lives of Polish DPs in the post-war world for better or worse. Britain's involvement in Poland's independence in 1918 had been championed in Poland, yet in Britain it was cast in a different light as Prime Minister David Lloyd George deemed that Poles were nothing more than 'children that gave trouble', claiming that 'Poland was drunk with the new wine of liberty supplied to her by the Allies'.[9] Although Britain's stance towards Poland could initially be perceived as negative, the situation was diplomatically fraught as fear that Britain would take Poland's side against Russia from 1919 to 1921 caused a bitter taste at home. After Poland had defeated Russia, however, the relationship between Britain and Poland grew closer. Britain's promise to protect Poland if it were attacked was upheld in 1939. Yet the special relationship that was meant to bloom between the two was abruptly brought to a halt as the British signed the Yalta and Potsdam agreements and ignored the principles of the Atlantic Charter. Polish DPs felt betrayed by the British, and this chapter therefore seeks to understand the British role in the creation of this pocket of Polonia. The inability of military officials and welfare workers to understand the diversity of Poles in exile was, at best, ignorant.

Polishness between the partitions and *Niepodległość*

The Second Polish Republic was formed at the end of the First World War as the Prussian, Russian, and Habsburg empires fell and the dreams of Poles who had been championing a free Poland for over a century were finally realized. The creation of this new and free Poland took place amid a backdrop of infighting, border disputes, and yet more war, this time with neighbours to the east. While some Poles who had previously left under the nineteenth century's Great Emigration came back to Poland to help with the task of spreading Polishness across the newly formed nation-state driven by a binding patriotic duty, Britain looked on with ambivalence bordering on distaste. Amid cries that Poland was 'a farce', 'a historic failure' and, according to Lloyd George, had 'won her freedom not by her own exertions but by the blood of others', Norman Davies asserted that 'rarely, if ever, has a newly independent country been subject to such eloquent and gratuitous abuse'.[10] *Niepodległość*, or independence, became synonymous with the Second Polish Republic. It was the culmination of Poland's poetically inspired Romantic tradition central to the deification of bards such as Adam Mickiewicz. Polish nationalism, it seems, was derived from a developed character, part of a personal identity, which flourished in opposition to suppression from the partitioning powers.

The Poland that emerged from the end of the First World War and the collapse of the partitioning powers was by no means a homogenous nation: it was multinational and multi-confessional. The end of the partitions left a legacy of individual rule. Aside from having eighteen registered political parties, multiple administrative centres, three legal codes, an army that could be commanded in one of four languages, and six currencies in circulation at once, it was also almost impossible to travel the length of the country by rail.[11] Officially the legal rights of all citizens, irrespective of origin, nationality, race, language or religion were protected by the Little Treaty of Versailles. Signed on the same day as the Treaty of Versailles, the Little Treaty (or Polish Minority Treaty) granted Poland independence and protected the freedom of all its peoples. In practice, however, Poland was directed towards becoming a nation-state, and those who were not self-declared Polish were equally fervent about their identity, be it Jewish, German, Belarussian or Ukrainian.

National censuses in 1921 and 1931 showed that the Second Polish Republic was dominated by Polish-speaking, Roman Catholic, ethnic Poles who accounted for just over two-thirds of the population. In an area that would come to push the concept of Polishness as a national identity with specific signifiers of ethnocultural belonging, it is hard to ignore the fact that almost a third of the Republic was largely comprised of non-Poles with their own sets of beliefs, traditions, and languages.[12] Although the censuses had their uses, the results cannot be accepted without reservation due to the former census entirely missing the regions of Upper Silesia and Vilnius with many in other regions describing their considered nationality as merely 'local' or '*tutejsi*' ('from here'), and the latter accused of forging returns to minimize the presence of a distinct Ukrainian community along the eastern borderlands.[13] Of course describing their nationality as 'local' was very telling in itself. After years of border disputes, ongoing occupations by armies, wars, collapsing partitions, and migratory movements, many simply did not want to tell a Polish official conducting a census that they did not consider themselves Polish, whereas others may have thought of themselves as both Polish and Ruthenian, or Polish and Lithuanian. In an ethnographer's recorded oral interview with a shoemaker in Kaunas in 1885, the shoemaker said that his 'tribe' was Catholic. When pressed for detail and asked whether he was a Pole or a Lithuanian, he replied that he was both. The researcher, dumbfounded by this answer, pressed further: 'That is impossible. You have to be either one or the other', and the shoemaker replied, 'I speak Polish, and I also speak Lithuanian'.[14] These blurred lines between various nationalities and cultures continued into the *Niepodległość* years, Catholicism sometimes being the only link to their 'tribe' that was worth noting for people like the shoemaker.

Upper Silesia and Vilnius were also contentious areas of Polishness due to the former containing a large proportion of German-speaking inhabitants and the latter enduring an ongoing territorial battle as to whether it was Polish or Lithuanian.[15] These were classifications that would also be used to dominate groupings in the DP camps in 1945. Although a Polish liaison officer might deem someone from Vilnius to be Polish, as the capital was subsumed into the Second Polish Republic between 1920 and 1939, by 1945 the borders had changed, and Vilnius was Lithuanian. The Allies found these discrepancies between nationalities and citizenship hard to understand, especially when, for British and Americans in particular, nationality was synonymous with citizenship.

Consequently, the idea of Polishness was constantly in the making. It was an imagined community with often clashing and overlapping concepts of nationhood, religious affiliations, class divisions, mother-tongues and much more. Although Anderson intended all nations to be made up of imagined communities, for Poles the concept was much more tangible, as their very community was only held together by this constantly evolving and adapting concept of Polishness. The nuances of these varied peoples were lost amid the over-arching concept of Polishness that gradually came to be enforced throughout the period of *Niepodległość* which adhered to a concept of sacral nationalism entrenched in traditionalism. This was overwhelmingly prescribed to by the elites, the gentry, the intelligentsia, and the state itself as a means of overwriting the diversity of modes of self-identification with the uniformity of Polishness. Cultural sensitivities were further emphasized through a marked difference in economic stature: the primary social division was not linguistic or even religious, but economic. The population was predominantly made up of peasants and workers, with only a small minority classed as intelligentsia, gentry or bourgeoisie. This came to be seen as a remnant of feudalism that Poland was struggling to cope with as it very slowly industrialized its landscape. According to the occupational structure of Poland in the 1921 census, 64 per cent of the population were peasants, 10 per cent were agricultural labourers, and the remaining 26 per cent comprised professionals, intelligentsia, the industrial proletariat, entrepreneurs, and landowners.[16] Within this framework the population was constantly at odds with one another regarding their vision of the Polish nation now that they had gained independence. Using a combination of ethnocultural symbolism and intense religiosity, the intelligentsia influenced the thinking of the people (*lud*) by promoting their inclusion in this new Poland as a country that thrived on every ordinary Pole's contribution to its freedom.[17]

This raises a further point about the composition of Poland and the very idea of Polishness that was consolidating throughout the period of *Niepodległość*. Like many other migrations throughout the nineteenth and early twentieth centuries, people from partitioned Poland were forced to migrate for economic reasons. The main drive of the Great Emigration (*Wielka Emigracja*) at the end of the nineteenth century was primarily made up of those seeking economic opportunities who largely moved to Great Britain, France, and Belgium.[18] For the vast majority of the emigrants, the Poland they longed for while constructing their pocket of Polonia abroad was a land of memories, reminiscences of childhood, and inculcated familial beliefs. As strong as the connection might have been, the great majority of those who emigrated for economic reasons did not return. In Germany this amounted to a densely Polish and Masurian population in the west, particularly in the Ruhr valley.[19]

This picture of an ideal Poland and what it meant to be Polish was not formulated by the everyday folk, the peasants, the migrants, and those generally on the lower stratum of society. It was created by the 'great exiles', often escaping persecution after a series of failed uprisings throughout the nineteenth century, who fostered this idea of Polishness from outside the country. As Ernest Renan stated, 'a nation's existence is a daily plebiscite, just as an individual's existence is a perpetual affirmation of life'.[20] Choosing to take part in this nation and in the constant reaffirmation of where and what Poland is was a task often left to artistic and highly politicized artisans such as Adam Mickiewicz, Tomasz Zan, Juliusz Słowacki, and Zygmunt Krasiński. In exile they produced a 'national' culture that would have an everlasting effect upon the creation of Poland as an independent state in 1918. Therefore, when Poland finally claimed its sovereignty at the end of partitioned rule, Polishness was once again something that was repeatedly inculcated from above and not below. The majority of Poles held allegiance in spirit with Poland, but economic factors would soon drive migration westward once more. These same mechanisms were reinforced in the DP camps in the post-war years as Poles took on a very active role in the community, quickly erecting committees for every possible need. As one UNRRA welfare worker, Rhoda Dawson, stated, 'working with Poles was something like working with Jews; their own organization was exceedingly active'; yet it too was dominated by elites.[21] The creation, moulding, structuring, and reshaping of the pattern of Polishness was consistently led by elite Poles in the DP camps just as it had been throughout the partitions, predominantly by those in exile, and throughout the *Niepodległość* years by leading figures. It is hardly surprising that the period of 1945–89 has come to be known as the Second Great Emigration (*Druga Wielka Emigracja*).[22]

Gradually, throughout the twenty-one years of *Niepodległość* the idea of a stereotypical Pole, whose main attributes were a common faith and language, became the standard for understanding who was a Pole and who was an 'other'. Yet as Timothy Snyder claims, this hegemonic state was not fully recognized after 1918. He argues that it was only with the organized violence of the Second World War and through 'deportations, genocide, and ethnic cleansing' destroying entire areas and emptying 'multicultural cities' that the path towards modern nationalism was cleared.[23] The cultural construct of the Pole that had constantly been re-imagined since Mickiewicz's era was then set up in sharp opposition to the Nazi and Communist threats during and after the Second World War. Consequently the Poles found in DP camps were largely the product of these re-imagined concepts of Poles and Polishness. To fit the criteria, one had to proclaim undying love for a Poland that had only briefly existed, the product of increased ethnocultural homogenization, and, for some, had only truly existed in their imagination.

It was during these years of independence that the peasant-Pole came to be recognized as a key component of the struggle for a true Poland, and against the backdrop of the political and economic crises during the 1930s, Polish peasant parties gained strength and support. With a strong agenda driven by the elite's increased intellectual fixation on the 'rest' of society known as *chłopomania* (peasant-mania), these parties were mostly led by elites. The new peasant parties generated the idea of holistic inclusion in the construction of Poland, even though in reality the peasant masses had very little to do with politics. Parties often used the return of those who had emigrated during the nineteenth-century migration movements as a cause for celebrating Polishness, lauding them as true Poles who had returned to replenish the biological stock in the name of a truly independent and free Poland.[24] At the same time many poorer Poles, most of whom were at the lower end of the social strata and struggling with increasing poverty, were emigrating from Poland to surrounding European countries due to economic hardship.[25] Promises of land reform made by the *Polskie Stronnictwo Ludowe* (PSL), or Polish Peasants/People's Party, were greeted enthusiastically by those experiencing hardship. Even though over 2.5 million hectares were passed into peasant hands between 1919 and 1938, this did little to alleviate the increasing poverty and, despite these achievements, rural conditions deteriorated leaving many with the only option of migration.[26]

The elites in Polish society took an increased interest in the poor as economic conditions worsened; public writing competitions flourished as social memoirs became a new way of understanding a specific social group through a typical depiction of one person's situation.[27] These competitions, however, rarely penetrated the deeper social problems plaguing Poland. Class- and ethnicity-based conflicts, in particular, increased as the formation of Polishness became more insulated from peripheral ideas and cultures. As Katherine Lebow asserts, 'in many ways, the Polish citizenry that had come into being with independence was more notional than actual'. The gap between small urbanized elites and the peasant masses was a virtual continuation of social divisions in the pre-1918 period and, if anything, grew wider throughout the 1930s. It was as if the 'two closed worlds lived side by side: the upper and the lower [*góra i doły*]'.[28] Social memoirs, sometimes referred to as 'the Polish method' outside of Poland, flourished in the post-war era and were seen as a legitimate way of dealing with a traumatic past, some competitions drawing thousands of entries. They were also used to promote the idea of class-advancement brought about through post-war circumstances, often using social practices taken from *Niepodległość* for the benefit of legitimizing communism.[29] These memoir-based competitions also opened the floodgates to the wider Polonia, helping Poles exiled in the diaspora to commemorate their own sense of enforced victimhood.

Ultimately, conceptions of Polishness created during the partitions as well as throughout the years of *Niepodległość* were designed by elites to bring about territorial and political change. In the case of the former, Polishness was created by Poland's romantic bards, who eventually held an almost deified position in the latter's formation of a new independent state. These manifestations of true Polishness were consistently reinforced through infighting in Central and Eastern Europe, and no more so than during the Polish-Soviet war.

The 'Quarrels of the Pygmies' and the declaration of war

The inherent social and economic problems of a Poland basking in its newly acquired freedom after 123 years of partitions were entangled with other geographical, spatial, and ideological battles that eventually erupted as armed conflict. Six wars were fought concurrently between 1918 and 1921, but the war that had the largest impact within and beyond Poland's borders was the Polish-Soviet war.[30] The other wars were fuelled by territorial and border disputes, but the Polish-Soviet war was different; it was provoked by a clash of ideologies that threatened the very existence of Europe.[31]

Winston Churchill commented on the night of the Armistice that 'the war of the giants has ended; the quarrels of the pygmies have begun'. As Western Europe enjoyed peace and prepared the ground for the Treaty of Versailles, Poland, headed by Józef Piłsudski, prepared to prevent the spread of communism.[32] The British government, although sympathetic to Poland's hunger for independence, could not agree to Poland's annexation of territories such as Vilnius and East Galicia. Thus, due to a combination of factors in Britain including inadequate Cabinet support, a weakened economic infrastructure, and turmoil on the home front, the ever-dangling carrot of British assistance was never fully grasped. It was through the leadership of Piłsudski and his colonels that Poland succeeded in asserting their independence after the Miracle on the Vistula (*Cud nad Wisłą*), deifying Piłsudski after his death in 1935 to an extent that could only be matched by figures such as Mickiewicz.

The Miracle on the Vistula, however, did much more than save the people of Warsaw: it was another affirmation of the fruition of the Romantic concept of Polishness. Poland had defeated its former oppressors and thereby managed to consolidate its place in Europe. The British were equally relieved to have avoided armed conflict and still maintain a relationship with Poland. The British ambassador to Berlin at the time, Lord D'Abernon, summed up the collective sense of relief: 'The Battle of Tours saved our ancestors from the Yoke of the Koran; it is probable that the Battle of Warsaw saved Central, and parts of Western Europe from a more subversive danger – the fanatical tyranny of the Soviet'.[33] Piłsudski's colonels continued his legacy after his death, but his idea of a *Międzymorze* (intermarium) a federation of Central and Eastern European countries, was actively ignored by the larger Polish populace who adopted his rival's conception of an ethnically homogenous Poland (*Narodowa Demokracja*). Active opposition to Soviet dominance became an integral part of Polish identity leading up to the outbreak of the Second World War. Although the British were aware of Polish-Soviet tensions, interested parties often sent reports to the Foreign Office to dispel any myths that another war would break out between Poland and Russia. In 1927, A. G. Marshall, a tradesman travelling abroad, sent a memorandum to the Minister for Poland, Sir Max Muller, in Warsaw. Marshall claimed that there was a calmness in the Polish attitude towards Russia, and that 'the Poles feel, and rightly so, that they are far in advance of Russia'. Although Marshall had a vested interest in Russia for trade purposes, this memorandum reinforced an ill-informed viewpoint that Polish-Russian relations were improving. Marshall cited the primary reason as the lack of westernization in Russia compared to Poland and concluded that 'for many years to come the most stable factor in E.Europe [sic] will be Poland and not Russia'.[34]

In the foreign theatre, Colonel Beck, serving as Foreign Minister in Poland from 1932 to 1939, had spent the latter years in office conducting a balancing act to stave off Nazi and Soviet aggression. As the pieces began to tumble, Britain, with France's reinforcement of the Franco-Polish alliance from 1921, offered a guarantee to Poland on 31 March 1939 that they would do 'everything possible' to resist an attack by Germany on Poland's independence. Although this guarantee has been construed largely as an attempt to stop Hitler rather than as a gesture of friendship to Poland, it was the re-ignition of Poland and Britain's 'brothers-in-arms' status that would come to mean a great deal more in the post-war world. The Permanent Under-Secretary for Foreign Affairs, Sir Alex Cadogan, later admitted in his diary that the proclamation was no guarantee that Britain would help Poland, reminiscing that 'you might say that it was cynical . . . perhaps it was. But it *did* bring us into the war'.[35] When the Nazis attacked Poland, Britain declared war on Germany and Neville Chamberlain announced that Britain and France were fulfilling their obligations by 'going to the aid of Poland, who is so bravely resisting this wicked and unprovoked attack on her people'.[36] As news spread on 17 September 1939 that the Soviet Union was attacking Poland from the east before British forces were anywhere close to providing physical aid to Poland, the Chief of the Imperial General Staff, Sir Edmund Ironside, implored the War Cabinet to realize the seriousness of Russia's action. Alongside the Secretary of State for War, Lord Hore-Belisha, they expressed the view that 'the Empire was faced with a situation of grave peril . . . the country should be stirred to make far greater efforts and submit far greater sacrifices', but ultimately Britain would not go to war with the Soviet Union.[37] The Soviet occupation of Poland in 1939 held implications, although these were not entirely clear in 1939, of long-term border and population changes, with a prolonged period of resettlement. The *Niepodległość* years had officially ended. Yet the Polish spirit and the very conception of Polishness that had been shaped and reinforced during this period would have a much longer legacy.

Occupied Poland: The fourth partition

Poland fought against the Nazi invasion; however, resisting the sheer might of Germany's war machine was too much without physical Allied support. On 28 September 1939, Warsaw surrendered to German forces and the first mass of Polish refugees, primarily politicians and other elites along with the Polish government, crossed the border into Romania and continued to France. The division ran along the rivers Bug and San, with Nazi Germany taking the west side and the Soviet Union taking the east. The so-called fourth partition of Poland had begun, as Nazism and Communism conspired to totally extinguish the 'bastard of Versailles'.[38]

In the east, the Soviet Union split Poland into three: governance of the southern portion, containing Lwów, was handed over to the Ukrainian SSR; the central portion to the Byelorussian SSR; and the northern area, the Vilnius region, was transferred to the Lithuanian Republic before eventually being annexed by the Soviet Union.[39] The western part was split between the regions annexed by Germany: *Reichsgau Wartheland* (including Polish Silesia, Pomerania, greater Poland and the city of Łódź), *Reichsgau Danzig-Westpreußen* (including the port of Danzig/Gdańsk and its surrounding area) and the *General Gouvernement* of the Polish Occupied Territories to be headed by Governor General Hans Frank.[40]

After *Operation Barbarossa* in 1941, the whole of pre-war Poland came under Nazi rule. Each part of Poland, controlled by various Nazi and Soviet forces, witnessed unprecedented cruelty and terror. Villages were razed to the ground, families were separated, men and women were forced into labour, children were Germanized, and Polishness was suppressed once more, as it had been under the 123 years of partitioned rule. The terror knew no limits as the intelligentsia were massacred by Nazis and Soviets alike, concentration camps were erected on Polish soil, and throughout it all the Polish resistance, comprising the biggest underground network of the war, held on to its interwar identity, the very essence of their Polishness.[41] In direct contradiction to this, the Nazis carried out their *Generalplan Ost*, the ethnic cleansing and colonization of Central and Eastern Europe, with increasing veracity.[42] With the exclusion of those considered ethnic Germans, and justifying their action with the idea of racial supremacy, the Nazis divided those under their control into three groups: those targeted for extermination, those considered to be racially inferior but perhaps useful, and those fit for Germanization. The majority of Poles fit in the second group and they were sent to Germany either as forced labourers (*Zwangsarbeiter*) or to annexed territories to create space for German settlers (*Lebensraum*). Worse was to follow, however, as the Polish decrees (*polenerlasse*) of 8 March 1940 curtailed their political, economic, social and cultural rights.[43]

The redrawing of borders after Germany's invasion and the split during the fourth partition were not unwelcome to all. For many Germans in Upper Silesia this was a vindication of the 1921 plebiscite, and some welcomed Germany's control of the territory.[44] Similarly, for those in Vilnius, where ethnic Poles were estimated to have constituted between 79 and 91 per cent of the population in 1944, the opportunity to Lithuanize the city was too good to miss, and the majority of Polish-speaking inhabitants were snubbed by self-proclaimed Lithuanians or deported.[45] In places such as Vilnius, Lithuanization 'must be seen not only in the physical removal of Poles from the city, but also in the elimination of Polish civilization as the urban way of life'.[46] The Nazi *Volksliste* was created to determine which Poles were of suitably Germanic ethnicity to be productive members of the annexed *Reichsgau* territories. The first two categories of the *Volksliste* were classed as suitably German, whether actively or passively embracing their Germanic roots. The third category was seen as a diluted type of German who more closely identified with being Polish, yet to whom conditional German citizenship could be granted. The fourth group were classified as non-Germans, rebels with no ties to their German ancestry.[47] Many Poles from the *Reichsgaue* who were not suitably German, or who were unwilling to become Germanized, were sent as forced labourers to other parts of the Reich, while others were transferred to the *General Gouvernement* and Polish Jews were sent to the Łódź ghetto. Poles were ordered to leave the annexed areas with only a few hours' notice, as one Pole in Gdynia recorded, 'not only must I be ready, but that the flat must be swept, the plates and dishes washed and the keys left in the cupboards, so that the Germans who were to live in my house should have no trouble'.[48] In an odd reversal of fate, the descriptions of orders to leave their homes in the newly annexed German *Reichsgaue* would echo the experiences of Germans in 1945 as they were expelled to western Germany by 'returning' Poles who settled in the 'Recovered Territories' (see Figure 2.2).

Poles living under Nazi occupation were faced with grave economic and social problems, most linked in some way to the provision and acquisition of foodstuffs as rations became increasingly restrictive and economic opportunities limited. By April 1940, only a few food items were unrationed, and the average Pole received

Figure 2.2 Poland's border changes between 1939 and 1945. Source: Created by Samantha K. Knapton.

just 609 calories per day. It was not until the Four-Year Plan was approved, and bread rations dramatically increased, that Polish rations grew to 938 calories per day, although in the same period Jewish rations decreased from 503 to 369 calories per day.[49] Some agricultural forced labourers found themselves in a comparably good situation where their 'employers' allowed them to eat what they ate, but many resorted to stealing to keep starvation at bay. It became a no-win situation: if they were too weak to work the farmers beat or reported them; if they stole and ate food for strength and energy, the farmers beat or reported them if they were caught. Naturally many took the risk, and very few were caught.[50] For those in the labour camps the food situation was even worse, as the Polish labourer Józefa Zalewska Hodorowicz wrote: 'Food was always being stolen. I had a bag with *kasza* [buckwheat groats] that I kept with me all the time tied around my waist with a piece of twine . . . I was always hungry.' Hodorowicz's daughter recounted in her book that 'so many of my mother's most vivid memories during her forced labour years revolved around food – its absence, obtaining it, and holding on to it'.[51] When the British zone was unable to adequately feed its inhabitants a sense of déjà vu descended on the DP camps. Although sustenance levels in the DP camps under British administration never reached the same desperate situation as those in labour camps or occupied Poland, it triggered horrific memories for many Polish DPs, in particular young women who were unable to feed their children adequately. Yet as shown in the DP camps after the war, the spirit was not broken, as one DP proudly exclaimed, 'The very fact you managed to come to terms with the horror of these experiences and become creative humans again means that your internal power is great'.[52]

Although no Polish decrees were put into effect in the Soviet-dominated portion of Poland, they subjected the area to rapid Sovietization in the form of collectivizing farms and resources. Measures were immediately put into place to eradicate any Polish elements that might incite uprisings, with execution orders for political prisoners, army officers, the intelligentsia and most other members of society. The most famous example was the Katyń massacres between April and May 1940 of over 22,000 POW officers. In lieu of outright murder, four instances of the vast mass deportation of Poles took place between February 1940 and June 1941, in which conditions on the trains have been said to 'defy coherent language'.[53] The estimates are contested, and it is thought that anywhere between 320,000 and 1,692,000 Polish citizens were deported to the Soviet Union including Red Army recruits, concentration camp inmates, and POWs.[54]

Many Poles who had fled alongside their government ended up in Britain after the fall of France in 1940; while the Polish armed forces, although continuing to swear allegiance to Poland, operated under British control.[55] They enjoyed the same rights as Commonwealth soldiers and were soon joined by General Władysław Anders' army after he abandoned plans to fight alongside the Soviet army and, travelling via the Middle East, joined British forces in Italy.

Reprisals against the Poles for acts of resistance increased as the war intensified. There was little sense of uniformity in the *General Gouvernement* as terror was spread through hangings, mass shootings, deportations, rapes, arrests and seemingly random street executions. The *łapanki* (round-ups), random manhunts conducted by Germans in the streets, were particularly feared, as those taken were largely sent to the Third Reich to keep its ever-growing war machine going. Consequently, the *łapanki* soon came to symbolize the nullity of a Pole's worth.⁵⁶ Poles, along with other Slavs, were close to the bottom of the Nazis' racial hierarchy and were therefore treated as such, stripping them of any autonomy. Many Poles remember their time in Germany not as forced labourers but as slaves. After interviewing eighty former forced labourers about their experiences, Piotr Filipkowski and Katarzyna Madoń-Mitzner contended that slave markets were a very real and traumatic memory for many: 'having their mouths opened, their teeth inspected, their muscles palpated; being bought and paid for'.⁵⁷ Yet this cannot be said to be representative of all forced labour in Germany, as many – often hundreds – arrived at the train station of a small town and were placed in factories without such a rigorous selection process. Nevertheless, even one instance of being treated like slaves in markets bears repeating. Underpinning the Poles' subordination to the Germans were thriving theories of eugenics, racial superiority, and biological explanations of prowess throughout the Third Reich that classified Poles on par with Jews, the apparent *Untermensch* (subhuman or *podczłowiek* in Polish) of the world.⁵⁸ An extract from Directive No. 1306 issued on 24 October 1939 following a statement from Goebbels' Ministry of Propaganda, asserted:

> It must be made clear even to the German milkmaid that Polishness equals subhumanity. Poles, Jews and gypsies are on the same inferior level… this should be brought home as a *leitmotiv* and, from time to time, in the form of existing concepts such as 'Polish economy', 'Polish ruin', and so on until everyone in Germany subconsciously sees any Pole, whether farm worker or intellectual, as vermin.⁵⁹

The previously mentioned *Polenerlasse* were a prime example of the Poles' supposed place in the racial hierarchy, from which pure *Volk* (Germans) were to be protected at all costs. Although they relied on the Poles to keep Germany's supreme Aryan society operating, there was an ideological unacceptability in the mixing of the two races and relationships between Germans and Poles were strictly forbidden; if caught, Poles may have faced the death penalty. For many Poles this constituted a social separation as well as a sexual one, as *Rassenschande* (racial defilement) came to include anything 'that offended popular sentiment', including 'social intercourse'.⁶⁰ Filipowski and Madoń-Mitzner's interviewees emphasized how they were treated like 'air', like non-persons.⁶¹ The humiliation and degradation of those sent to concentration camps have been well documented and further illumination of their plight is not needed here.

Continual acts of resistance among the Polish population significantly helped the Allied war effort, the deliberate 'go-slow' (sometimes recorded as *Arbeitsbummelei*, or loafing) in the German factories intentionally slowed production, a punishable offence, but nevertheless occurred regularly.⁶² In the post-war period, this was often cited by Polish societies abroad as a reason for Polish equality with the Western Allies. In a 1947 memorandum sent by the Help Poles in Germany Polish Social Committee based in London to British and international authorities, it stated:

> Wireless messages from England and America continuously appealed to foreign workers in Germany to sabotage the work they did for the enemy. The Poles showed much discipline in obeying these orders, and in doing so sometimes risked their lives to a greater extent than many front-line soldiers. Continuous 'go-slow', direct sabotage of factory work, betrayal of many production secrets – such was the contribution to the war effort made by foreign workers, the Poles in particular.⁶³

Demobilized Polish soldiers living in underground resistance networks, some living in the forests, some helping others escape the *łapanki* and other forms of humiliation all accumulate into a sizeable resistance movement, most notably the *Armia Krajowa* (Home Army, AK). The Polish government-in-exile, residing first in Paris and Angers, and then in London, kept close links with the AK. The Warsaw Uprising, however, had an enormous cost, as 20,000 AK members and over 225,000 civilians were killed. Warsaw was reduced to rubble, and a city that had housed 1,289,000 people just six years previously had few inhabitants left. The timing of the uprising had been ill-fated and the situation poorly judged, and it had cost the Polish people dearly.⁶⁴ It also cost the Polish London government-in-exile greatly as it was seen as the architect of the uprising and the Allies were keen not to upset their new partnership with the Soviet Union. No one wanted to be reminded that the Soviet Union was hardly any less culpable of warmongering and abhorrent population controls than the Nazi enemy. The Americans and British considered it foolish to think that their new Soviet alliance 'should be upset for the sake of Poles'.⁶⁵ After the Warsaw Uprising in 1944, the majority of those captured were sent to POW camps and were only liberated by the Allies in 1945. Many of these former POWs took on leadership positions in the DP camps and, supporting the Polish armed services in Britain, used their position to influence Polish DPs on the issue of repatriation.

The bond between the British and Polish had been re-cast after the fall of France in 1940 and the amalgamation of Anders' army with the Polish Second Corps under British command, many of whom would create a distinctive Polish enclave in Britain after the war. The sense of betrayal when Britain and the Allies recognized the new Polish borders and rule of the Polish Provisional Government of National Unity in 1945 was much harder to bear for Poles who had fought alongside the British. To add salt to the wound, the oppressor of Poland's freedom was now framed in the post-war era as an ally, and the Poles were perceived to be making a 'nuisance' of themselves by interfering with Western diplomacy. These pent-up grievances and anxieties about Poland's future once the war had been won bore fruit when Britain provided very limited assistance during the Warsaw Uprising. The feelings of betrayal gradually culminated in active distaste for the British as Poles' love for Poland grew and the reality of the Poland they loved became a bittersweet memory.

And you call *this* freedom? The fifth partition

The war ended on 8 May 1945, but the sense of freedom was soon replaced by apprehension, as one DP exclaimed:

> We felt drunk with this freedom – almost dazed. We were like drunk people, or like children who suddenly found themselves in a new unknown situation and don't know what to do with themselves. As helpless as we were, we faced this immense joy. At once, we had the impression that it was only the brightest of dreams – deluding us with its brightness. We feared to look behind this delusion, we did not want it to disappear and see the torturer in his hated grey-green uniform.... These were the first days of happiness.... Slowly we got accustomed to this new situation. Life does not allow you to wonder too long. It brought us new troubles, new problems and it didn't let us be idle.[66]

The Poland that emerged from the Second World War was unrecognizable to many Poles. The borders were redrawn, and Poland had lost significant territory; the London government-in-exile was unsure of its political position; the Polish army was under orders to demobilize against its will, and millions of Poles had been dispersed throughout the Third Reich. Alongside the chaos of destruction, the elation of liberation, and spontaneous romances commencing for no other reason other than that they could, confusion reigned supreme, as Józefa Zalewska Hodorowicz recounted:

> When the war was over we didn't know what to do. We were stranded, left completely to our own devices. No one telling us what to do, not even the simplest rations to eat. Thousands of people from all walks of life were meeting up on the roads. 'Where are you going?' 'What should we do?' We were like small wandering tribes trying to find a home.[67]

Józefa was one of millions who suddenly found themselves liberated from forced labour in agriculture by advancing Allied armies. Yet, the rules had changed overnight, and no one knew what to do. Like many other Poles, Józefa and her husband wanted neither to stay in Germany and work for the Germans nor go back to a Poland they no longer considered their own. Consequently, they turned to the Allies for help, and like many others they ended up in abandoned and partially bombed-out buildings in the British zone awaiting the chance of resettlement.

Poland had changed more during the six years of war than it had over the previous century. The ethnic homogeneity that was developing during the *Niepodległość* years had been relentlessly accelerated during the war. Ethnic minorities were almost a thing of the past as throughout the war Jews had been systematically murdered, those considered eligible according to the *Volksliste* had been removed and placed in Reich territories, Ukrainians and Byelorussians had been incorporated into the USSR, and ethnic Poles from the east had been brought to central Poland to replenish 'stock' that had been sent to Germany for forced labour. The ideal of a Roman Catholic, Polish-speaking, culturally homogenous society had almost been realized. Social structures were decimated, as the majority of Poland's intelligentsia had been executed by the Nazis and the Soviets alike. The very composition of Polish society was radically different. Although much of the peasantry remained, the urban population (Jews, bourgeoisies, intelligentsia) had largely been destroyed or evacuated, making their way across borders to join former forced labourers in Germany. The war had sped up the process of ethnic homogenization while simultaneously decimating the social composition of Polish society, the majority of those left to rebuild Poland and repopulate the 'Recovered Territories' in the West were considered true Poles – the *lud*.

The poet and novelist Adam Zagajewski who was deported with his family in 1945 from Lwów to Gliwice (formally Gleiwitz in Upper Silesia) recounted in his essay 'Two Cities' that most of Gliwice's inhabitants 'were deported from the east. They were fresh emigrants; but it was not the emigrants who had left their country, it was the country that had simply shifted west, that's all. And they along with it'.[68] As the First World War had sought to shape borders to fit populations, the end of the Second World War sought to shape populations to fit borders, and unfortunately for Poland this meant the displacement of millions.[69]

Throughout the war relations between the British and the Polish government-in-exile had been strained. Poland had become 'an inconvenient ally'. Through fraught negotiations in Tehran with the Soviets, Churchill spent much of early 1944 trying to persuade the Prime Minister of the Polish government-in-exile, Stanisław Mikołajczyk, to accept the Curzon line, thereby handing Poland's eastern provinces to the Soviets. In compensation Poland would receive land to the west which was rich in minerals and industry, and perhaps also the historic port of Danzig; Churchill summarized that the Poles 'would not do so badly'.[70] The British tried to convince Poland that this was the best course of action, ascertaining that it was in their best interests as the land to the east was 'mixed' and therefore incompatible with the concept of an ethnically homogeneous nation-state, arguing instead that Poland would be strengthened by the loss of these minorities.[71] Yet the biggest fear was the creation of a puppet government controlled by the Soviet Union. During a Cabinet meeting in January 1944, when asked whether 'the Russians really want an independent Poland? Or had they in view a puppet Government?', Foreign Secretary Anthony Eden replied, 'there were increasing signs which pointed in the latter direction. [...] It was noticeable that the Russian Government appeared to continue to modify their attitude towards the Polish Government and that that attitude showed a progressive stiffening'.[72] Mikołajczyk eventually accepted the Curzon line in the hope that it would prevent the occurrence of further concessions that could result in uneven Soviet influences in Poland. He was unable, however, to convince the rest of the Polish government-in-exile to accept that the eastern territories had been lost and resigned as Prime Minister in November 1944.

Churchill arrived at Yalta in February 1945 with the intention to do his best for the Polish cause, although his vision did not match with the government-in-exile. Ultimately, Britain held little sway as it had been weakened by a decline in its global status and was overruled by Stalin's rigidity and Roosevelt's indifference at the meeting. Relations began to sour with the government-in-exile as Britain saw Tomasz Arciszewski, Mikołajczyk's successor, as difficult and unrealistic in his demands. Objectively, Poland had been betrayed by her British ally; however, the relationship was much more complicated than outward appearances made it seem. With the benefit of hindsight Britain's position may appear callous, yet the government-in-exile had made certain assumptions to its detriment. Primarily, it had continuously conflated Britain's appreciation of its active, eager military participation with the reward of diplomatic influence. The government-in-exile believed that fighting courageously and fearlessly alongside the British would afford them a say in the post-war world among the Western Allies, and this proved to be their greatest error. As Anita Prażmowska asserts, 'they hoped by being brave and selfless they would gain British respect, support or at least gratitude. They achieved none of this. The only lingering positive impression created by the Poles was of reckless heroism'. While the Poles needed long-term commitment against the Soviet Union with Britain as her ally, this was often construed as Poland pushing Britain to 'support the Polish case irrespective of British priorities'.[73]

Churchill repeatedly tried to convey the importance of friendly relations with the Soviet Union, requesting that the Poles adopt a realistic attitude that would not provoke harmful and dangerous consequences for themselves or for Europe as a whole. Although there are accounts of Churchill's sympathetic and duty-bound view of the Polish plight, he also felt that the Poland that emerged from the Second World War would, by necessity, have to be politically and territorially acceptable to the Soviet Union.[74] After the announcement at Yalta in February 1945 that Poland's borders were to move westwards, many questioned how the concession of Poland's territory, the redrawing of boundaries, and the possibility of a re-imagined and decidedly communist government did not encroach on the principles of the Anglo-American Atlantic Charter, which had been held up by the United States and Britain to the world as a blueprint upon which the post-war world should be built. Indeed, Britain actively ignored the first three articles of the Atlantic Charter and when questioned why the Charter's principles were not applied in Poland's case regardless of Churchill's ostensible commitment, his reply was simply that 'the Atlantic Charter is a guide, not a rule'.[75] Arciszewski and his government-in-exile readily espoused the attitude of the 'betrayed ally'. As Poland was actively excluded from protection, trampling on the sovereignty granted to them by their allies in 1918, the re-birth of Polish nationalism grew to create a highly politicized Polonia. The end of the war was meant to be a period of re-birth for Poland; instead its independence was stifled and its national identity, formed through imagined communities both in the British zone and elsewhere, was impeded.

As the principles of the Atlantic Charter were being ignored, the Polish Second Corps in Italy under General Anders saw no reason to continue fighting for a Poland that no longer existed. Luckily, they were persuaded to continue and went on to play a major part in numerous offensive manoeuvres. Yet in British circles it was felt that the government-in-exile did not represent the average Pole anymore; it did not understand their wants or needs, and as free and unfettered elections had been promised in Poland, for now, the Soviet-backed Polish Provisional Government would work best. The British who had assumed that the majority of Poles resident in Britain, as well as those serving alongside the armed forces, would want to return to Poland, had severely underestimated their hatred for the Soviet Union and communism.[76] After the announcement of the terms agreed at Yalta, Anders flew to London for a meeting with Churchill, where he threatened to withdraw the Polish Second Corps from Italy. Eventually dissuaded by the government-in-exile's President Raczkiewicz he and his troops dutifully continued to fight, but their spirit was broken. Anders recorded his troops' reaction to the news from Yalta in his memoirs:

> There was a violent reaction in the army as the men realized the great injustice that had been done to them. Each had trusted that at the end of his struggles, toil and suffering, he would be able to return to his own country, his family, his cottage, his trade or his piece of land; now he knew that the reward for his efforts and his comrades' sacrifices was to be either further wandering in alien lands, or a return to a country under foreign rule.[77]

After the Allies officially recognized the Polish Provisional Government of National Unity as Poland's legal government, the London-based government-in-exile headed by Arciszewski was officially made redundant. It became the cornerstone of the post-war exile mission, however, and was a symbol of Polishness that had been carried throughout the war by all Poles, regardless of background. In the post-war world they amassed in the assembly and transit centres of Europe with a common vision of the Poland they had been fighting for, and it was not the one the Allies had presented them with.

From May to September 1945, Germany's occupied zones concentrated solely on the repatriation of Western and Soviet DPs. The repatriation of Poles had been forestalled until the Allies' binding agreement with Stalin to prioritize all Soviet DPs, using force if necessary, was complete. This proved to be a calamitous error. Many Poles wished to return home in May 1945; however, by September the numbers of Poles wishing to repatriate had been severely reduced. One of the principal causes was the Allies' official recognition of the New Polish Provisional Government in Poland on 5 June 1945. The thought of installing anything but the London-based government-in-exile was abhorrent for many Poles, in particular those who had served alongside the British in the army. Anders' army was particularly against a return to a communist Poland, and among the very few who did return, reports of unfair treatment, random arrests and jail sentences were common. In May 1945 Anders could be found visiting various DP camps, transit centres, assembly centres, and makeshift installations, spreading 'anti-Soviet propaganda':

> All Poles know that this is not liberty yet, it is not the victory yet. I have to tell you that the situation in the Country is terrible. Already officers are being shot, especially those from the Home Army. Everyone who had contact with the Home Army is sent to Siberia. None of us have access to Poland while Soviets rule there. After crossing the border everyone is at best arrested according to the Soviet rules. Who wants to come back – let him come back. It is his right. My duty is to warn you.[78]

Throughout Poland the mood was equally despondent. Those who had remained and suffered the harsh conditions of Nazi and Soviet rule were once more to be subjected to a life under another power. The British and Polish did not share the same vision of a post-war world. British priorities at home certainly outweighed Polish worries over Soviet rule in Poland. The end of the six years of warfare was not the end of suffering for the approximately 5,000,000 Poles abroad: the end of the war brought another interregnum period that could only end once the Poland of the *Niepodległość* years was restored. The ideal of a post-war Poland, and therefore the very concept of Polishness in the DP camps, that was presented was thus a composition of pre-war elite rhetoric with a heavy focus on anti-Soviet views coupled with wartime experiences that culminated in this expression of sacral nationalism and took root in the British zone in strong opposition to their former Allies. The active opposition to accept any form of Poland unlike that of the *Niepodległość* years was fervently advocated in the camps alongside the 'betrayed ally' rhetoric. It was an exceptional community formation based on the principle that, as Keith Sword states, the majority of those outside Poland's borders in 1945 'experienced the irony of being on the winning side militarily and yet – in political terms – also defeated'.[79]

Conclusion

By mid-1945, the very concept of Polishness was being vigorously reinforced using popular concepts rooted in the nineteenth-century Romantic tradition. The cross-pollination of various ideas were woven together piecemeal throughout the years of *Niepodległość* to give a definition to something which seemingly had no definition to give.[80] The great Polish poet Adam Mickiewicz's conception of a Pole was not synonymous with the ethnically homogenous conception sought in the twentieth century. Mickiewicz, a Pole and a Lithuanian, opened one of his most famous epic poems, *Pan Tadeusz*, with the words *Litwo! Ojczyzno moja! ty jesteś jak zdrowie!* (Lithuania! my Fatherland! You are like health to me).[81] Yet the Poles of Polonia dispersed throughout the world at the end of the Second World War saw their Polishness as equivalent to that of the great Adam Mickiewicz. He was a true bastion of what it meant to be Polish, enduring the suffering and the exile, and many chose to neglect his stance against ethnic homogeneity. Poland's iconic leader of the *Niepodległość* era, Józef Piłsudski, was similarly in favour of a return to the Polish-Lithuanian commonwealth structure, *Międzymorze*, which his rival, Roman Dmowski, actively pushed aside in favour of his policy of *Narodowa Demokracja* after Piłsudski's death in 1935. The one obvious theme repeated in all imaginations of Polishness was blunt resistance to outside intrusion, specifically from the east. The country's long and difficult history with Russia was a defining element that came to constitute the very core of Polishness, particularly for Poles in exile and was readily pushed at non-elites by the elite DPs in the camps to secure their resistance and establish a community. The struggles to understand who was Polish, where Poland was, and indeed what constituted a Pole all merged together throughout the oppressive Nazi and Soviet occupations. For many who survived the unrepentant pogroms and deportations in the eastern zone under Stalinist rule the scars were psychologically inflicted and they would carry them into the DP camps of Germany.[82] This mental imprisonment found consolation in the creation of new Polish enclaves that offered sanctuary from the years of physical and mental torture. They also acted as a release from this oppression: a place where Polishness, in culture, language, religion and many other ways could blossom unhindered.

To the British, the creation of the new Poland in the post-war era was the 'necessary evil' that would ensure a lasting peace.[83] Britain was preoccupied with its loss of status as a leading global power throughout the war. Its crippling financial situation only further exacerbated Foreign Office officials dealing with the increasingly unrealistic demands of the government-in-exile. The British were not sympathetic about their sufferings. In this context pockets of Polonia began to grow, feeding on reminiscences of the *Niepodległość* years and over a century and half of cultivated cultural symbolism that expressed and represented their Polishness. The very idea of Poles finding themselves under Russian rule again was unthinkable. Quickly the idea spread throughout the DP camps that 'they would rather be dead in Germany than alive in Russia'.[84] This deeply ingrained and almost visceral reaction to Russians, communists, and the new Polish Provisional Government became a common foundation for Polish DPs in the British zone. Indeed, Julian Niemcewicz's verse spoke to many of those who found the Poland they loved so dearly ripped from them:

> Wygnańcy, co tak długo błądzicie po świecie,
> Kiedyż znużonym stopom spoczynek znajdziecie?
> Dziki gołąb ma gniazdo, robak ziemi bryłę,
> Każdy człowiek ojczyznę, a Polak mogiłę
> [O exiles, whose worldly wanderings are never complete
> When may you rest your sore and weary feet?
> The worm has its clod of earth. There's a nest for the wild dove.
> Everyone has a homeland; but the Pole has only a grave.][85]

In contrast, the British largely felt they had done their duty. They had gone to war for Poland, had been its faithful ally and had secured their freedom. The Poles' refusal to return home and alleviate the pressure on British resources was construed as an act of greed.[86] Increasingly, the British proclivity for thinking of Polish DPs as peasants looking for an economic opportunity in the West grew. Adding to the maelstrom of burgeoning grudges, distrust and suspicions between the Poles and the British was the introduction of UNRRA, championed as the bastion of post-war international cooperation and humanitarianism. The welfare workers, the 'adventitious assembly of do-gooders' as Morgan put it, were thrown into a volatile situation they could not possibly have been imagined or understood beforehand.[87] Upon entering the camps in post-war Germany, many Poles found that the preceding years of war and destruction had not only devastated the Polish landscape, ripped it apart and placed it under a former oppressor's rule but had also degraded the strength and purity of Polishness itself. The concepts of Polishness that had grown throughout the pre-war years were now sullied with wartime acts of humiliation, degradation, and repeated accusations of their biological and cultural inferiority. In the camps, the remnants of Poland's elites worked quickly and efficiently to erect camp committees to discuss every aspect of Polish life. They drew heavily on a specific conception of Polishness, which was heavily informed by nationalism and Catholicism to ensure that those Poles who remained in the west were forming the Second Great Emigration.[88] Ultimately, their refusal to return to a country they no longer conceived of as home was an act of resilience in the face of British pressure to alleviate the problems of a ruined occupation zone which was perennially understaffed and overcrowded.

3

'Little Poland' in Germany

Life in Polish displaced persons camps

Introduction

Between 3 and 4 June 1945 Rhoda Dawson, a British UNRRA worker, wrote to her friend in England after attending a garden party hosted by the US Army in Erlangen. She felt uneasy as one of the only 'Britishers' and doubly uncomfortable about the luxurious rations they were able to consume among the ruins of Germany, telling her friend, 'I long to see a plain quiet Englishman and some plain English chocolate'. Dawson and her UNRRA team were on their way to Munich to begin their work with DPs. Although the party was a welcome distraction, the US Army men belittled UNRRA's importance, repeatedly stating the training was useless and the DPs would be gone soon anyway. While mindful of the task at hand, even Dawson lamented that 'what we fear now is that the D.P.'s [*sic*] are going home at such a rate that our work will be over in a few months'.[1] She need not have worried. A day later, the Polish Provisional Government of National Unity was officially recognized by the Allies as the ruling government of Poland. This caused widespread apprehension among the Polish DPs wishing to repatriate. After the Potsdam Conference a month later, the Polish borders were redrawn and Poland was effectively shifted 150 miles westward, and with it even the most optimistic DPs became anxious.

In an attempt to reduce animosity and fighting between DPs, they were divided by nationality and/or ethnicity as the Allied armies fought their way through Germany during 1944 and 1945. Consequently, they were concentrated in particular areas, and by September 1945 Polish DPs were the most visible group in Germany's three western zones of occupation, totalling 816,000.[2] In the US zone of occupation, Wildflecken DP camp (sometimes referred to as *Durzyń* by the inhabitants) contained 20,000 Polish DPs. Undoubtedly Wildflecken was the largest singular Polish DP camp in Germany; however, the archipelago of Polish DP camps in the British zone formed the ostensible 'Polish zone of occupation', also known as 'Little Poland', with Maczków as its capital. Although only containing 5,000 'Polish' DPs, Maczków became the centre of Polish DP activity as the 'camp' was not a camp at all, but rather the entirely requisitioned German town of Haren on the Ems river. Symbolically, Maczków was the embodiment of Poland and Polishness carried forward from 1939 as the inhabitants were loyal to the London government-in-exile and rejected the new Polish Provisional Government of National Unity as a legitimate governing body. The infusion of sacral nationalism alongside the physical construction of this 'imagined community' gave Maczków a unique identity. Conversely, it also sparked animosity and hostility towards foreigners in the area leading up to the present day as memories of expulsion alongside the creation of Maczków have not subsided.

Although the grouping of nationalities/ethnicities was the same across the three western zones of occupation, the requisitioning of an entire town that was only nominally under UNRRA care in the British zone solidified the unique position of Polish DPs. This chapter looks at the creation of Polish enclaves in the British zone of occupation, and in particular Maczków and Wentorf. Although Maczków only contained half the number of Poles compared to Wentorf, its impact on Anglo-Polish-German relations is significant. Through the use of archival and personal collections, this chapter charts how these Polish DP camps were governed and by whom, while also emphasizing the lasting impact of these 'temporarily housed' foreigners on German towns soon after the war's end. Lastly, it also analyses British humanitarian workers' attitudes to Polish DPs in particular, and how this helped to shape the daily life in the camps as statistics turned into people.

Maczków: 'Little Poland' on the Ems

As those such as Józefa Zalewska Hodorowicz found themselves suddenly freed among the ruins of Germany without a plan or direction, one special enclave in the British zone materialized that would become a hub for the Polish life. Maczków and its inhabitants kept close ties with the London government-in-exile, members of the AK, and Anders' army, and it soon became the symbolic heartland of Poland in the British zone. Between 18 and 19 May 1945, two Military Government Detachments were ordered to help Germans in Haren evacuate, and by 22 May the Polish First Armoured Division had arrived together with sixteen female members of the AK to help register, process, and house DPs. The first transport of 262 Poles arrived in the city at 2.40 pm; twenty minutes later a column of trucks carrying about 1,000 Poles arrived; at 10.35 pm another 250 DPs arrived at the railway station.[3] The transports kept arriving and the Poles, totalling 4,000 by the following night, settled into the town. On 24 May, Major Gilmore of 701 Military Government Detachment issued instructions for the Haren (Maczków) camp, opening by saying 'all facilities within the town are for the benefit of the Polish population as a whole'.[4]

Maczków quickly became the informal capital of a series of Polish camps that comprised 'Little Poland' in and around Emsland. The creation of Polish microcosms under British control became typical as the largest number of Poles were found in the British zone and their organizational ability was exemplary. For example, Wentorf DP camp which housed nearly 10,000 'Polish nationals' by September 1945, was 'controlled' by Military Government Detachment 220, consisting of seven Polish liaison officers, seventeen British officers, two Belgian officers, eight members of the Friends Ambulance Unit, four UNRRA teams, and two DP assembly centre teams.[5] Maczków, however, was different. Although the army and UNRRA ostensibly controlled 'DP camp Haren', they had little practical effect on its functioning. Indeed, Maczków took on a life of its own. As Polish enclaves grew from mid-1945 onwards it was common to see Polish DP camps comprising 5,000 or more DP Poles, and these *polskie skupiska* (Polish clusters) grew to the point that their own administrative machinery was necessary to function. One of the major follies of UNRRA's provisions for employees to deal with DPs in 1945 was a lack of language training, which proved detrimental to the whole organization's cohesive functioning. Rhoda Dawson's language training at UNRRA's Jullouville centre in France consisted of learning the Polish alphabet and writing down how to pronounce the letters phonetically (see Figure 3.1). Needless to say, when confronted with thousands of native speakers, each with their own slight accents and dialects, knowing the alphabet was not of much use.

A little Poland that contains Poles is run by Poles and is for Poles would naturally need Polish-language administrative machinery, and where better to recruit than from the DPs themselves. Britain, on her own initiative, had given over Haren to the Polish First Armoured Division and the Polish First Independent Parachute Brigade as a temporary settlement. It was an easy way to group and register Poles and provide sustainable living arrangements without actually having to deal with them. This drew sharp criticism, however, from members of the British 21st Army group, as accusations of 'behaviour worse

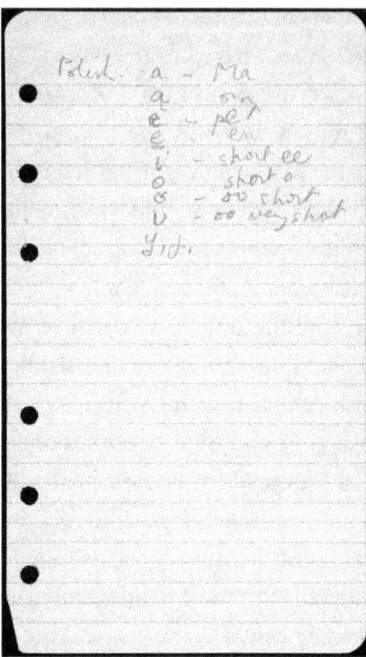

Figure 3.1 Rhoda Dawson's Polish-language training at Jullouville, France. Source: Imperial War Museum.

than the Russians' were made about the Polish First Armoured Division and civilians alike. It was only by emphasizing Maczków's temporariness that these concerns were quietened.[6] It became a dominant point of contention, however, in British-Soviet relations as the British adviser to Moscow, Sir A. Clark Kerr, levelled accusations that towns such as Maczków and Osnabrück were creating a new Polish state on German land. Kerr claimed that the towns 'were turned into camps in which Polish fascists gather all the Poles liberated from the Germans' and were creating a base for action against the new Poland and the USSR.[7] Kerr was worried about opposition. As Maczków enjoyed British military protective status and maintained close links with the London government-in-exile, the diaspora was free to express Polish identity and culture (or Polishness) away from the watchful gaze of the new Polish government in Warsaw. Unsurprisingly, Maczków became a hub for Polish cultural life in the British zone.

The inhabitants of Maczków were anti-Warsaw and pro-London; their loyalties lay with the government-in-exile and questions were asked among the military government about whether the Polish forces should be allowed to stay in control, particularly when their total strength numbered close to 21,000.[8] Although the British military oversaw the whole operation, they felt as though this experimental town of Polish DPs, ex-POWs, and active/ex-servicemen could cause a permanent problem on German soil. The leading British military governors and UNRRA, however, acknowledged that repatriation was the main goal regarding Polish DPs; places such as Maczków were inherently temporary. To further forestall fears, an entire system of governance was soon formalized, including a Polish town council with an elected mayor and magistrates, and administrative departments for the police, education, public health, food, and housing. On 14 June 1945 Haren, having already been named 'little Lwów' for a few weeks, was renamed Maczków by the Polish First Armoured Division in honour of their commander, General Maczek.[9]

The physical construction of the imagined community

This microcosm of Polish society thrived from this point, and by the end of June 1945 Maczków boasted primary and secondary schools, four bakeries, a butchery, a theatre, a publishing house, a hospital, a police station, a fire brigade, a Roman Catholic parish, and the beginnings of a youth scouting movement. An extract from the *Maczków Daily* of 24 June 1945 reports that the town was publishing 200 copies of its daily newspaper (there would be more if not for the lack of paper), and there were aspirations for cinemas, leisure clubs, libraries, shops, and much more. The sacral nationalism of Polish society had found its place in Maczków with over 100 wedding ceremonies by the end of June 1945 adorned with pre-1939 Polish flags and an abundance of red ribbons, flowers, and eagles.[10] The inhabitants became vehemently protective of their town, proclaiming in the *Maczków Daily* that 'Maczków is such a town as Warsaw, Poznań or Lwów, the fact that it is in a foreign land and a bit smaller is not of great importance'.[11]

Although Polish associations sprang up across Europe after the war, the strongest, The Polish Union of Germany (PU, *Zjednoczenie Polskie w Niemczech*) was formed in Maczków. It became an umbrella organization for all Polish organizations in Germany and Austria, often helping to cover the welfare gaps that UNRRA and voluntary societies could not fill. It relied on donations, largely from a Polish association headquartered in Great Britain (*Społeczny Komitet Pomocy Obywatelom Polskim w Niemczech*) and conducted financial transactions using cigarettes; a most welcomed supply in Maczków after numerous inhabitants were found to be 'smoking weeds wrapped in newspapers'.[12] Above all, however, the PU declared that every Pole, regardless of citizenship status, 'who lived in a DP camp was automatically a PU member'; those outside merely had to register.[13]

Maczków, as the capital of little Poland, became an idealized version of Anderson's concept of 'nation' to all Poles in diaspora. The nation, in this case Poland, was a set of imagined political communities that were both, as Anderson contends, 'inherently limited and sovereign'. In the post-war years, the Polish nation to those in diaspora and particularly to those in the DP camps of Germany were bound by these imagined communities that contained an infinite number of members spread across the world.[14] The concept of imagined communities is used here as the people who belonged to this Polish community no longer identified with a fixed geographical location, but rather with a people, many of whom were spread so far and wide that it would be impossible for them all to meet and know each other. This reclaiming of national identity and invocation to supplant geographically defined nationalism with diasporic nationalism was one of the backbones of the administration in Maczków. Anderson's concept was intended to describe all nations, but its application to a collectivity of mini-diasporas formed under unusual circumstances is exceptionally fitting.

In an essay on nationalism, George Orwell stated that 'nomenclature plays a very important part in nationalist thought', going on to describe how countries who have often had to fight for their independence 'usually change their names'. The Polish DPs' acquisition of an area that was 'for the benefit of the Polish population as a whole' necessitated the name change from Haren to Maczków to validate their enclave.[15] Maczków was not the only large Polish DP camp whose name changed: Wildflecken in the US zone was renamed *Durzyń* after a Slavic tribe, the *Durzyńcy*, which settled the area 1,500 years ago. The renaming of these camps and installations became an important and common trait of Polish DP camps, and although the British did not officially object to the name change they never recognized the camp as Maczków but rather consistently referred to it as Camp Haren. UNRRA appeared conflicted and chose to cover all bases, using both names in correspondence, for instance 'Team 162, Haren/ Maczków'. Yet for all intents and purposes, Maczków was a little Poland in the heart of Germany that had, through the displacement of Germans, created a sanctuary for displaced Poles and a hub for the continuation of pre-war Polish culture.

No other Polish installation in Germany could compare to Maczków. It was of unsurpassed quality which had grown from the Polish DPs' own industriousness in reinvigorating *their* Poland on German soil.[16] As one DP, a former concentration camp prisoner proclaimed, 'it appears to me as a just fortuity that we had to start rebuilding our life here where those who ruined it came from'.[17] Indeed, the Polish Red Cross made sure that Maczków's hospital had operating facilities and up to 200 beds, in addition to a specific orphanage for Polish children (*Dom Dziecka*): both were significant contributions given the limited supplies across Europe at the time. Of course, as in many other Polish DP camps there were various administrations that developed into political parties. In particular circles, former political prisoners scrutinized the 'validity' of new members, as their suffering had afforded them an almost privileged status. According to Łuczak, they therefore felt that they deserved 'additional rights' in terms of social welfare 'compared to "other" DPs'.[18] This stance created a double standard in the DP camps, with former political prisoners treated almost as aristocracy, continuing to wear their striped uniforms honourably. This was rarely contended by 'ordinary' Polish DPs, and those considered asocial were actively snubbed.[19]

Maczków was also the hub for something that came to dominate the lives of Polish DPs across Germany: education. The town quickly established primary and secondary schools, vital as many children had not received any education throughout the war and many were barely literate. Between 1945 and 1948 Maczków's schools enrolled 680 students, a third of which were registered as DPs, under a quarter were ex-POWs and AK members, and many were still active soldiers.[20] As teachers' associations had been running covertly throughout the war, aided significantly by the AK, an established number of teachers was already able to help to educate the Polish youth once adequate facilities were ready. Numerous Polish teachers' organizations were created throughout the three western zones of occupation as a priority, and naturally the heads of all of these chose to gather in Maczków in June 1946 to create the Central Committee for Schools and Education (*Centralny Komitet dla Spraw Szkolnych i Oświatowych*).[21]

The physical construction of the imagined community, often fused with sacral nationalism, was quite visible in Maczków by the end of 1945. Indeed, thanks to the administrative machinery, educational and medical facilities, and numerous small businesses, this microcosm could boast one of the most successful local economies in western Germany at the time. It was precisely because the British occupiers and UNRRA's machinery stepped back from governing Maczków that this was able to happen. As will be shown, UNRRA was a much-vaunted and celebrated organization from its outset, but it was also dreadfully hindered by stifling bureaucracy that often caused more harm than good. Consequently, when Maczków's UNRRA team leader, Paul Rousseau, took a back seat to Maczków's Polish inhabitants the town was able to work cohesively much quicker than other DP camps in the area.

'Betrayed Ally' or 'Troublesome Nuisance'?: Post-1945 Anglo-Polish relationships in the camps

Maczków became something of legend throughout Germany, as well as to all Poles living in Poland and the wider diaspora. Many who joined the town later in 1945 were extended family members of the servicemen units stationed in Maczków, taking advantage of chaotic borders and the lack of official British and UNRRA control over the camp. This microcosm, however, could not last. The dissolution of Maczków came about due to numerous factors. First, Maczków and the surrounding area suffered a severe flood in February 1946, causing some to leave but more importantly, keeping others away. Secondly, the UNRRA commander in charge of Team 162, Paul Rousseau (a Belgian) thought of fondly by Maczków's mayor and citizens alike for his relaxed approach, stepped down in mid-1946. He was replaced by Thomas Jamieson (British), who became known for his formal execution of UNRRA policy and was deeply disliked. Thirdly, with UNRRA's repatriation of Poles from September 1945 the population gradually dwindled, with the biggest depopulation due to the announcement of the Polish Resettlement Act in Britain (1947) and the simultaneous order to demobilize the divisions stationed in Maczków (May 1947). The vast majority of those from the Polish First Armoured Division and Polish First Independent Parachute Brigade chose not to return to Poland; some stayed in Germany and were subsequently excluded from the Homeless Foreigners Act in 1951. Many, however, chose to join the Polish Resettlement Corps in Britain along with Anders' men. Lastly, on 10 March 1947, the Municipal Council of Maczków received an irrevocable order from UNRRA Team 162 to hand over sixty-five houses to their German owners. The reversal of 1945 was coming into effect.[22] Poles who had replaced the Germans being evacuated in 1945 were now being evacuated themselves and replaced with the same Germans who once lived there. By 1948, the inhabitants of 'the capital of Little Poland' had dissipated, some to new countries, some to Poland, and many to other DP camps in the British zone. The town was Haren once more.

The situation in Maczków was unique. A town run entirely by its inhabitants with strong links to the pre-war Polish government, now living in exile in London, and the Polish army – in particular units under the command of Władysław Anders and Stanisław Maczek. Yet another notable camp in the British zone, Wentorf, contained roughly twice the number of Polish DPs (10,000). It too was a 'thriving community of liberated people' which boasted 'hospitals, Churches, schools, workshops, shopping centres, broadcasting studios, cinemas, newspaper offices and varied welfare centres'.[23] In contrast to Maczków this camp was fully under British army and UNRRA care. Two personal collections spanning 1945–7 at Wentorf alongside official records from The National Archives emphasize the relationships between Polish DPs and those in charge in the camp. The two memoirs provide distinctly different experiences, one from Major R S Lawson, a seasoned British army officer, and the other from Liselotte Becker, a young German girl working as a secretary to British officials. As their residence at Wentorf spanned a similar time period and their paths often crossed, the complementary memoirs provide an illuminating insight into the camp's daily workings, individuals, and processes for dealing with DPs.

One of the themes that recurs in Lawson's account of life at Wentorf is the hierarchy of DPs that formed in the camps as a whole. He details how Polish DPs who were known to be ex-POWs were 'brought into the camp to act as camp police and to save-guard [sic] the interests of the community', and seemingly were never challenged by the other DPs.[24] Similarly, a committee was set up in the camp to ensure 'special privileges' for ex-concentration camp prisoners. This was a theme that ran throughout Polish DP camps. The war had completely decimated Poland's social order, and in its place a social hierarchy was built within the DP camps based on wartime experiences. Many Poles had earned titles: for instance, those who had been in the Home Army and/or took part in the Warsaw Uprising were known as *akowcy* or *akaczki* (an abbreviation of *Armia Krajowa*, AK), Poles from Maczek's First Armoured Division were *maczkowcy*, those under Anders were *andersowcy*, women from the auxiliary women's services became *pestki*, and Poles who had fought in September 1939 against the Nazi invasion were *wrześniowcy* (Septemberists). Their titles were then coupled with their wartime experience, those who had seen the most severe conditions (e.g. as political prisoners or ex-POWs) were at the top of the hierarchy and those who had a relatively 'easier' experience as forced labour on farms, in particular the peasants, at the bottom. This created a new and reinvigorated sense of community that allowed for social mobility within a new framework; class differences were, however, still apparent.[25]

During the conclusion of *A Brief History of Wentorf Displaced Persons Camp*, Major Lawson mapped the life of a child DP born in the camp, showing that at every step of the way from ante-natal care, to education, to vocational training and jobs, a full life could be led at Wentorf.[26] Lawson's point is that the camp is so vast, well-organized and staffed that a whole life could be lived there, but, he concludes, it should not be. He emphasizes instead that Poles should wish to 'return to their own soil and once again take up their pre-war role of being good citizens of Poland', rather than remain in a DP camp. Written in 1946, it is hard to believe that Lawson did not know of the ongoing issues with repatriation, particularly as UNRRA geared up to run incentivizing schemes to entice (or some say bribe) the Polish DPs back to Poland by offering food parcels.[27] Although Lawson ostensibly played a rather major role in the camp, as Public Safety Officer, his history of Wentorf only demonstrated the positives. As a memoir, Lawson is presenting the camp as he wished others to view it.

Liselotte Becker, however, details her experiences in a rather different way. Although quite thoughtful and contemplative of individuals and their actions throughout her diaries, Becker appears only to talk about Polish DPs, Polish officers, and Polish women negatively. They either taunted her (for being German), forced her to clean ('the Poles notice I avoid their company'), or married British officials (with insinuations of 'poor reputation[s]').[28] What is most striking, however, is the adoption of British language towards Poles that is often found in British military records. In particular, after hoisting a Polish flag in place of the Union Jack, Becker describes the Poles as 'troublesome'.[29] Although this may not sound like a grievous error, this language has been replicated across Foreign Office, Home Office, and War Office memoranda when referring specifically to Poles. The same negative and discouraging language is not found in references to Balts or Ukrainians. The repeated use of unfavourable phrases such as 'troublesome' and 'nuisance' indicates the fragile Anglo-Polish relationship in post-war Germany and, by proxy, German administrative assistants working for British officials. The 'betrayed ally' rhetoric that took root in everyday conversations between Polish elites in exile cascaded down to Polish army members at the end of the war and gradually filtered into the camps with them as they were demobbed.

Among welfare workers, however, the views of Poles and the passage of time are reversed. Rhoda Dawson, for instance, begins her earlier memoirs talking about Poles negatively; it is only as her memoirs continue towards the end of her service with UNRRA that she becomes much more positive. This odd back-to-front of attitudes and language use among officials in predominantly Polish DP camps can be attributed to one primary factor: interaction. This may seem simplistic, but as is the case with many xenophobic or negative opinions regarding races or peoples, they are often formed from ignorance and lack of contact or familiarity. For welfare workers in the camps, their tasks were to interact with the DPs, as well as liaison officers and other officials, as a matter of course. The more familiar they were, the less of an 'other' Poles became. The opposite was true for

British officials. Many, although working diligently at their tasks such as Becker's boss Major Pyle, were often unused to interacting with the DPs, liaison officers or PWXs on a regular basis and they soon became a 'nuisance' or 'troublesome' due to their mere presence. Indeed, as the presence of these people was directly linked to the British official's prolonged stay in Germany, and particularly within DP camps, animosity grew. Lawson appeared to be somewhat of an exception. As detailed in his own *Brief History of Wentorf* as well as in Becker's diary, Lawson was often viewed as one of the most empathetic and friendly officials at Wentorf. As Public Safety Officer he was somewhere between the desk-bound officials such as Major Pyle (often in charge of logistical sections, such as transport and labour offices) and the welfare workers on the ground. His status of being 'in the middle', however, afforded him a much more holistic view of post-war DP camps in British-occupied Germany.

'Mechanically Pigeonholed': Humanitarian workers and Polish displaced persons

Throughout humanitarian workers' memoirs a pattern gradually formed when talking about DPs. In the first instance they were referred to as statistics or elsewhere 'like a swarm of bees'.[30] Only after the initial masses had been divided into groups, and humanitarian workers transferred from training or transit centres to DP camps, did names and faces become perceptible. In particular, as more permanent groups of DPs were established the relationship between humanitarian worker and DP grew more amiable. As one UNRRA worker in the US zone noted, perceptions of DPs could change quickly as 'statistics turned into people and the people turned into friends'.[31] Quaker relief worker Margaret McNeill mentions the human faces that grew from this mass of once unidentifiable people, and concluded early on in her relief work:

> The Displaced Persons themselves were, until I met them, nothing more to me than a phrase: a phrase stamped with scientific detachment, suggesting a mere alteration in the distribution of Europe's population, a convenient label for one of the confusing legacies of the War. Unrelated to oneself, the phrase remains impotent.[32]

Welfare workers undoubtedly developed attachments to DPs, and those such as McNeill who were used to conducting welfare and relief work attached faces to names quicker than others. Dawson, for instance, took longer to warm to the

DPs as she had previously decided that welfare work was not really her thing. Pettiss also admits that by having no concept of who these people were, or why geographical origins mattered so much, her ability to relate to the DPs was scuppered from the outset.[33]

Life in the camps, however, could be equally taxing and chaotic for the welfare workers. Rhoda Dawson's first few days at Rosenheim DP camp were eventful, and she stated 'the DPs look just like the pictures' she had seen back home. As her UNRRA team and the army competed to requisition the sparse housing available for their own use, Dawson tried to care for a mixture of DPs from eighteen different nationalities, none of whom spoke English. The chaos gradually calmed as the camp became a series of cubicles made out of hanging blankets to achieve that little bit of privacy for each DP family. The only consistent focus for all was food, as she playfully wrote: 'I also went round with an interpreter announcing that children and pregnant women could have extra milk at 5 o'clock. There will be a great many pregnant mothers and one or two pregnant men.'[34] During her initial stay at Rosenheim, however, Dawson often laments the hopelessness of the situation as the DPs just 'keep coming' as 'one just can't consider them individually. They are like grains of sand.'[35] Numerous references to DPs' 'loss of personality' are present in welfare worker and military workers' diaries and memoirs. Kathryn Close, an UNRRA worker in the British zone, upon returning to the United States, wrote a piece for the *Survey Graphic* in November 1946 titled, 'They Want to Be People'. Close's aim was to dispel any myths to people in possible resettlement countries about the remaining DPs in the camps, particularly surrounding Balts, Ukrainians, Yugoslavs, and Poles. The opening quote, 'If I could only go some place where I could be a person and not a DP', was attributed to a particular Latvian DP. As Close asserts, however, similar words were continuously spoken by Poles, Ukrainians, and others as 'behind it was the helpless frustration of a person for whom life is suspended, whose daily lot is waiting, whose tragedy is that his waiting has no goal'.[36] DPs frequently spoke of being referred to as a number, another statistic, and not as an individual.[37] Yet, from 1946 onwards, instances of welfare workers' perceptions changing towards the DPs became more common as their personal accounts started referring to 'their DPs' by affectionate nicknames, and a recognition of individuality grew.[38] Dawson, Cooper, McNeill, Pettiss and others record multiple instances of this happening and, as Pettiss happily declares, 'the DPs were losing their anonymity for me, becoming individuals with faces and stories'.[39] Others, such as Close, were adamant this needed to be put to the public too, closing her piece in *Survey Graphic* stating: 'These people are not statistics, or just DP's, but real flesh and blood – *and what are they going to do?*⁴⁰

There were repeated attempts by welfare workers to understand the Polish DPs, but trying to function within the military's rigid hierarchy on a daily basis was challenging enough. It was only after considerable experience with the Polish DPs that welfare workers were able to understand Poland, and therefore the DPs themselves. Poles drew unwanted attention at first, but soon the Polish character came to be viewed favourably, as one welfare worker stated:

> They were a paradoxical people. Their camps were nearly always in greater or less degree ramshackle and squalid, yet they showed a deeper, more artistic sensitivity than any other D.P.s. They were often overwhelmed with a forlorn misery, yet no D.P.s could laugh so gaily, or what was more, so laugh at themselves. They respected their Church and counted honour something to be defended to the death, yet they earned for themselves a reputation for drunkenness, dishonesty and cruelty. They were often hopelessly lazy and unreliable as far as steady routine work went, but in a crisis they would, at the eleventh hour, rally and work with unparalleled speed and determination.⁴¹

Attitudes towards the Poles reflected UNRRA's paternalistic approach which sought to infantilize the DPs, making them dependent on UNRRA and other non-governmental organizations (NGOs), a perennial issue for charities and relief organizations throughout much of the twentieth century. This was the crux of the problem, however, as UNRRA, dominated by Americans from the outset, was often lambasted for overly subscribing to the new social scientific methods developed in the United States regarding welfare. As UNRRA consisted of multiple nationalities, the American approach to welfare was relatively new to many. As Dawson recounts, even in Jullouville their practice was corrected by the UNRRA trainer Arnold-Forster, who declared 'it was not so suited to Europeans'.⁴² On the other hand, UNRRA workers drafted from the army such as Marvin Klemmé believed UNRRA to be too soft. On his first day he recalls, the UNRRA offices had the 'atmosphere of a Communist headquarters' with many people who 'had that starry-eyed look which is usually associated with people who have visions of radically changing the world'.⁴³ The army in general viewed UNRRA and their fellow NGOs' work as destructive to the 'rehabilitation' of a human. Battle-hardened British officials rigorously perpetuated the 'tough love' stance as opposed to nurturing, arguing that using the soft-handed approach with DPs would only result in increased idleness and dependency. In the British zone, Polish DPs were often caught somewhere in the middle.

In Maczków, however, the relationship between the director of UNRRA Team 162, Paul Rousseau, and the Polish inhabitants was not viewed as paternalistic but rather fraternal. Unlike other large Polish camps, the presence of British military officials was severely limited as most tasks were carried out by the Polish First Armoured Division. UNRRA welfare workers worked alongside Poles, setting up hospitals, distributing supplies, repairing homes and furniture, rather than being in charge of them. When Rousseau retired from UNRRA Team 162, the inhabitants and the mayor of Maczków sent him cards and personal letters of thanks, often lovingly decorated. It was a parting of dear friends, not a paternalistic separation forged by dependency. The extent to which Rousseau interacted with the ordinary Polish inhabitants of Maczków is as questionable as the interactions between camp leaders and inhabitants in other camps. Polish was not a widely known language throughout Europe, and English was undoubtedly the language used most by the British military, UNRRA workers, and members of NGOs when dealing with DPs. Consequently, most DPs who had direct contact with team directors such as Rousseau would have been educated and have some knowledge of English, and most would have belonged to Poland's elite. Therefore, Polish education became critically important due to the severe level of illiteracy among the Polish DPs.[44] After Rousseau retired Jamieson took over UNRRA Team 162. A former military man, he treated the DPs more like soldiers rather than dependants. The town's weekly reports certainly did not evidence any paternal or fraternal love between Jamieson and the Poles.[45]

Conclusion

The archipelago of Polish DP camps throughout British-occupied Germany were a long-lasting feature of the post-war landscape. By officially recognizing the new government of Poland on 5 June 1945, however, the Allies prolonged the stay of many DPs in the camps. When the borders were officially changed after Potsdam a month later, this solidified the resolve of many not to return to the new Poland. Consequently, many viewed their situation as one of statelessness. Something that was never recognized by the Allies. As Poland did indeed exist, and was welcoming of repatriates, statelessness was not an option. To many in the camps, however, the idea of returning to a land that was formerly East Germany or part of the new Soviet Union was also not an option. As this idea grew within the camps, attempts to root oneself within a diasporic community in Germany became commonplace. Places like Maczków were not only created to stabilize a community in turmoil, but they became a necessity for many as they suddenly lacked a geographically defined homeland that matched their pre-war ideals. Therefore, the physical construction of the imagined community became the only tangible remnant many Polish DPs were left with as they scrambled to resettle outside of Poland's new borders.

The Anglo-Polish relationships in the camps gradually fell apart during the immediate post-war years as a tendency to speak of Poles as a 'nuisance' became commonplace. As was seen earlier in this chapter, the recurring references to Poles in unfavourable terms also had an impact on the local Germans, exemplified here through Liselotte Becker. In the wider community too, however, Polish DPs taking over large areas of previously German land was predictably unwelcome. Haren's extreme case of evacuating an entire town and dispersing them into the surrounding area was met with anger that has lasted up until the present day. In other areas too, Germans feared reprisals from former forced labourers and Allied soldiers alike. Welfare workers often detail attempts to requisition German houses, with some owners begging UNRRA to take it to stop any further destruction, as one owner pleaded to Rhoda Dawson:

> Please, madam, take my house. Take my house. Here, where you have had lunch. The soldiers BREAK EVERYTHING. With a woman here, it will be better, please, madam, take my house. The Poles have taken everything. The officers . . . oh, the officers!⁴⁶

The Anglo-Polish-German relationships in the immediate post-war years were fraught. The British, Poland's ostensible 'brothers in arms', were caring for Polish DPs on the very land former aggressors had held them captive, and suddenly the Anglo-German power roles were reversed. This, understandably, led to some ill-feeling in communities that had been herded together by virtue of their birthplace, regardless of which nation they identified with. In the midst of these larger issues that confused place of birth with national identification, humanitarian workers attempted to work with only basic knowledge of these peoples' language, religion, and culture. Many, such as Pettiss, struggled to understand why geographic origins mattered so much. Others only came to understand later as physical reminders were placed in camps themselves. One American UNRRA worker, Kathryn Hulme, eventually realized what she was asking of the Polish DPs, imagining that half of the United States had been 'ceded to a foreign power – for example, everything from the Missouri River to the Pacific Coast, with about 38,000 square miles of Canada tossed in as recompense'.⁴⁷ The intricacies of what post-war Poland and Polishness meant to the DPs was something that only came to be understood through frequent interaction in the camps.

Rhoda Dawson's personal collection, bursting with postcards, scraps of paper, and photographs from Polish DPs, vividly expresses the affinity she developed for 'her DPs'. From the beginning of the diary-come-reflective-memoir *The Stagnant Pool*, it was clear she did not think much of Polish DPs, often referring to them as 'Polish dogs' or the occasional 'dirty old Pole'.[48] Quickly, her mind changed, as did her writings. Dawson's diary soon became filled with admiration for the Polish dedication to tradition, particularly tied to the sacral nationalism that was often displayed in Polish DP camps as festivities were readily adorned with religious and nationalist symbolism alike. Throughout her time with UNRRA she found herself taking up numerous welfare positions in camps across the British and US zones of occupation, but almost always with Polish DPs. A staunch advocate for literacy and artistic expression, her collection attests to the amount of time she spent procuring Polish songbooks and painting materials, pastimes she believed would be a form of rehabilitative counselling.[49]

Yet welfare workers such as Rhoda Dawson were only one half of the administrative machinery in DP camps. The military were the other half. The carers (welfare workers) and protectors (military officials) had to work in tandem to meet DPs' needs, but their relationship was strained from the outset. Maczków was free of these issues due to its own self-governing nature; however, DPs at camps like Wentorf found life much more restrictive as UNRRA and the military in particular vied for control over the camps.

4

'Carers' and 'protectors'

Encounters between the British military, humanitarian workers, and displaced persons

Introduction

The words 'displaced person' came to be emblematic of the Second World War as the sheer volume of those displaced was staggering. The Allies knew it was essential to heed the all-too-recent lessons of history and to create an organization, or organizations, capable of handling the mass of DPs who would be found throughout Europe and Asia once the fighting stopped. By mid-1942, Sir Frederick Leith-Ross, as the newly appointed chairman of the British-run Inter-Allied Committee on Post-War Requirements, had started to press the importance of international cooperation in the post-war world through a large and specifically designed relief organization which would operate alongside voluntary organizations.[1] Yet it was not until the Allies jointly released press statements concerning Hitler's extermination of Europe's Jews on 17 December 1942 that public outcry demanding that something must be done pushed the issue of refugees to the forefront of post-war Allied planning; UNRRA was the result.[2]

The United Nations Information Organization's pamphlet *Help the People to Help Themselves*, created in 1944, stated that 'there were few wasted words in the UNRRA pact; its spirit, devoid of frills and formalities, was one of honest realism'.[3] UNRRA was destined to become more than mere 'soup kitchen charity'. Its creators, imbued by the spirit of international humanitarianism, hoped that UNRRA would become a global model for future endeavours at the end of its short life. It was a departure from previous norms; a new precedent was set. Although UNRRA was to have a limited lifespan, its creators recognized it to be a watershed moment in international cooperation. As its first director general, Herbert Lehman declared to the US House of Representatives:

> If UNRRA succeeds, the world will know that international cooperation is possible, that common interests can be stronger than separate differences. Having done it once, the United Nations will have more confidence that they can do it again. The habit will have been formed.[4]

Alongside forming this new habit, UNRRA devoted half of its mission to ensuring lasting recovery for all those it helped through 'rehabilitation'. The provision of material needs was taken for granted, but, as UNRRA stated, 'men do not live by bread alone'.[5] Within the camps, however, understanding what 'rehabilitation' constituted was largely subjective. As will be seen, seemingly each welfare worker and military official came into the camps with their own preconceived ideas, contributing to fractious relationships. This chapter uses archival and private records to look at life in the DP camps in the British-occupied Germany. The British zone is often neglected in the current historiography as numerous rich and readily available memoirs of UNRRA welfare workers from the US zone have largely dominated research on DP experiences and relationships in camps.[6] This chapter will question who oversaw these camps and how the division of responsibility between the DPs' 'carers' and 'protectors' often coincided with a division of gender. Within this layered framework, Polish DPs, welfare workers, and military officials found they had to navigate the new structures of the post-war world. The policies which led to the creation of a hard core of DPs who were increasingly resentful of the Allies are discussed alongside the inability of the British to understand who Poles were in 1945, as well as how the very concept of 'nationality' had changed beyond recognition for many Central and Eastern Europeans. When determining who constituted a 'good' or a 'bad' DP, both UNRRA and the military would consider how amiable the DP group was on the whole. As Polish DPs resisted repeated interventions from both their carers and protectors they remained a 'bad' DP group for the duration. The strained relationship between the two caused complications for the DPs, and in particular Poles as the attribution of negative labels often came about as a result of biases and conflicts between the two dominant organizations. Indeed, attaching the 'nuisance' label to Polish DPs seemed to be a common ground upon which UNRRA and military workers agreed. This, in turn, affected the DPs themselves and how they looked upon their 'ally', eventually causing a more permanent DP camp community to form.

The impetus behind and creation of UNRRA

Before the humanitarian crisis that faced the Allies in 1945, the end of the First World War saw tens of thousands of people renouncing their nationality or being stripped of their citizenship to become Europe's stateless. Those classified as stateless persons after the First World War – mostly Turks, Greeks, Armenians, Russians, and Bulgarians – were those in need of care and legal protection as they had been made vulnerable by shifting borders and expulsions. Although the nation-states of Europe were relatively new, the concept of people who belonged to no nation was strikingly novel. In the post-1918 era, the League of Nations sought to create protection for those who had been declared stateless. This led to the creation of Nansen Passports in 1922 as the first international identity document that could be used in place of a passport.[7] It was the difficulties that this group of earlier refugees had presented that prompted the Allies to recognize the necessity of creating organizations that would assist such people legally, physically, mentally, and in any other capacity to restore peace in their troubled lives. Additionally, it led the way for a more permanent solution to problems concerning those seeking asylum, protection or refuge as the Allies came to recognize the permanence of groups such as these as a result of increasing tensions between nations and during conflict.

Although an organization already existed to deal with certain categories of refugees, the Intergovernmental Committee on Refugees (IGCR), the need to create something all-encompassing became urgent.[8] US and British delegates met in 1943 at Hamilton in Bermuda. The conference was called to discuss what was to be done with Jewish refugees who had been liberated by the Allies but remained in Nazi-occupied Europe.[9] The outcome of the conference was a clearer focus on refugees' need for sustenance, repatriation, and possible resettlement once hostilities ceased.[10] To ensure that these needs were met, UNRRA was formally signed into existence on 9 November 1943 at the White House in Washington, D.C., with a total of forty-four member nations. At the same time the IGCR underwent a major re-organization to account for the creation of UNRRA and was subsequently given government funding for the first time to help complete its task.[11] The distinction between the two organizations, however, needed clarification. Tommie Sjöberg concludes that 'the most important difference between the two organizations' tasks was that UNRRA was not mandated to deal with those DPs who for various reasons did not wish to be repatriated'.[12] As the numbers of those unwilling to repatriate grew, however, the mandate shifted. A memorandum dated 25 June 1945 stated that although the IGCR was to take care of 'non-repatriables' and was ultimately in charge of their eventual resettlement, there would also be an extension of UNRRA's duties with regard to 'persons who, though not immediately repatriable, may be regarded as potentially repatriable': in other words, the Poles.[13]

As discussed, Polish DPs, ex-POWs, soldiers, and all other classifications would come to argue that the Poland they had been presented with at the end of the Second World War was not their Poland. They did not recognize it as their home, and many felt they could not return. It was UNRRA's job to ensure every Pole was encouraged to return to what the Allies perceived to be Poland, and mounting pressure from UNRRA policymakers weighed heavily upon the welfare workers on the ground. The influence UNRRA had on the Polish DP population can be discerned by looking at who UNRRA was, why they were needed, the complications with the practical application of policies and why they were perceived to be inadequate by their contemporaries.

Each of UNRRA's forty-four contributing nations donated 1 per cent of their total national income to the cause, making Britain and the United States UNRRA's largest contributors and earning them the title 'UNRRA's real parents'.[14] UNRRA established its headquarters in Washington, DC, and its European Regional Office in London, appointing senior officials such as Sir Frederick Leith-Ross to take on its daily operations. Former governor of New York Herbert H. Lehman was hand-picked by the American president Franklin Delano Roosevelt as the first director general of UNRRA, a decision apparently made in haste without proper consultation with other Allies.[15] UNRRA had three director generals in its lifetime, all of whom came from the United States as a condition of their participation in order to avoid another League of Nations fiasco.[16]

As well as the appointment of an American to administer the organization, UNRRA consisted of a Policy Committee and a Council. The Council, comprising all forty-four nations, met twice a year whereas the Policy Committee was to consist of the Four Great Powers (China, the United States, Britain, and USSR) which ultimately made the majority of decisions directing the distribution of relief and implementation of policies.[17] It is important to understand that the meaning of UNRRA's second 'R' was debated throughout its lifetime with far-reaching implications for the DPs under their care. In UNRRA's *Help the People to Help Themselves* pamphlet one of its founding fathers, Dean Acheson states unequivocally, 'Post-war reconstruction was not its function; its limit was relief and such material rehabilitation as might be found essential to relief'.[18] In practical terms, the separation of rehabilitation and reconstruction was poorly defined leading to unending confusion throughout UNRRA's lifetime.[19] Some UNRRA workers understood 'rehabilitation' to be synonymous with relief; others viewed it as a means of agricultural and socio-economic reconstruction; and others still thought of it as psychological rehabilitation. The outlook of British UNRRA welfare workers working throughout the three zones was very reminiscent of Victorian traditions similar to those of colonizing missions.[20] Fraught with financial problems, the British zone focused on cost-effective self-help and psychological rehabilitation by providing very little material assistance and encouraging 'civilised and democratic values'.[21] Dean Acheson later lamented in his memoirs that 'the word [rehabilitation] had no definition: rather it was propitiation by the unknown'.[22] This lack of clarity caused widespread resentment among the British public once it became clear only fifteen months into UNRRA's existence that a drastic overhaul of its administration was needed if there was to be any hope of it achieving its goals.[23] Commander Robert Jackson was given the task of finding 'top men' where none were available. The war was still going on after all. Jackson, unlike the media, did not blame Lehman but rather recognized that 'inferior staff and administrative inefficiency all helped to give the dog a very bad name'.[24] UNRRA's poor organization in its formative years became an example of how the co-construction of aid operations dealing with a newly formed international humanitarian organization and the long-established military government were stifled before they even began. This had lasting consequences for those under its care as administrative quibbling obscured the real task at hand.

UNRRA, unique in its formation to deal with the aftermath of war, was constantly hindered by events outside its control. First, all the figures for relief and rehabilitation had been estimated based on the assumption that the war would be over in 1944. Consequently, the funding was inadequate, and Europe was increasingly devastated between 1944 and 1945. The Great War had left behind a legacy of horror, needless death and vast destruction; yet at the end of the Second World War the enormous displacement of people, the crippling of industry, and continuing hostility towards the Allies brought about a very different situation to that which UNRRA had prepared for. The organization never fully recovered from the shambolic administrative machinery of its first year, and consequently the forty-four contributing nations became increasingly apprehensive of continuing to provide funds for an organization that was a veritable money pit. The administration only briefly recovered under Commander Jackson. By mid-1946, most saw it as a failure and were happy to let the burden of its task weigh it down.

UNRRA was a 'necessary evil': UNRRA, SHAEF and managing the camps

As planning and reality were mismatched due to the war's length, UNRRA inevitably suffered from another problem: overpromising. This exacerbated the military and UNRRA's difficult relationship. After the drastic overhaul of its administration in 1944, UNRRA readied itself to help those in need once the hostilities ceased, although, rather problematically, it was impossible to know when this would happen. As the war continued throughout 1944 and into 1945, UNRRA's urgency about readying the teams to descend upon Europe appeared to be waning. In the meantime, something had to be done with DPs wandering through Europe trying to find a way home, as it was evident that their high numbers could hinder military operations and impede efforts to bring the war to a close. To combat this escalating problem the Supreme Headquarters Allied Expeditionary Forces (SHAEF) created its Refugees, Displaced Persons and Welfare branch.[25] It was created to stem the flow of refugees attempting to 'self-repatriate [which] might result in pillaging of freed areas' and could break down 'governmental authority . . . perhaps leading to revolutions and revealing Allied incapacity to deal with Europe's ills'.[26] Primarily its objective was to gather any persons without a home or refuge and place them in camps. In the interests of practicality, and to prevent friction between various groups, it was determined that this would be done according to nationality or ethnic group, a policy later continued by UNRRA when it was finally able to enter Germany in April 1945. Classifying who was Polish and by what criteria, however, was a task that the Allies could not comprehend. At the beginning under SHAEF, Poles were classified as Poles if they claimed to be Poles. It was only later that the varied nuances of Polishness began to surface and the whole organizational structure started to quake under the pressures of screening, as will be discussed in the next chapter.

SHAEF did its utmost to ensure that DPs were washed, clothed, fed, sheltered, and deloused with DDT powder. The scale of the operation dealing with Germany's DPs was overwhelming, and most UNRRA workers leaving the jubilant training centres in France were unprepared for the chaotic sight of the camps that greeted them.[27] Numerous UNRRA employees' journals commented extensively on their disbelief on entering a DP camp. Claiming there was no sign of Western standards of civilization, with excrement covering the floors of each room and couples fornicating anywhere they could. Men and women had, for the most part, been segregated for months and sometimes years while engaged in forced labour or housed in concentration camps. When liberation came and the DPs freedom was restored the prevention of venereal diseases became problematic as the rush of sexual freedom and euphoria further strained the limited medical supplies. In the small district of Soest, the number of cases of STDs reported increased from around ten per year to fifteen per week.[28] The occupiers showed a lack of concern about individual welfare, and the only way to combat these problems was compulsory hospitalization where 'vaccination measures were enforced by withholding ration cards in cases of non-compliance'.[29] In the explosion of euphoria that followed the cessation of hostilities, the body became a thing of power after being enslaved for so long. Poles could choose how they used their bodies, when they used them, and for what purpose, as they had been unable to do so throughout the war due to various restrictions. As Katarzyna Nowak notes, the camps took on a carnivalesque 'world turned upside down' akin to the medieval Feast of Fools wherein social hierarchies are reversed and 'for a brief moment, what was repressed may thrive, the ruled may rule, the sacred is humiliated, and the profane is elevated'.[30] After the initial euphoria subsided, the consequences became plain, with venereal disease and illegitimate children common. Many Poles were shunned for their exploits, as promiscuity, and especially with non-Poles, was viewed as un-Catholic, and subsequently un-Polish.[31]

It was clear that there was much to be done to bring order into Germany's DP camps. UNRRA was in charge of looking after DPs in the camps, performing welfare tasks, and preparing them for eventual repatriation. Initially, the Poles in the camps did not intend to stay in the British zone for longer than a few weeks after the cessation of hostilities. Due to earlier agreements between the Allies at Yalta and Potsdam, however, Soviet DPs had been given priority for repatriation, causing a suspension in Polish repatriation until the summer of 1945.[32] From this point onwards, Polish resistance to repatriation festered. Some UNRRA workers commented on the Allies' vital decision to prioritize Soviet repatriation, stating that as a result 'we've missed the psychological moment as far as the Poles are concerned'.[33] Some believe that had the Poles been able to repatriate en masse at the end of the war, accompanied by jubilant fanfare and patriotic fervour, the situation would have been entirely different by September 1945. The Poles were in a reluctant state of suspension in the camps waiting for their repatriation to begin.

The camps were set up hastily using any prefabricated building classed as inhabitable. In British-occupied Germany just over 200 DP camps existed, the majority containing Poles. Although some, such as Braunschweig and Bottrop, were solely Polish camps, others, such as Greven and Augustdorf, held a mixture of various Central and Eastern European nationalities, although they were increasingly dominated by Poles by September 1945.[34] The operations of the camps themselves were complicated, however, with two dominating forces in charge: UNRRA and the Allied military.[35] The difficult relationship between the two was exacerbated in the British zone due to a lack of financial resources resulting in inadequate food supplies and minimal staffing. The formation of the camps' infrastructure, how the camps were run on a daily basis, and the competing ideologies imposed on the DPs by the two dominating forces all contributed to the formation of a more permanent Polish DP group. Although the duties of the UNRRA staff and military authorities were meticulously divided and assigned on paper, like many other aspects of the post-war world, in practice this became impossible to implement.[36] Private and administrative sources often vindicate the view that both UNRRA welfare workers and military personnel were resentful of one another throughout their time governing the camps. This continuous discord between the carer and protector negatively impacted the Polish DPs themselves; too busy meticulously attending to their bureaucratic duties, UNRRA and the British military government failed to see the hard core of Polish DPs forming as a result of poorly implemented policies.

The *SHAEF Guide to Displaced Persons in Germany* (revised and released in May 1945) stated that the welfare and repatriation of United Nations DPs was the highest Allied objective and that detailed procedures were to be followed, including housing them appropriately, separating national groups, grouping family units together, ensuring access to Repatriation Officers, and encouraging recreational activities to dissuade idleness.[37] The Allied military were at first unwilling to accept UNRRA's help and instead longed for partnership with familiar relief agencies, in particular the Red Cross, to take care of Europe's DPs.[38] The Red Cross did continue to play a fairly prominent role, albeit subordinate to the Allied military and UNRRA. The Polish Red Cross (*Polski Czerwony Krzyż*) came to symbolize an exceptional part of DP life, later continuing its efforts under the title of Relief Society for Poles (*Towarzystwo Pomocy Polakom*) and trading almost exclusively in cigarettes.[39] SHAEF viewed the task of repatriation as their burden, causing the military to become 'collectively contemptuous of [UNRRA's] personnel' believing that involving a civilian organization such as UNRRA 'would create a security hazard'.[40] Some military officials were against UNRRA entirely: as Proudfoot asserted, 'it was generally felt that military commitments were best discharged by military personnel, working under military orders, and equipped from military sources'.[41] Once official estimates had been made of the numbers expected to require repatriation, however, SHAEF conceded that outside help would be essential to get the job done; UNRRA was a necessary evil. UNRRA's primary responsibility was established as the care and maintenance of Europe's DPs, and at the first council session multiple resolutions were passed to ensure that DPs were all treated fairly and equally. Due to a shortage of staff and a severe problem with overpromising, however, the required number of UNRRA teams fell drastically short of those agreed by Lehman and the Allied military.

In February 1945, UNRRA had promised 250 full teams, later increasing this number to 450 full teams to work with the military as SHAEF cleared the path towards Berlin. Yet it was not until the end of 1945 that these numbers were reached, and this failure became known as the 'origin of the perpetual muddle that never got straightened out'.[42] Consequently, the occupying military forces and other volunteer relief agencies were required to bulk out the numbers.

The relationship between UNRRA and the military

The tense relationship that developed between UNRRA and the military authorities caused practical problems, including adequately administering relief, encouraging rehabilitation, and organizing repatriation. The noticeable animosity at all levels of the UNRRA and military hierarchies led to the implementation of a series of ad hoc policies in the camps that only proved to impede repatriation attempts and further increase tensions. Yet the interdependence of the two authorities was key to the day-to-day running of the DP camps in the British zone. Initially, UNRRA was made subordinate on the principle that during active warfare it was imperative that the military government had total control of the theatre of operation. This principle, however, continued during peacetime. The DP camps remained under military care, and control could be delegated to a civilian organization at the behest of a commanding officer. In reality, this meant 'a severe limitation of UNRRA's supposedly vast scope and promise . . . UNRRA was 'at best a "junior partner"'.[43] There was no question that cooperation between UNRRA and the military was essential; however, the physical composition of each side meant their views were often diametrically opposed. This was habitually attributed to the military's inherent lack of understanding of UNRRA's role, and especially the problems associated with DPs and refugees. Yet both shared one definite goal: 'to maintain order and hygiene in the Assembly Centres'.[44]

The military and UNRRA representatives operated in markedly different ways in the camps. The human element was sometimes lost to the more military minded, and there was a perceptible inability among military staff to understand what the aid programme really required of them other than providing food, shelter, and transport. Many were frustrated at having to care for these people. Military officials also frequently complained about the UNRRA workers they had to deal with, accusing them of being dumb, corrupt, naïve, and inefficient. Indeed, Rhoda Dawson's own recollections in *The Stagnant Pool* are not wholly complimentary of her UNRRA team. After a lecture from an American SHAEF member of staff she lamented:

> From his description the work sounds terrific and I fear a little for my team. We have no doctor, Mina is dreamy, slow and rather nervous (thirty-three, looks a young twenty-four), the Director is <u>tres gentil</u> but so far shows no special brilliance; I feel horribly nervous and my back is a nuisance.[45]

The acronym UNRRA had been attributed various meanings, primarily by Red Cross workers, jesting that UNRRA really stood for 'You Never Really Rehabilitate Anyone'.[46] Consequently, many UNRRA welfare workers' testimonies are not shy of voicing their distaste for military men who lacked even the most basic empathy. Of course, having experienced years of warfare it is easy to understand that many of these men were utterly exhausted, especially compared to the newly trained and enthusiastic UNRRA workers. Yet the DPs themselves did not treat all British military personnel with disdain: some created lasting relationships with strong bonds. It is significant, although not surprising, that while UNRRA's composition was fairly equal in terms of gender distribution (40% of the Displaced Persons Operation by June 1946 in Germany was staffed by women), the vast majority of welfare positions were taken up by women, while many of the military officials in positions of authority in the camps were men.[47] This gender contrast often added to the already diametrically opposed ideals of how the DPs should be looked after in the camps.

SHAEF's original plan recognized the need for closer arrangements with UNRRA to look after refugees if it was to take over from the military at the end of the hostilities. Yet after SHAEF was terminated on 13 July 1945, the Allied agreements 'specified unequivocally that UNRRA, in spite of increased responsibility, was to remain in a subordinate relationship to the military authorities who would exercise sovereign power in enemy territory'. As a result, it is argued here that UNRRA was unable to fully carry out the task for which it was initially created due to the military's reluctance to relinquish control over the DPs and their care. Proudfoot succinctly sums up the relationship between the Allied military and UNRRA: 'the civilian and the soldier were as oil and water, and dependence on the military was resented to the end'.[48] Of course, this comparison generated further difficulties once soldiers were required to take on responsibilities that were previously designated as 'civilian duties'. Due to UNRRA's shortage of staff, many were plucked from the military lines and amalgamated into the organization, causing further tensions.

UNRRA suffered from serious structural difficulties from the beginning, largely stemming from its endless subordination to the Allied armies. As a consequence, the inability to perform to the best of its ability had a detrimental effect on the DPs themselves. Reports flooded in of UNRRA installations being treated as army camps. Armed military personnel guarded the camps, curfews had been implemented, food was restricted, work was being demanded, or denied, and so forth, all of which culminated into a depressingly anti-climactic view of liberation for the DPs.[49]

In the British zone, wartime bombing had had a particularly damaging effect on the housing infrastructure, and there was heavy reliance on former concentration camps, foreign labour camps, and other installations which could provoke unwanted memories. Indeed, many were one and the same. In the small district of Soest in the middle of Nordrhein-Westfalen, where slave labourers had been used for work on the *Deutsche Reichsbahn* and for two other companies, the transition from concentration camp to DP camp was barely discernible.[50] The DP camp did not last long, as requisitioning amenities from the surrounding German houses was barely enough to keep the camp going and most of the DPs were moved on to other camps in the British zone.[51] In a 1945 article in *The World Today*, the set-up and organization of Esterwegen DP camp in Lower Saxony is described as an average example of what one would come across in a DP camp. The camp mostly housed Russians, with a smattering of Poles, and was 'enclosed by three sets of wire (one of them electrified) and a high brick wall'.[52] It was overcrowded and showed signs of being subject to unhygienic conditions that had only recently been alleviated by a bar of soap. Reports such as these made it clear that the need for UNRRA was greater than the military was willing to recognize. A possible corrective to this situation, it was thought, would be to place an army official in the UNRRA fold.

During 1945 it became apparent to Polish DPs, caught in the midst of this infighting between UNRRA and military personnel, that this could work in their favour. As UNRRA focused on the improvement of Poles through 'rehabilitation', camp leaders used the ineffective relationship with the military to encourage the Polish establishment of active organizational committees. The principle of self-governance was readily accepted by Poles who were particularly anxious to re-form organizations similar to those that had existed before the war. The military's inability to intervene in the creation of these organizations soon began to irk those eager to repatriate the DPs. In Maczków, exceptional levels of organization took place to ensure that Poles were provided for. To UNRRA workers in 1945/46 this was a boon for UNRRA's founding principles of helping the people to help themselves. Once a more permanent group of DPs became visible, however, it became harder to disband these camp communities and follow through with UNRRA's dominant aim: repatriation. Not all military personnel in charge of the Polish DP camps lamented this self-organization. At Wentorf, the Public Safety Officer R S Lawson and the rest of Military Government Detachment 220 welcomed it, but admitted that repatriation was nevertheless the real aim.[53] As in Maczków, other Polish DP camps evolved once the British had designated a 'high-ranking Pole' to form an ethnic enclave. Wacław Sterner, a former AK officer who had participated in the Warsaw Uprising, was charged with such a task and his insights into how the camps operated provide a useful perspective from within the Polish community. After his liberation he was granted the title Commandant by the British military authorities and put in charge of Buchhorst, later renamed *Kościuszko*, a hastily erected, primarily Polish DP camp of wooden shacks and a partially destroyed brick factory. To Sterner it resembled a huge 'Gypsy camp' with an inordinately high number of women. Like many Poles he was grateful at first for small mercies, such as toilet paper.[54] Soon he came to resent the military authorities, and determined that other DPs were suggesting Germans should be removed from villages to make way for Poles, believing that the Poles had suffered enough, and now the Germans should be their slaves.[55]

There was a continual attempt to delicately balance the scale of DPs' self-governance while they received aid from UNRRA and protection from the military. Most of the time, however, the balance could not be negotiated adequately, leading to multiple complications when implementing repatriation policies.[56] Kanty Cooper, a member of the Quakers' Friends Ambulance Unit, recollected that when she arrived in the British zone in 1946 to help with relief and screening, she was simultaneously shocked by the level of devastation and infuriated by the living arrangements. Both DPs and Germans were living in shambolic constructions while the military lived in great comfort. As a member of an NGO she was assigned the same courtesies as the military officers, and claimed:

> We lived in great comfort, we lacked nothing, our accommodation was more than adequate. According to army instructions, an officer had to have a room to himself and not more than four could share a bathroom. If the house were large and there were only one or two bathrooms, bedrooms remained empty.[57]

Kanty was particularly aggrieved to be living in relative luxury while those she was there to help struggled for the basic necessities. From a German's point of view, houses were being requisitioned for officers and DPs; from a DP's point of view, they were being requisitioned for Germans. This bred resentment among the camp communities. Somewhere in the middle, UNRRA and NGO workers were sorting, classifying, and 'rehabilitating' the 'human debris' of war.

The military government, Lieutenant General Sir Frederick Morgan and attitudes towards Polish displaced persons

In September 1945, Lieutenant General Sir Frederick Morgan was appointed Chief of Operations for the UNRRA mission in Germany. Morgan accepted the appointment stating that 'to my simple military mind a touchingly humble request for one's services made personally by a Secretary of State was, whatever the consequences, hardly to be denied'.[58] Morgan threw himself into the task, much to the appreciation of Commander Robert Jackson who had spent the previous months untangling the mess of red tape that UNRRA had bound itself in. Although Morgan and Field Marshal Montgomery clashed on the operation of UNRRA, it was agreed that 'UNRRA would take over the running of the DP camps but would remain dependent on the military for law and order, security and transport'.[59] Appointments such as Morgan's, however, were a cause of contention between UNRRA and the military. It was believed to be a source of much 'heart-burning among the rank and file of the UNRRA staff' as they watched UNRRA cherry-pick Allied military personnel in substantial numbers and place them in key positions.[60] It was thought, perhaps, that these positions were best filled by civilians to further disentangle the UNRRA-military administrative apparatus. Yet the war had already claimed 'the best and brightest' who were engaged in active service, in the administrative field or filling governmental positions. As Proudfoot argues, due to a severe shortage of manpower when recruiting 'UNRRA's needs were to be met primarily by a limited number of welfare specialists, over-aged adults, persons physically disqualified from military service, and women'.[61] It therefore became apparent quite early on that army officers would be required to fill the key positions in UNRRA once they had been relieved of duty as the human resources available to UNRRA were deemed unsuitable. Notably, however, those recruited from the military often took administrative roles rather than welfare positions, causing what Silvia Salvatici terms as the 'masculinization of relief work'.[62] This was yet another indication that the division of carer and protector was gendered in the DP camps. Interestingly, this division also extended to other British "zones" housing Polish DPs, such as the camps in colonial East and Central Africa. In particular, when discussing the British-Polish connection that had followed the Polish DPs across the Middle East and into British colonies in Africa, Jochen Lingelbach states: 'The welfare of women and children was seen as a task for women, whereas the overall responsibility lay in the hands of male administrators with military ranks, clearly reflecting the Gendered roles of "caring" women and "protecting" men'.[63] The terms 'carer' and 'protector' also applied to the roles filled by Polish DPs themselves; women as the national image of *Matka Polka* (Polish Mother) charged with caring for the nation's children, and men as their (and the nation's) protectors.[64] The replication of these roles among those in charge of the camps – the military, and UNRRA – only exacerbated DP attempts at self-governance as the hierarchal system of 'carer' and 'protector' were put in place, once more infantilizing the DPs.

Additionally, the difficulties of repatriating Poles were often exacerbated by British prejudice. Morgan believed that UNRRA's goal of repatriating DPs could be achieved with relative ease, unless the Poles refused to return home. Unfortunately for Morgan, the latter came to dominate UNRRA's repatriation programme and caused considerable outrage among many of the British military officials and UNRRA workers. Poles were viewed much less favourably than other DP groups, Morgan himself marvelled at the cleanliness and structure of Baltic DP camps, but found the Polish DP camps much less favourable. In his diary he remarked:

> One could see here very clearly the superiority of the Balt over the Pole, from the point of view of civilization, though it was interesting to see that the Poles here have evidently learnt a lot from living cheek by jowl with the Balts. I went into several of the Polish rooms and in none of them did one meet with the smell of long dead dog that is so typical of most other Polish settlements that one has visited.[65]

Morgan seemingly had previously compared the smell of a Polish DP camp to that of 'a zoological garden ... after the animals had been dead for a fortnight'.[66] Many other members of the military, regardless of whether they officially worked for UNRRA, came to similar conclusions. The years of repetitive Nazi propaganda accusing Poles of being slovenly, lazy, work-shy, and inferior also seemed to find a place in the British mindset. It is important to remember that the prejudicial assumptions underpinning Nazi racial policy were also common in other societies at the time, including Britain and Poland.[67]

In one instance, while boarding repatriation ships at Travemünde, a port near Lübeck, on 21 October 1946, Poles were subjected to thorough searches of their belongings. When Schepanik (according to anglicized notations) was asked to produce a certificate of ownership for an item, it was ignored and claimed illegitimate. After a scuffle and the threat that he would be shot, he showed the scrap of paper, written in German, to the chief of the CCG Port Control: 'German Police in Hamburg, no. 34 certified that the man SCHEPANIK, inhabitant of POLASKA Camp, Lubeck/Schwartau, (Schwartauerallee, 50/51) had exchanged his wristwatch, make "DOCKSE" for a bicycle make "UNION" no. 99329.' The chief ignored this, however, and demanded nothing less than a certificate of ownership signed by either a full army colonel or an UNRRA team director which also stated that 'the article had been obtained by the DP with the money he had earned in GERMANY'.[68] Other Poles had radios and cigarettes confiscated with no justification given. Although this is not surprising as cigarettes and radios were two of the most sought-after items on the black market in Germany at the time. Polish DPs such as 'Schepanik' would not have had access to the ordinary means of trading with money, and frequently used an exchange system. Yet the British military, doggedly specific about authorized certificates of possession, were unwilling to accept or recognize that paying for goods with money, earned in Germany no less, was not possible for many Polish DPs.

The expansion of the black market, often selling UNRRA goods, was one of the areas in occupied Europe where the Allies had very little control, and in many cases were actively involved themselves. The confiscation of bicycles is perhaps the lesser of two evils contained in the report from Travemünde. The condition of the ships, much like those of the 'cattle cars' transporting ethnic Germans under *Operation Swallow* defied coherent language. Krysz, a Polish repatriation officer inspecting the ship, had 'the impression of seeing revived pictures of the inside of slave ships'. The poorly lit upper and lower decks had no lavatories, windows, or receptacles of any kind if one were to get seasick. Indeed, the set-up was reminiscent of the camps from which the Poles had recently been liberated, with racks of bunks no more than two and a half feet between them, three tiers high and in absolute darkness. There were no fire precautions, and the entire ship was stuffed with wood and straw. If a fire had occurred there was no doubt as to what would happen.[69] In a series of curt replies, the British military addressed the travelling conditions of the ship by stating, 'the deterioration of amenities can only be attributed to the repatriants themselves, as a whole, if not the specific party travelling on this occasion'.[70] The onus was put on the Poles, even though the amenities mentioned could not be changed by any amount of regard for cleanliness.[71] The British military was unwilling to accept the conditions were of its own making and, perhaps worse, did not care that Poles were subjected to these concentration-camp-like conditions. The accusation that the conditions were of the Poles' own making is repeatedly echoed throughout Morgan's diary, often with comments on the Poles' laziness and lack of cleanliness. After visiting Hersfeld DP camp he wrote:

> One saw how almost hopeless the Pole is. These people were just sitting about and had been sitting about for months without doing anything at all, and they made trivial complaints with regard to the food, which I thought was ample and very good.[72]

Morgan's position at UNRRA was called into question after a press conference in Frankfurt am Main on 2 January 1946. At this conference he referred to a 'positive plan for a second exodus of Jews' from Poland, stating that 'all of them were well dressed, well fed, healthy, and had pockets bulging with money'.[73] Shortly after he had made these inappropriate comments, newspapers and US correspondents contacted UNRRA's director general, Herbert Lehman, in support of Morgan and his position.[74] Herbert metaphorically slapped Morgan on the wrist and ordered him not to mention matters unrelated to UNRRA's task in Germany, praising his 'deep concern for his work and his desire to return to carry it forward'.[75]

Morgan continued to carry out his duties as Chief of Operations for the UNRRA mission in Germany for a brief period, but after giving an 'off-the-record' address to correspondents at UNRRA's Fifth Council session in Geneva, the new director general, Fiorello LaGuardia, eliminated his position in Germany. In his autobiography, Morgan claims that LaGuardia summed up the matter by saying, 'You know, General, I believe you were the wrong man for this job from the start'. Whether or not Morgan's attitude towards the various ethnic DP groups can be taken as indicative of shared attitudes among Allied military personnel and UNRRA teams is not easy to discern, and further investigation is required. Morgan certainly had his prejudices. Yet as correspondents for American newspapers in Germany argued, his observations on the Jewish DPs flooding into the US and British zones of occupation, and his slanderous comments about UNRRA's corrupt organization in Geneva, were not a great departure from the truth. As has been suggested numerous times elsewhere, UNRRA's administration was viewed as corrupt almost from the outset, as such an altruistic venture even with the best intentions could only achieve so much in times of crisis.⁷⁶ Morgan later commented in his autobiography that his 'off-the-record' address signified that 'the curtain had went up on the last act of the tragi-comedy [that was] my United Nations service'.⁷⁷

It is important to acknowledge that many felt that UNRRA had done the best it could under the circumstances. The organization had seemingly been beset with the misfortune from the start. As one reporter noted, UNRRA 'had accumulated the red tape of 40 nations, but it would be truer to say 40 countries had tied UNRRA up in their red tape'.⁷⁸ Morgan's case is significant in terms of understanding the military and UNRRA's perceptions of Polish DPs. As Chief of Operations for UNRRA in Germany, his main priority was officially supposed to be UNRRA, although he was clearly a military man above all else. Morgan later branded UNRRA workers in his autobiography an 'adventitious assembly of silver-tongued ineffectuals, professional do-gooders, crooks and crackpots' many of whom were 'seeking to atone for draft-dodging'. He blamed UNRRA's ineffectual work on the international formation of its ranks, complaining that he had 'dealt with a mixed bag before but never with a receptacle of "all sorts" such as was UNRRA in Germany', which made any unifying force or idea impossible.⁷⁹

In Morgan's autobiography, his views on DPs in general were favourable. He showed commitment to providing them with sufficient relief by reversing previous measures that had proved detrimental, and tried to further their rehabilitation by promoting UNRRA as the source of not only physical but also psychological help, which had been lacking before Morgan's appointment. Morgan recognized that the need for rehabilitation was about 'helping the people to help themselves' through encouraging various activities such as the formation of amateur theatre groups and educational groups to enhance their future job prospects.⁸⁰ Although this concept was anchored in the foundations of UNRRA's welfare guide, it was all too frequently ignored by military personnel unwilling to fulfil what they perceived to be a civilian role.⁸¹ On the other hand, from early on in his chapter relating to UNRRA, Morgan is critical of Polish DPs as a whole and clearly distinguishes between them and other nationalities similarly to his distinction between Jews and 'other DPs'. This ideological (and Morgan would argue, often physical) separation of Poles and Jews from 'others' was an unhappy continuation of wartime policies. Although practices were not carried out anywhere near to the same malicious extent, they were still an unfortunate reminder of the separation of these groups from 'others'. In the 'hierarchy of empathy' Poles were very close to the bottom, and this proved to have lasting consequences.⁸²

Forming a bond: UNRRA welfare workers and Polish displaced persons

Amid the chaos of post-war Germany, often referred to as the *Trümmerzeit* (rubble time) due to the complete lack of cohesive infrastructure and means of supply, UNRRA's altruistic individuals were trained to help those whom they had seen in newspapers looking desperate and wanting. DPs, comprising a hodgepodge of nationalities, vying for attention and for recognition of the fact that the hardships they had endured were unique, significant, and tragic, became the sole charge of UNRRA welfare workers. Poles, the biggest group after Soviet DPs had been repatriated, were easily the most visible, and due to their situation were perceived to be needy. Yet despite their vociferous claims, this afforded them neither special treatment nor special recognition. Wacław Sterner comments that many Poles viewed themselves as victims of the Third Reich and felt that they deserved compensation as the Allies were obviously rich. He writes that Poles thought in collective terms: 'we first opposed'; 'we fought for London'; 'we have suffered the longest'. He summarizes the Polish DPs' case ironically declaring that it 'would be a deep ungratefulness of Englishmen if they would not give us fair compensation for all this'.[83] Sterner, as a camp commandant, is frustrated by the Polish attitude towards the British and believes many Poles used it as an excuse not to work in the camps. From the welfare workers' point of view, however, all were to be treated the same, and the task was to be carried out with efficiency. Rhoda Dawson opens her notes on the organization's training programme at Jullouville in France stating, 'I have a chart of the ideal D.P. Camp to copy out, but our job may not take long as the main D.P.'s [*sic*] should be home by July and all should have left by next March'. As soon as Dawson was introduced to a member of SHAEF, however, she was told to disregard everything she had been taught at Jullouville because conditions were constantly in flux.[84]

UNRRA's first team arrived in Neustadt in the US zone in April 1945; they were greeted by utter chaos and highly unsanitary conditions. After a month, basic order was restored. It became evident at this time that the military's cooperation was fundamental if UNRRA's goal of providing relief and rehabilitation to millions of DPs across Germany was to be achieved. Indeed, as a YMCA worker believed, 'without the military then, it would have been an utter shambles'.[85] The teams generally consisted of thirteen members: director, deputy director, clerk-stenographer, supply officer, mess officer, warehouse officer, medical officer, nurse, team cook, two welfare officers, and two drivers. Although the need for more UNRRA teams became increasingly apparent, a 'make do' attitude prevailed, and 'spearhead' teams were composed of no more than seven team members.[86] According to some welfare workers, the spearhead teams of seven members were frequently also a figment of the planner's imagination. UNRRA teams' first task was to take over the military's efforts at clothing, feeding, sheltering, and delousing. Their second task, however, UNRRA's second 'R', was much more complex.

UNRRA workers had become increasingly irritated by their fellow Westerners' 'ethnocentrism or sheer ignorance' about DPs and cultural differences.[87] Dawson makes it clear in her private papers that this lack of rehabilitative measures was not necessarily always the fault of UNRRA's system, blaming the lacklustre efforts of the UNRRA employees themselves. Indeed, the level of care DPs received was certainly affected by such a fractured view of the task at hand. Increasingly, as the job became repetitive and monotonous, UNRRA workers were even less inclined to help rehabilitate the hard-core DP population that remained, namely the Poles. UNRRA workers' descriptions of their time in Germany as welfare workers often complain of the frequency with which they were moved about. This heightened feelings of ineffectualness as time constraints and sudden relocation, often with less than twenty-four hours' notice, caused distress. A charitable disposition and humanitarian goals were not enough for UNRRA workers to perform to the best of their abilities, and a growing sense of frustration with the administration can be seen in personal writings by mid-1946.[88] Consistently, this frustration is of two kinds, the military's apathetic view of DPs, and UNRRA's overwhelming bureaucracy coupled with a growing disillusionment with welfare work.

Many workers themselves often lamented the overly bureaucratic nature of UNRRA's organization from the outset. Silvia Salvatici argues that rival bureaucratic models were simultaneously being put into place, as in 'European assembly centres old and new methods, practices and objectives coexisted, interplayed and mingled'.[89] On the one hand, UNRRA wanted to be recognized for making international humanitarianism a modern profession. On the other hand, the organization's administration was run along lines similar to those of previous attempts at international humanitarian endeavours. It was rigid and overly bureaucratic, with a complex hierarchical tower.[90] Additionally, it was felt that any new model of relief and rehabilitation envisaged because of UNRRA was going to be hampered by the presence of ex-soldiers in UNRRA's ranks. Ralf Hodge, who worked for UNRRA in the British zone, resigned over his inability to carry out his work due to military interference. He stated that the army's caste system was stifling UNRRA, commenting that 'UNRRA seems to have become a heaven for demobbed who insist on perpetuating military titles, following army procedures and socializing on rank basis'.[91] Hodge was not alone in his inability to work in these parameters, other welfare workers found the overly bureaucratic model cripplingly uncompromising.

Rhoda Dawson became particularly disheartened over the bureaucracy of UNRRA. In December 1946, she states that she has had a 'rather too recent realization of what this work requires - a careful study of directives because each one may contradict the last; four copies of every letter, margins to begin fifteen spaces from the left-hand edge and subdivisions of subdivisions numbers (a), (b) and (c)'.[92] Dawson prefaces her private papers *The Stagnant Pool* with a statement that one of her friends, 'a crippled woman of considerable ability and great charm, who longed to clear up the human debris left about Europe' had shamed her into applying to UNRRA, even though she had concluded that social work was not her thing at all after working continuously in welfare positions throughout the war years. Although she was not initially enthusiastic at the notion of another welfare position her attitude changed upon reaching France. Beginning in May 1945, at the Jullouville training facility her hopes of helping those most in need throughout Europe grew. The Arnold-Forster lecture series had made her see the altruistic potential of UNRRA.[93] When discussing her work with UNRRA between 1945 and 1947, however, there is a perceptible deflation in attitude towards her job.

In June 1945, Dawson was sent to her first posting, a Jewish DP camp named Rosenheim. This was followed by a series of moves to other camps, frequently establishing connections with UNRRA colleagues only to lose them due to constant movement. This happened all too often, resulting in fractured UNRRA teams without cohesive rehabilitation policies.[94] Although Dawson was largely moved around in the US zone, this was typical of UNRRA welfare workers in all three of the western zones. Similarly, Iris Murdoch, who worked in UNRRA's European regional office in London before being transferred several times, was also disillusioned by UNRRA's administrative body. She later wrote that UNRRA was 'rather too full of inept British civil servants (me for instance), uncoordinated foreigners with Special Ideas and an imperfect command of English. The result was pretty fair chaos. V[ery] many noble-hearted good-intentioned – drown in the general flood of mediocrity and muddle'.[95] From both sides of the administration, the field and the office, the stifling bureaucracy and overshadowing military all helped to sour UNRRA's reputation.[96]

Another point of contention for Polish DPs in the British zone was the restriction of self-established committees that served any purpose other than the daily running of the camps.[97] Although the US zone used the active New

Deal welfare model coupled with the ideal of American democracy, the British and French zones were more restrictive. Again, Maczków was an exception to the rule. Due to Britain's financial restrictions, their zone was unable to provide vast material assistance, and instead relied on building civic and moral values. According to Anna Holian, by 1945 the idea that refugees could be legitimate political subjects 'had fallen decisively out of favour', largely because it was believed that political exiles could only add to international conflicts.[98] This was something the British wished to subdue in their zone, which contained two strong political exile communities of Poles and Jews.[99] The solution for the Jews was, for the British, a mystery in 1945. The solution for the Poles, however, rested heavily on repatriation, as the British believed they had a homeland to return to and were merely exploiting the Allies, UNRRA, and the NGOs for economic reasons. The British went further than most to promote repatriation, and while distrust grew among the military-minded, welfare workers warmed to them and their distrust was more readily directed at the military and UNRRA rather than at the DPs themselves.[100] Just before Dawson was sent to spend a month in a German hospital, a member of the Polish Red Cross thanked her for her help:

> [. . .]because I, apparently alone among Welfare Officers, treat D.Ps as human beings. This depresses me slightly as it follows inevitably that one cannot be popular both with D.Ps and with one's superior officers, and it really does not mean that one does a good job, by UNRRA standards. For one is obliged to work impersonally, according to directives and with filling of many forms, to get things done properly.[101]

Dawson and many other welfare workers found the increasing restrictions placed on their ability to perform their welfare tasks oppressive. By the end of 1945, it was becoming clear that the Poles in particular were unwilling to repatriate en masse without assurances from the Allies that fair and just elections would be held in Poland. They continued with their welfare tasks in the camps, following SHAEF's order that UNRRA follow the Ford Assembly Line system: each person has a duty as a cog in the machinery but 'the cogs don't fit'.[102]

Ultimately the welfare workers and military officials were ill-equipped to deal with the huge number of Poles in their midst and knowing exactly who could be classed as a Pole was the cause of numerous headaches. The introduction of strict screening procedures in 1946 presented a more defined method of identifying the various nationalities and, naturally it was accompanied by a system to expunge 'undesirable' elements.[103] The mess of administrative paperwork created by UNRRA's hierarchy for processing DPs was a cause of endless confusion and frustration. Although the Allied military and UNRRA were the dominant forces in the DP camps, NGOs were essential to the task of screening. The Council of British Societies for Relief Abroad (COBSRA), an umbrella organization created in 1942 dedicated to social work and relief from suffering, was also required to follow UNRRA directives, including the recording of individual DPs and their nationalities.[104] The attempt to segregate DPs based on nationality or ethnicity in 1945 began in earnest. Once the dust had settled, and the vast majority of DPs had returned home by September 1945, those who remained were viewed as a burden, and eligibility screening was introduced to whittle their numbers down further.[105]

Conclusion

The relationship between the British military and UNRRA caused numerous problems when they were trying to implement policies in the camps. The inability and unwillingness of the military government to recognize the importance of a welfare worker's position in the camps caused policies aimed at rehabilitating DPs to fall flat before they even started. Many fine ideas died at birth. Dawson frequently complained about UNRRA's training centre being filled with ex-soldiers who relished telling civilians what to do with DPs but were reluctant to show them how. As stated in SHAEF's *Guide to Displaced Persons*, 'speedy repatriation remains the chief objective', and consequently efforts at rehabilitation, whatever the connotation, fell by the wayside. There was an inherent misunderstanding between the two dominant forces in the DP camps about what the DPs needed, and what was to be supplied. With most Polish DPs struggling to accept the reality of 1945 and its consequences for Poland, the British carers and protectors were trying to persuade them to return to a land that was viewed with suspicion by many.

The level of empathy with the DPs was clearly split between the carer and the protector, as was the gender division. The British military was overwhelmingly dominated by men, whereas the UNRRA welfare workers were primarily women under male control within the UNRRA framework. The classic gendered spheres that had existed before the war permeated the DP camps as well. A male UNRRA worker was likely to be not a man who had decided to take up relief work but one who had been drafted from the military and, like Marvin Klemmé, saw the organization as shambolic, ineffectual, and too soft on the DPs. Although this had a bearing on how receptive the DPs were to different groups, there were other factors at play in the camps that disassociated the Poles from their apparent allies.

UNRRA's work was hindered by a significant lack of political and geographical understanding of Europe, its history, and the recent formation of nation-states such as Poland. The British military and UNRRA workers bickered incessantly over the implementation of policy in the camps. In particular, the degree to which DPs were looked after and in what capacity, and who bore this responsibility. They often failed to fully understand the fundamental characteristics and composition of the DPs. Indeed, when Balts and 'Slavs' were housed together in the British zone all manner of fighting ensued to the perplexity of the inexperienced UNRRA and military government officials.[106] They were left scratching their heads in bewilderment as to why these similar people would not and could not get along. This became a virtual glue between the various officials in the camps, as they jointly castigated the Poles for their unwillingness to get along with other DPs. Had the officials taken the time to recognize almost any aspect of Polish history, a more thorough understanding might have developed.

UNRRA was poorly equipped to give history lessons to the wealth of workers it had to deploy across the world in an unnaturally short space of time. Klemmé was also ignorant of wartime circumstances, accusing Poles of laziness and greed. He argues that most working in Germany were not forced to labour at all and the majority worked voluntarily, simply continuing their pre-war foreign labour practices. He justifies their work in Germany by listing the benefits of working in a stronger economy, claiming that 'the German government had even gone so far as to work out an elaborate insurance and social security system for these people'. He sees nothing wrong with conscripted labour, predominantly because he considers it voluntary and for mutual gain.[107] In reality, by 1 March 1940 only 4 per cent of foreign workers in Germany were working voluntarily.[108]

If Klemmé, a former soldier, believed this it is likely that the thoughts of UNRRA's welfare workers, drafted primarily from the British and American home-fronts, were certainly under the same false impression. The presumption of an inherent Polish character was established. Working with and alongside Polish DPs, UNRRA welfare workers realized that they were not so different from themselves. It was only when attempts to repatriate the Polish DPs had picked up pace significantly that many UNRRA workers took the time to educate themselves about Poland, as well as the version of Poland they were asking the DPs to return to.

5

'No special obligation ... We did not take them to Germany'

Repatriation and resettlement of Polish displaced persons

Introduction

Throughout the summation of her memoirs, Rhoda Dawson is saddened by the turn UNRRA had taken against the DPs and by the winter of 1946 laments that 'welfare comes last, the main object is repatriation, in other words; "We've paid for you long enough, now get out".[1] The repatriation of Polish DPs was ostensibly no more difficult than that of other DP groups. To Polish DPs in British-occupied Germany, however, repatriation was inextricably linked with a growing fear of what awaited them in Poland. Yet in Britain and to British minds, this amounted to nothing more than the illegitimate rejection of repatriation for economic gain, further fuelling a negative perception of Polish DPs in the camps. The ideal of Anglo-Polish 'brothers in arms' had certainly hit on hard times. Britain, largely preoccupied by its own international standing and preventing the spread of communism in Germany, disregarded Polish appeals from those in the camps and in London to prioritize resettlement opportunities over repatriation. The Allied point of view was that Ukrainian and Baltic DPs could claim non-repatriable status, but not Poles; they were merely stalling. Laura J. Hilton's assertion that Polish DPs 'were the group that had the weakest basis for claiming non-repatriable status' may have been applicable to those resident in the US zone; however, those in the British zone had more than enough reason to choose to stay in a DP camp rather than return to Poland.[2]

As the repatriation figures waned among Polish DPs, UNRRA sought to boost them via various means; from official operations, such as *Operation Carrot*, promising extra food and using UN-sanctioned newsreels, to the banning of all recreational activities thereby enforcing idleness and boredom. Exhausting ways to encourage repatriation were coupled with a change in organization as this chapter looks at the period leading up to the IRO takeover in British-occupied Germany. As UNRRA bowed out from its European operations, it handed over the DP camps to an organization primarily aiming for resettlement rather than repatriation. In doing so, this chapter highlights how integral UNRRA and the IRO were to changes in policy and the shift from repatriation to resettlement, as well as how these ideas were enacted and received on the ground by welfare workers and DPs alike.

Alongside the shift in focus and organization, discerning how and why Poles were suddenly being accepted onto European Volunteer Worker (EVW) schemes across the globe, such as *Operation Westward Ho!* and *Operation Black Diamond*, with particular focus on Poles being accepted to Britain between 1946 and 1949, will be addressed. The treatment of Poles resettled in Britain under the Polish Resettlement Act (1947), including their dependents under *Operation Pole Jump*, and those who came to Britain as part of the EVW schemes also provides a glimpse into the post-war alliances that effected Anglo-Polish relations. The division between civilians accepted under EVW schemes and those who were demobbed within the Polish Resettlement Corps (and later resettled) highlights another area of division and hierarchy among the Poles themselves; a division fuelled by British policies. At the same time, within the camps 'screening' became a daily reminder of dividing lines between camp communities as procedures became increasingly rigorous in an effort to weed out 'quislings' and contributed to a further ethnic homogenization of camp communities. Simultaneously, Polish DP camp communities carried out their own methods of 'screening'. Based on a mixture of pre-war conceptions of morality coupled with wartime service, Polish communities determined levels of 'Polishness' (*polskość*) resulting in rejection or acceptance within the camps. For many, being screened by their 'carers' and 'protectors', as well as their own communities was exhausting and dehumanizing.

The combination of a shift in the carers' position to that of administrator and the rigorous screening procedures introduced in the camps eventually led to a state of apathy among many DPs. This was the result of a delay in offering resettlement opportunities to Polish DPs due to pressure from Warsaw to forcibly repatriate and UNRRA's focus on repatriation, as well as the British government's proclivity to prefer Baltic and Ukrainian DPs over Poles. Emphasizing how and when these resettlement opportunities evolved for Polish DPs will help to address the increasing antagonisms between those in the camps with varying priorities.

Repatriation became synonymous with Rehabilitation – but for whom?

UNRRA's second R (Rehabilitation), was plagued with uncertainty from the organization's inception. Even after deliberation and an official meaning was ascribed to the word, leading members were still in dispute over its connotation.[3] In the camps, and among UNRRA staff in particular, 'rehabilitation' came to mean whatever they deemed relevant to the situation they currently found themselves in. As mentioned in the previous chapter, the popular acronym of UNRRA's name, 'You Never Really Rehabilitate Anyone', became a well-known substitute.[4] Planners envisioned an organization that would remedy numerous post-war afflictions, beyond merely filling empty stomachs. During the war, ideas about how rehabilitation should and could be carried out were dependent on the individual's perception of the area of most need. To some, this meant the physical rehabilitation of the human being. Relief, to some extent, covers this by providing food, shelter, medicine, and clothing. Yet many were aware of needing to see rehabilitation as a recovery of both the body and the mind. Although post-traumatic stress disorder (PTSD) was yet to work its way into the welfare workers' vocabularies, notions of shellshock and trauma from the First World War were becoming well known. Some, however, also thought of rehabilitation in a spiritual sense. The experiences of war had certainly shaken any notion of religious belief or inner peace in many; however, it was predominantly welfare workers working on behalf of the Red Cross and Friend's Ambulance Service that thought of rehabilitation in this respect. To Rhoda Dawson, it was all of the above. A person, once broken by war, needed to be mended in every way. Yet other understandings of rehabilitation still abound as ideas of rehabilitation and reconstruction were often used interchangeably. For the military, this could mean the rehabilitation of institutions, and for governments, the rehabilitation of destroyed land and infrastructure. 'Rehabilitation' was the *mot du jour*, but a specific meaning was never determined.[5]

By September 1945 there remained 816,000 Poles in the three western zones of occupation in Germany. According to Malcolm J. Proudfoot, Polish DPs accounted for the majority of DPs in each of the western zones of Germany after 30 September 1945, making 79 per cent of the British zone's total DP population. Although Poles represented the highest percentage in all three zones, the British zone accommodated the majority of Polish DPs (see Figure 5.1). Consequently, when problems with repatriation arose, the British zone was hardest hit.[6] As Chief of Operations for the UNRRA mission in Germany, Morgan stated that

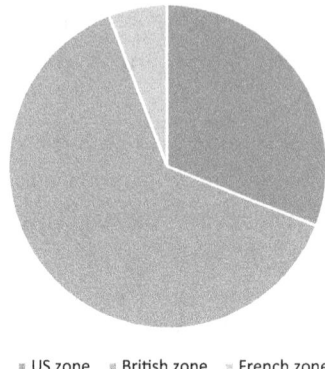

Figure 5.1 Percentage of total number of Poles in three western zones of Germany. Source: Created by Samantha K. Knapton.

'almost everything depends on the solution of the Polish problem. If the Poles agree to go home, and there is every likelihood that the vast majority of them will, the whole thing is comparatively simple'.[7] Unfortunately for Morgan the combination of events between May and September 1945 caused the Polish repatriation to stagnate.

The steadfast refusal of Polish DPs to repatriate seemed trivial to many of the British military officials and UNRRA welfare workers. This resulted in Poles falling firmly into the categorization of the 'bad' DP described by Woodbridge, one that was not as easily malleable as the Anglo-American post-war planners had hoped. Yet, even a basic understanding of who was classed as a Polish DP was often incomprehensible to the staff trained by UNRRA. While training at Jullouville, Dawson jotted in her notebook: 'Eastern Poles – may if let free by Soviet, opt for West Poland. If Russian Liaison Officer decides that Eastern Pole is Soviet Citizen he must go back'.[8] According to Dawson's notes, UNRRA was to forcibly repatriate Poles who were originally from east of the River Bug, the territory that had now become part of the Soviet Union. This was incorrect and the implementation of such a policy could have dire consequences for those forced to repatriate to a country they never belonged to in the first instance. Confusion at all levels of UNRRA's infrastructure, and certainly in the army, meant that policies were inconsistently applied.

In a SHAEF memorandum from June 1945, a discussion arose concerning what to do with those remaining in the camps as, according to the DP Branch in London, the '"sludge" if allowed to remain in the camps would rapidly become sour'.[9] The document proposes sorting the DPs in the camps into those who are certainly repatriating, and those who were not. Even at this juncture it was known to be impractical to carry out such a task before the Soviet DPs had been fully repatriated. The DP Branch, however, thought those remaining would pollute the minds of those wishing to repatriate. Animosity was already growing between British troops and the Polish DPs in the camps who were eagerly awaiting news of life in the new Poland.

By September 1945, Polish DP behaviour had been called into question by British military officers. There were numerous attempts to continually try and reinvigorate the 'brothers in arms' rhetoric within the camps, reinforcing assertions that the British and Polish could work together peacefully and amiably in the post-war world.[10] Although as we have seen this was largely ignored once it became clear the Germans were a more pressing priority outside of the camps than the Poles within them. Soon the propaganda used by Warsaw was being adopted by the British as the British Foreign Office encouraged repatriation on the basis that the Polish DPs needed to return to Poland to make it 'healthy' again, and there cannot be a 'healthy and restored Poland without the Poles themselves to do the job'.[11] Some British divisions threatened to 'get tough' with the Polish DPs, claiming to withhold food, clothing and other necessities, but this was met with scorn by the British Army of the Rhine HQ.[12]

To further encourage repatriation in the British zone, and therefore to aid 'rehabilitation', measures were put in place by British officials and UNRRA targeting Polish DPs. In the British zone this amounted to restricting newspaper circulation, refusing entry of any Polish DPs returning to the camps, and the introduction of Warsaw's own Polish liaison officers.[13] These were used in combination with bigger schemes launched by UNRRA to encourage Polish DP repatriation across all zones, such as *Operation Carrot*. The British zone, however, was particularly desperate for the Polish DPs to repatriate for a number of reasons. First, they were the most sizeable group and therefore perceived as a drain on the already dwindling resources in Germany. Secondly, the continued presence of Polish DPs in the British zone emphasized an unwillingness to conduct forcible repatriation, and therefore exacerbated relations with the Soviet Union. As Cold War tensions increased, the British in Germany came to view the Poles as an easy way to show good faith to the Soviet Union – if they could get them to repatriate. The implementation of policies to ensure this took place, however, were met with limited success. The British officials, instead of looking inward, blamed the Polish DPs for their steadfast refusal to repatriate and interpreted it almost as a sign of disobedience.

By the summer of 1946, the British perception of Poles was unfavourable. A Foreign Office telegram to Berlin on 4 July 1946 describes the situation in the British zone as unsatisfactory. It accused Poles of a tendency to cause disturbances and requests a more thorough screening procedure so that only those who would otherwise be in personal danger are allowed to remain in the camps. Point five of the telegram, however, unambiguously states what the British expected of the remaining Polish DPs:

> The rest of the D.P.'s would be informed that they must now choose between going home, settling in Germany on German rations or finding themselves other emigration possibilities (if they can). We cannot help with the latter. We have our hands full with Polish armed forces. We should add that the exact date at which D.P. camps will be terminated cannot be stated now, but the present state of affairs cannot continue indefinitely. D.P.'s would be well advised to return before the hardships of next winter. We should explain frankly that we cannot afford to keep them much longer at expense of taxpayer, that we are under no special obligation as we did not take them to Germany, that there is no work for so many in Germany in its present condition and that they should return home where there is a shortage of manpower.[14]

The Allied Control Council in Berlin agreed, stating that 'after a suitable interval to allow our announcement to the Poles to become known, we should begin to empty and close the camps'.[15] It appeared the British no longer regarded the Poles' unique plight as their concern. They increasingly felt burdened, particularly in a financial sense, and a solution was needed immediately. At this juncture UNRRA, led by LaGuardia, put *Operation Carrot* into full effect with the aid of a bombardment of pro-Warsaw literature. The British were growing weary and tired of their responsibilities and, although they had helped to create the very conditions that had led to the Poles' refusal to repatriate, they had effectively disowned their 'plucky little ally'. The Foreign Office's interpretation of the situation was that Britain was not wholly responsible for the Poles, as they had not brought them to Germany in the first place, and therefore were 'under no special obligation' to care for them. This sentiment is typical of the growing resentment felt towards the remaining DPs in mid-to-late 1946 as the British government and military were facing sharp criticism from the British public due to the introduction of bread rationing at home and the ongoing problems with food supplies throughout their occupation zone. The bad winter of 1946 suspended most repatriation transport to Poland, and by this time the British military knew that UNRRA's operations were to be discontinued by the summer of 1947. With this in mind there would have to be a final push for repatriation.

The relationship between the Polish DPs and the British were even more strained as they were viewed as a paradoxical people, longing for home but refusing to repatriate and subsequently confusing welfare workers and military officials alike. As Margaret McNeill stated, it permeated everything: 'the ally who had been so praised and had become so disliked. The Polish D.P.s coupled an intense admiration for all things British with a piqued disappointment that the British did not help them more'.[16] Within their own communities, Poles were also being scrutinized for their loyalty to the pre-war government, now the London government-in-exile, which was reinforced through the strong presence of London-appointed Liaison Officers. As 1946 progressed, untangling the British and UNRRA definition of 'rehabilitation' from repatriation became increasingly difficult as the Polish communities themselves took little notice of Allied priorities.

The duality of being 'screened' by UNRRA and the Polish community

Due to their lack of official papers, DPs could readily assume any identity they wished in the immediate post-war period. Morgan commented that 'by 1945 the production of false identity papers in Europe had become almost a major industry'.[17] The initial rush to sort and classify the DPs into camps meant that identification procedures were virtually non-existent. In addition, UNRRA workers were unfamiliar with their long and awkward-sounding names, often misspelling them on identity cards without heeding the warnings of the Red Cross, which was all too familiar with the need for specialized staff.[18] Indeed, language instruction for UNRRA employees, as illustrated by Dawson's Polish-language notes (see Figure 3.1), was limited at best. When talking about the French-occupied Germany, Laure Humbert's research found similar issues as she argues that 'while DPs were often multilingual, relief workers often only spoke French, German or English'.[19] Only a handful of voluntary relief societies, coming under the umbrella of the Council of British Societies for Relief Abroad (COBSRA), gave language instruction to potential welfare and relief workers in preparation for working in post-war Europe. Francesca Wilson, a Quaker relief worker who had considerable experience with relief work during the First World War and Spanish Civil War, helped set up training centres and promote language instruction as she deemed it vital for effective relief work. The languages available for instruction, however, were often limited to mainly

French or German, with Serb-Croat, Greek, and Polish taught at one time or another, but not consistently.[20] Other agencies under the COBSRA umbrella focused on Yiddish language instruction, in the hope that any Jews, regardless of mother tongue, would be able to understand some Yiddish.[21] UNRRA, however, was a representative of multiple nations, staffed by civilians and ex-military personnel unfamiliar with foreign languages who found it increasingly difficult to communicate with the DPs under their care.

UNRRA workers and military personnel often felt overwhelmed by the task of screening the DPs; however, as screening determined their eligibility for aid, it too became a necessary evil. The disquieting comparison of screening for DP eligibility and earlier screenings to be placed on the Nazi *Volksliste* weighed heavily on the DPs' minds. Many welfare workers and military officials, when defining who was a Pole and what determined their Polishness, were confronted by inverted notions of nationality. Someone who spoke Polish could be on the *Volksliste* but those who were not on the list might not speak Polish if they were from Silesia, Vilnius, or East Galicia.[22] In 1945, the SHAEF guide established the importance of creating friendly and amenable living situations, claiming it was essential to clearly make the standard better than that of their former enslaved or imprisoned status, while also encouraging self-government and recreational activities to reduce idleness and boost morale.[23] Yet the process of registration and later, screening, made most DPs feel they were constantly being interrogated, inevitably heightening their dislike of the Allies and lowering their morale.[24]

As the end of 1945 approached, DP numbers dropped while UNRRA team numbers increased – more time could now be devoted to screening. UNRRA's Fourth Council Session in March 1946 put Resolution 92 into place, creating a necessary system of identification for all DPs, directing UNRRA personnel 'to complete the registration of all displaced persons in assembly centres and to compile data concerning their skills, previous experiences and other qualifications for employment'.[25] Although these details seemed harmless enough, they were accompanied by rigorous written and verbal tests of the DPs' claimed nationality. These tests were often conducted by young soldiers with a clear lack of interest in or understanding of their task and supervised by an UNRRA welfare worker. The same process was also being carried out among the German population with similarly poor consequences. The British rather quickly put the Germans in charge of their own screening (aka, Denazification); the same trust was, however, not applied to the DPs. As Gerard D. Cohen argues, although this was a joint venture between UNRRA and the military there was a clear divide between their perceived roles, as 'UNRRA workers were trying to ascertain the identity of refugees [yet] the investigation and eviction of suspected "security threats" remained the prerogative of military personnel'.[26] It was through these screening procedures that UNRRA workers were first able to provide assistance not directly linked to welfare activities.[27] After a few problems were encountered between the three western zones due to divergent screening procedures with different cut-off dates, it was agreed that UNRRA should take on the task of creating a questionnaire that could be used in all three zones.[28] By the end of 1946, all of the DP camps in the western zones had been screened and few were found to be ineligible for UNRRA care. The US zone had the highest expulsion rate at 10 per cent.[29]

The journalist and writer Gitta Sereny was an UNRRA welfare worker. Although Austrian by birth she was classified as an American UNRRA employee and worked in both the US and British occupation zones. As in many other aspects of her life, Sereny excelled at her task, especially reuniting children who had been captured by the Nazis for Germanization with their biological parents. Morgan praises her in his personal diary as a 'remarkable girl, aged 25 . . . speaks 7 European languages fluently and has knowledge beyond her years of European affairs . . . Here at last is one of the type of which UNRRA or anything like it should be exclusively composed'.[30] In her reflective work, *The German Trauma*, Sereny records being excited at the prospect of being a member of the screening teams, as this would also allow her to weed out suspected war criminals who were falsely claiming DP status according to UNRRA regulations.[31] Yet she proved extremely unpopular with other personnel due to her own interpretations of the eligibility guidelines and her outspoken attitude towards the military, and she eventually left in October 1946. Shephard argues that Sereny's interpretation of the guidelines would find that in one camp 'between 15 and 20 per cent of the Poles would be found ineligible, mainly as collaborators or as members of the Wehrmacht'.[32] Sereny never fully adhered to the official guidelines. She believed that a large proportion of Eastern DPs would have had no choice in their participation in labour throughout the war. Whereas others, who were apparently not being penalized, were granted DP status without further investigation, making the guidelines redundant.[33]

Rhoda Dawson comments on how the screening process in the camps, although born of necessity, was often 'cruel for the muddled, neurotic people, who immediately saw in it another threat of forced return to terror'.[34] Although weeding out war criminals, collaborators, and *Volksdeutsche* was an essential task, Dawson argues that there was no consistency in screening on the part of the military or UNRRA workers. Many of the military officers who carried out the screening had only been given a few days' training and were generally disinterested in the whole process as another task that they believed should be the sole responsibility of UNRRA. The additional language barrier was particularly difficult to overcome, as too few liaison officers were available to attend screenings. Although many DPs were forbidden to talk to unscreened DPs after taking the tests, some candidates were found to have the answers to all the questions written on their hands upon entering the examination room.[35]

Poles were considered a difficult group. Many had worked in German agriculture in the pre-war era and the military personnel found it hard to identify who was eligible for UNRRA's care. Contrary to those classed as DPs, the pre-war Poles were predominantly part of a wave of economic migration and were therefore not 'outside the normal boundaries of their country by reason of war'. Consequently, many Poles who arrived in Germany for work in the late nineteenth and early twentieth century were also deemed fit for Germanization by the *Volksliste*, and were therefore ineligible for UNRRA care.[36] Once it was made clear that most of the Poles remaining in the camps in 1946 were unwilling to repatriate, expressing '"valid objections" to returning to Communist Poland', they were immediately granted DP status.[37] By 1946, when the screening procedure was being rigorously implemented, Polish liaison officers were largely thought to be sabotaging Warsaw's Polish Repatriation Mission as the majority were loyal to the London-based government-in-exile.[38] While it is possible that a great number of Polish DPs were ineligible for UNRRA care, the biased opinions of the Polish liaison officers would certainly have influenced the results of the screening procedure. The task was rather fruitless when it came to Polish DPs, as the disinterest of those in the British zone in adequately determining who was Polish as well as their ability to do so was all too obvious. Only those considered *Volksdeutsche* by the Polish liaison officers were denounced.

UNRRA's official historian, George Woodbridge, was cynical about screening, especially when it involved the screening of Slavic groups. He summarized his concerns over the validity of the procedure:

> For the Slav nations there were two classes of displaced persons: good and bad. The good should be helped. The bad should not. The test of whether an individual was good or bad was whether he wanted, actively and quickly, to return to his area of origin.[39]

By this time most of the Poles had refused to repatriate on numerous occasions, and with adverse reports filtering into the camps via liaison officers, newspapers, and personal letters, their reluctance to leave the relative comfort and safety of the DP camps became understandable.[40]

While the military government and UNRRA attempted to screen the Poles to weed out undesirable elements, the Poles conducted their own screening in their community. Tadeusz Nowakowski describes the neurotic and muddled masses that Dawson refers to as the 'flotsam and jetsam of the battlefields and concentration camps', afflicted with 'barbed wire complex', many mindlessly wandering and muttering to themselves as they were 'slaves of habit, afflicted with prisoners' psychoses of all kinds'. Nowakowski's main character, Stefan Grzegorczyk, in his book Camp of All Saints (Obóz Wszystkich Świętych), is loosely based on his own experiences throughout the war. The main story, based in 1947, centres around Stefan, a former member of the AK known as the 'Avenger', who became a history teacher at the school in Papenburg DP camp, a position Nowakowski himself held in Maczków. He then fell in love with and married a German girl, Ursula. The townspeople were up-in-arms:

> 'If it were a civilian it would be bad enough, but a fellow who won a star during the Warsaw Uprising!'. . . 'I wouldn't have minded if he'd given her a bastard, some little Hitler – without publicity, of course, discreetly – I'd have gone along with that. After all we're only men, *errare humanum est*' . . . 'Grist to the Communists' mill! If Warsaw learns that our veterans marry German girls, we'll cut a fine figure in the eyes of oppressed Poland!'[41]

In the fashion of Romeo and Juliet, Nowakowski's protagonists were eventually separated by their respective communities' disgust at their relationship as the pressure of societal values eventually became too much to bear. Apart from the love story, Nowakowski painfully details the broken psyches of his fellow DPs, former forced labourers, ex-POWs, and former concentration camp prisoners:

> In the street he [the protagonist] often saw respectable ex-prisoners fall into a panic at a sight of a police officer. Like sneak thieves they would make for the next doorway, vanish around corners or hurriedly cross to the other side of the street. Others, unasked, would insist on showing their personal papers, hastening to identify themselves, infected as they were with the camp madness of passes, certificates, permits, and ration cards.[42]

Screening awoke in DPs' painful memories reminiscent of *Volksliste* interrogations throughout the war. Yet, the Allies, forever committed to an ideal and blind to the consequences, continued the screenings without a second thought. Initially, ex-POWs and DPs were separate categories even though many UNRRA workers complained they could not tell them apart; from 1946 onwards the two groups were amalgamated as DPs. Although various classifications were ascribed to individual DPs by the military government and UNRRA, the Polish communities had their own hierarchy. As previously mentioned, many Poles used their wartime experiences to create a new social hierarchy in the camps; the harsher the wartime experience, the higher ranking and more 'Polish' they were deemed to be in DP camps. One signifier of this 'Polishness' (*polskość*) was firmly based on pre-war Polish conceptions of morality ranging from how religious one was to how chaste. The ideals of heroism, stoicism, chastity, and religiosity converged in the camps to create an idealized version of who was Polish. This was often in stark contrast to how many experienced the liberation and immediate post-war life as Katarzyna Nowak described a world turned upside down.[43] Yet, the excesses experienced shortly after liberation were shocking to the exiled Polish elites who sought to curtail these excesses, and 'reassert the primacy of marriage to save Poles from further moral and physical "degeneration".'[44]

Maczków's high proportion of former political prisoners constituted the elitist circle. Artists and doctors were still highly respected and revered, but the war had changed how Polish DPs viewed social status. Again, the Purple 'P' became significant as a badge of honour and Polish suffering that could not be suppressed by the Germans: as one DP remarked, 'Today we keep these triangles, taken from behind the barbed wire, among the most cherished souvenirs'.[45] Indeed, if one wore the 'P', eligibility for aid was all but taken for granted. Kruczkiewicz claims in his memoirs that some concentration camp prisoners continued to wear their striped 'pyjamas' as a signifier of intense suffering that afforded them a higher place in the Polish DP camp community. The reality for many was that UNRRA could not provide clothes fast enough, and many were trapped in the same attire they had been forced to wear throughout the most painful period of their lives: the alternatives were donated clothes, which were often impractical, or an SS uniform.[46] 'Imprisoned' within their former attire, they changed its connotation: 'brothers dispersed throughout the world and a grey-blue piece of striped fabric is our flag. . . . Today we are not looking back to dwell on our suffering, but we want to shout that what has already happened cannot happen again'.[47]

Eventually the screening process was abandoned in the US zone due to complications between UNRRA and the army, and soon the British zone followed suit.[48] Apart from the psychological damage caused by the screening procedure, as in most economic and social organs in Germany in the immediate post-war period, corruption was rife. False identity papers were all too common, camps were saturated with them, and by 1946 most military staff and UNRRA workers were keen to return home rather than painstakingly interrogate those who remained. The screening of DPs can be compared to the screening of Germany's own population through the Denazification procedure. The similarities are overwhelming and just as time-consuming, and the outcome equally shocking and disappointing.

The last push: *Operation Carrot* and the beginning of the end for UNRRA

When Fiorello LaGuardia took over as director of UNRRA in 1946, he immediately pursued a tougher line towards Polish DPs, focusing on the increasingly problematic and exacerbating issue of repatriation. The culmination of his efforts was *Operation Carrot* wherein any Pole who volunteered to repatriate to Poland was given sixty days' worth of food rations. These bulk parcels were set up as displays in camps and the Polish DPs were ordered to walk past them; for an individual this amounted to 90lbs of food, and for a family of four 376lbs.[49] Morgan commented in his diary as visiting politicians observed a group of Poles readying themselves for repatriation to Poland, the 'poor misguided wretches' but at least it made the day 'less disappointing' for the politicians.[50] *Operation Carrot* was advertised alongside a Soviet-commissioned newsreel, *Return to Homeland*, as UNRRA and the Allies went all out to encourage as many Polish DPs as possible to repatriate.[51] Soon, however, messages from those who did accept the 'bait', as UNRRA worker Kathryn Hulme termed it, trickled back to the camps complaining about delayed or non-existent food packages.[52] Although also accompanied by a large bi-lingual informational booklet addressing common questions titled *What Every Citizen Should Know*, the operation had limited success (see Figure 5.2).[53] To compound Polish experiences further, LaGuardia took an even tougher stance as policies flipped from generosity through food and information, to repressive coercion through boredom: 'Effective October 1st 1946, all educational, recreational and other cultural activities are to be discontinued in all camps caring for one hundred or more Polish Displaced People.'[54] This decision essentially crushed any rehabilitative measures put into place in the Polish DP camps and made it clear they were no longer welcome.[55]

Apart from the obvious immediate result, the rising repatriation numbers, *Operation Carrot* and the ban on all recreational activities had a distressing effect on the Polish DPs. Prior to October 1946, they had realized that the British did not look upon them as equals; however, with the implementation of these policies their attitude changed from disappointment to active disgust of their

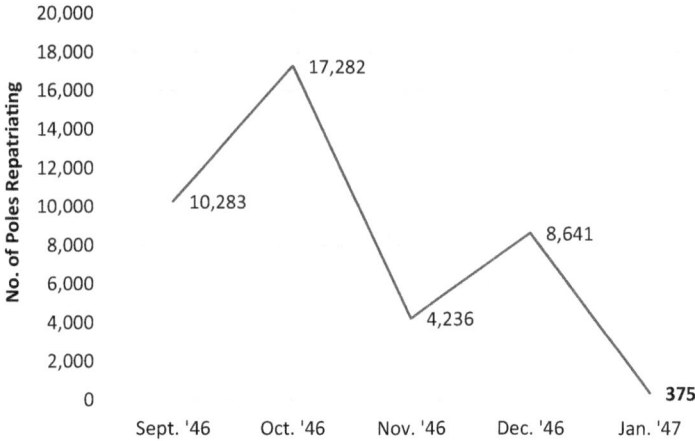

Figure 5.2 Poles repatriating from the British zone of occupation, October 1946–January 1947. Source: Created by Samantha K. Knapton AN, AJ-43-60, 'British Zone in Germany: Agreements between the UNRRA Intergovernmental Committee and the Military Authorities, Correspondence, August 1945–February 1946' – DP/PWX State Reports, 28 August 1946–29 January 1947.

former Allies. From this point onwards the Poles' contempt for the Allies was palpable in the camps. The British in particular were readily compared to the Soviet propaganda machine running in Warsaw. Complaints about only being perceived as a statistic and addressed as an acronym aroused equally vociferous protest. Welfare workers similarly found this label unworthy of its purpose, as McNeill recounts one of her fellow Quakers saying, 'I *hate* the phrase D.P. . . . it's insulting to reduce people down to two letters which might stand for anything'.[56] The reduction of millions of people to two letters had obvious effects on self-esteem and self-identification as a caesura point in 1945 caused psychological problems that were evaluated for years to come.[57] When the separation of Polish DPs gathered in the camps became an official policy, it conflicted with the hitherto followed policy of grouping DPs by ethnicity or nationality. UNRRA, and by consequence the Allies, were making life as unbearable as possible to enforce repatriation. As the president of the Polish-American Congress, Karol Rozmarek, contended: 'UNRRA has embarked on a course to make life so miserable for Displaced Persons that they will accept repatriation as the lesser of two evils'.[58] Yet, for many, repatriation was not a possibility and for those in the British zone in particular resettlement had been, up till then, an illusion.

UNRRA's Fifth Council session was held in August 1946, around the same time as *Operation Carrot* peaked. By now, it had become clear that insurmountable problems existed over issues of repatriation and resettlement, and an end date for European operations was determined. The Inter Governmental Committee on Refugees (IGCR) had been charged with the task of resettlement since 1943, whereas the task of repatriation had only been given to UNRRA in 1945, following numerous policy changes. Due to some over-complicated clauses built into the IGCR's mandate in 1943, it was unable to help most of those left in Germany, namely the Eastern Europeans. As Tommie Sjöberg argues, 'while the eastern bloc maintained that their nationals should be repatriated, by force, if necessary, the western powers claimed that they should be given the status of refugees and be resettled in the west'.[59] The West, however, did not concede to pressure from the Eastern Bloc and resettlement opportunities began to flourish in the form of the EVW schemes, although not everyone was eligible for resettlement.

UNRRA was to be terminated on 30 June 1947 due to 'the simple fact that not one of the contributing nations had made any provision for U.N.R.R.A. for 1947'.[60] According to Commander Robert Jackson, its 'functions were transferred to the Food and Agricultural Organization, the World Health Organization and the International Refugee Organization'.[61] These three organizations were charged with carrying out the duties for which UNRRA and the military had hitherto been responsible. The British public's view of UNRRA had become negative since its inception in November 1943. Few newspapers reported the closure of its operations with a fanfare similar to that which had accompanied its creation. UNRRA had been foreseen as the culmination of humanitarian efforts that would pioneer international cooperation in the post-war era. Instead, a legacy of bureaucratic inefficiency, increasing financial burden, and black marketeering had made their mark on the British psyche. The rise of economic self-interest eclipsed the British public's desire to be part of a truly international humanitarian cause, especially since the introduction of bread rationing in 1946. In the United States, Congress found it increasingly difficult to continue financing an unpopular and seemingly failed enterprise: the United States had contributed 72 per cent of UNRRA's total budget, and public opinion was turning against the organization. Commander Jackson believed that the centricity of US public opinion and its influence on governmental decisions was integral to UNRRA's continuation in Europe, a concept alien to British officials as public opinion was not as vital when it came to British government funding. Jackson further blamed Fiorello LaGuardia, UNRRA's second director general, for publicizing UNRRA's failures in order to remove himself from his post so that he could see out his retirement in peace. Jackson, believing that 'although it is true that the provision of economic aid to restore Europe ... is beyond the capacity of any one nation, it is equally obvious that very little can be achieved without the full co-operation of the United States', argued that LaGuardia had knowingly sent the organization to its grave.⁶² Due to the United States' dominant financial backing UNRRA had no option but to terminate its operations when funds were no longer available. The British people had consigned themselves to prolonged rationing to help fund the organization and its aims and could surely not afford to make a further contribution.

UNRRA's bad publicity and impending termination were two of the main reasons why the British Foreign Office, as well as the IGCR, felt the need to promote the usefulness of Polish DPs as genuinely hard-working souls; resettlement was now the primary target. This led to the creation of EVW schemes which selected DPs from those who had applied to live and work in Britain. UNRRA's task had been to create a screening process for those wishing to take part in the scheme in order to aid the all-encompassing goal of rehabilitation by any means possible, no matter how temporary the intent. Like other recipient countries such as Australia and Canada, however, Britain was particular about which DPs they were willing to accept.⁶³ Baltic DPs were heavily favoured for work schemes as they were thought to be generally well educated; many already spoke English, and were perceived to be the closest, genetically, to other Westerners.⁶⁴ Additionally, Balts were, from a 'moral standpoint' thought to top 'the scale of probity, ahead of Yugoslavs, Hungarians and Poles'.⁶⁵

Although the practice of eugenics has been made infamous by Nazi Germany it was also thought of as a much broader issue that became fashionable in the United States and Britain throughout the first half of the twentieth century. As asserted by Teitelbaum and Winter, eugenics is best understood in Britain at this time as a term for national improvement of *race* (meaning nation) and was understood as 'the science of the improvement of the genetic stock of the human population', as well as being used as a means to aid peaceful assimilation of other nationalities into society.⁶⁶ The 1949 Royal Commission on Population report stated that Britain was only to welcome immigrants into its well-established society on a large scale 'if the immigrant were of Good Human Stock and were not prevented by their religion or race from intermarrying with the local population and becoming merged with it'.⁶⁷ In practice this meant that only Baltic DPs were encouraged to live and work in Britain as part of the EVW scheme. Poles, on the other hand, were viewed as peasantry with unclean habits, often lacking appropriate etiquette, and therefore placed at the bottom of the list for employment.⁶⁸ Their precarious position in the DP camps in Germany left them in limbo as nationalist policies took priority. The Poles' only options were to leave the camps and fend for themselves in Germany or repatriate to Poland.

Eventually, as the British realized that the EVW quota could not be filled with only Balts and Ukrainians, Poles were also accepted alongside others.[69] Although some Poles ended up settling in Germany, a significant number started a new life in Britain, where many had trouble integrating.[70]

At Cabinet level in Britain, the acceptance of EVWs, and their subsequent integration into British society was perceived to be primarily for economic advancement and not as a means of implementing the humanitarian principles UNRRA was founded on. The cause, in short, had become selfish.[71] UNRRA's numerous failings since its creation may also have influenced the British decision to terminate the short-lived organization. Its inability to deliver what was promised caused British public and governmental opinion to become increasingly hostile; above all they were unwilling to make any further financial contribution.[72] Dean Acheson recounts in his autobiography that UNRRA was to be 'wound up' due to weak staff and weaker leadership; more importantly, he concedes 'the supplies turned up all too frequently on the black market, but, far more serious, the bulk of them . . . went to the wrong places and were used for the wrong purposes'.[73]

As the new decade approached, Britain shifted from immediate post-war humanitarianism to the protection of national interests. The humanitarian principles on which UNRRA had been founded were discounted as the need to rebuild home economies, and Germany's economy for trading purposes, took priority. It was not until 1953 in Britain and 1955 in Germany that the increasing need for labour caused both countries to look towards migrants again. By 1948, the majority of those who accepted positions on the EVW schemes had settled in the country they travelled to, some integrating much faster than others. The EVW scheme, like other schemes designed to rehabilitate or resettle the remaining DPs, came about due to an ill-defined policy regarding the DPs' stance in Europe and the shifting attitudes of the nations concerned. UNRRA had become overwhelmed with the sheer number of those needing help, the lack of resources available to them, and the inconsistent orders given. Although the EVW scheme was initially promoted as a stop gap measure before repatriation, it provided many DPs with their final destination.

One of the main aims of UNRRA's mission was the repatriation of Europe's DPs; however, as tension increased between the United States and USSR it became harder to send DPs back to eastern territories. Contemporary critics argued that apart from UNRRA's well-established label as an ineffectual and over-bureaucratic hotbed for black marketeering, its activities were ultimately brought to an end 'when the US government decided that continued repatriation to the Eastern bloc was assisting its Cold War rival'.[74] The progression of the Cold War and the creation of Bizonia effectively forced Britain to agree with the US decision to cease UNRRA's operations and hand over the DP problem to the newly formed IRO. The durability of the IRO's repatriation efforts was short-lived and the organization quickly turned to resettlement instead, continuing the EVW scheme in Britain until 1949.[75] Additionally, many employees who had transferred their allegiance from UNRRA to IRO appeared to have lost faith in the humanitarian ideals that once characterized their jobs, and this brought about further, unforeseen problems. Kanty Cooper worked on behalf of the Quakers as an intermediary helping with resettlement. She recalls as the IRO screened DPs and the CCG controlled the Displaced Persons Assembly Centres (DPACs) there were numerous instances of petty quarrels superseding the primary goal. In one instance, while helping 300 DPs onto a Canadian lumberjack scheme, Kanty remembers the IRO team director was a Polish colonel, 'a despot, a man who loved power and was determined to boss the English DPACs team running the camps'. This vying for power over DPs and NGO workers like Kanty caused repeated problems throughout her stay in Düsseldorf, and she recalls their continual efforts to belittle one another to DPs and 'outsiders' as the relationship grew sour.[76]

Repatriation to resettlement: European Volunteer Worker schemes from *Operation Westward Ho!* to *Operation Black Diamond*

There was no strong basis for Polish migration to Britain prior to 1945. Germany, France, and the United States had been the receiving countries throughout the latter half of the nineteenth century as well as before and after the First World War. It was only with the establishment of the Polish Resettlement Corps (PRC) in 1946 that a large-scale migration of Poles to Britain occurred.[77] Those eligible were members of the Polish army that joined the PRC with a view of eventually demobilizing. Once it was realized that many were unwilling to return to Poland while the pre-war government remained in exile, former soldiers were accepted in Britain under the Polish Resettlement Act (1947) while many of their dependents joined them as part of *Operation Pole Jump*.[78] The Resettlement Act and *Operation Pole Jump*, alongside the restrictive Distressed Relatives Scheme (begun in August 1945), offered little chance for those in the DP camps of Germany to resettle in Britain as the criteria often limited eligibility. Britain's

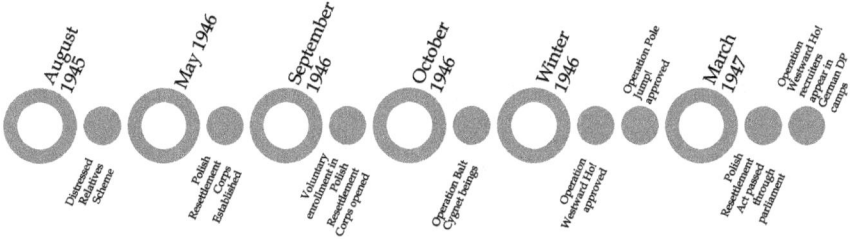

Figure 5.3 Timeline of resettlement schemes in Britain. Source: Created by Samantha K. Knapton.

reluctance to accept Polish DPs as migrant workers (and potentially permanent migrants) was also due to fears among government officials of ghettoization.[79] Poles were quickly becoming a large and visible minority group in Britain; consequently any opportunity to stem the flow of Poles swelling these numbers was taken (see Figure 5.3).[80]

The EVW scheme began in Britain with *Operation Balt Cygnet*, the first of the former DPs arriving in Britain on 19 October 1946.[81] At first the 'cygnets' were sent to work as orderlies in British sanatoriums, but as demand for such workers increased their duties soon carried them to regular hospitals as well. After much deliberation, and with a very specific set of guidelines, the Ministry of Labour expanded the scheme so Baltic EVWs could work in all forms of care. As the EVW scheme grew in significance with the increased need for DP labour in Britain it expanded to include *Operation Westward Ho!* which was formed in the winter of the same year, even though the initial reaction by British politicians was that resettlement in Britain was as likely as 'resettlement of the refugees on the mountains of the moon'.[82] Arguably UNRRA's goal of clearing the DP camps as quickly as possible was the driving force behind the expansion of the initial *Balt Cygnet* operation. *Operation Westward Ho!* entailed the recruitment of an estimated 100,000 DPs, specifically Balts and Ukrainians, needed to fill positions in industrial and agricultural industries suffering from labour shortages. Margaret McNeill wrote of the elation at her camp near Brunswick in the British zone when *Westward Ho!* was gleefully announced by 'Collie' (Captain Collins). It was only after carefully reading over the announcement that many of the British officials, UNRRA workers, and Quakers realized the order would cause great consternation, least of all for its explicit exclusion of Poles with no explanation. To make matters more confusing, the order also stated that 'Soviet Ukrainians' would be accepted, but not 'Polish Ukrainians'.

In order to avoid forced repatriation, during the months immediately after the cessation of hostilities the majority of Ukrainians had claimed Polish nationality. Now, having to admit this falsehood, they presented themselves to the Ministry of Labour recruitment officer as 'Soviet Ukrainian', as did any Pole who could speak Ukrainian. In one instance, according to McNeill, two staff members, Dr Pilak (Polish) and Fierek (Ukrainian), tried to determine the nationality of one particular DP by speaking to them in both languages. The upshot was that neither could determine the DP's nationality as:

> he came from a district where the two nationalities were inextricably mixed; and when a language test was tried, Fierek declared the man spoke Polish with a marked Ukrainian accent, and Dr. Pilak cocked his head and said he spoke Ukrainian deplorably interlarded with Polish expressions.[83]

Eventually, the matter was only settled after a curt interjection by Collie, whereupon he determined the man would be considered Ukrainian if sent back to Poland, and therefore at risk. To give him a chance at resettlement, they decided, 'he'd better be Ukrainian here too'.[84] Eventually, realizing the target could not be filled by Balts and Ukrainians alone the scheme opened up to include Yugoslavs, Hungarians, Bulgarians, Czechs, Slovaks, and Poles. According to a Polish periodical circulated in the camps, *Dziennik Polski* (Polish Journal) on 17 July 1947 the first Poles, fifty-six girls, arrived in York as part of *Operation Westward Ho!*.[85] At first, the government's major preoccupation was how successfully the DPs could assimilate into British society. According to Tannahill, however, the chance to alleviate Britain's labour shortage while also 'helping to solve the refugee problem ... was too good to miss'.[86] While the recruitment may have helped the DP situation abroad, it was not initially led by humanitarian considerations.

Newspaper articles on EVWs indicate the differing receptions these labourers received in Britain. On the one hand, the *Baltic Cygnets* alongside other domestic workers and industrial labourers were well received. Newspapers boasted about how successfully these foreigners had integrated, stating for instance that '[al]though still a foreigner, he would become "our foreigner"'.[87] Other newspapers were also appreciative of their eagerness to work as transition camp administrators, confirming the EVWs would do the 'dirty jobs' the British would not.[88] On the other hand, the view of agricultural workers was often presented as rather hostile, as due to the seasonal nature of farming 'the scheme was costly and disappointing'.[89] Yet, it was Polish EVWs that appear to have attracted the most criticism, as local newspapers regularly reported on negative behaviour, accusing Poles of being lewd and dangerous.[90] In Spey Bay Aleksander Rybicki, a

Polish EVW, was imprisoned for lewd behaviour as he had entered the bedroom of a sleeping eighteen-year-old girl and 'assaulted the student by attempting to put his arm around her [however] after she slapped his face he left' and was quickly ejected from the property.[91] In another example, a Polish worker in Wooler, Northumberland, named as Tadousz [sic] Bruszawski, was sentenced to six months' imprisonment on nine charges of larceny amounting to £41-6 (shillings). They determined Bruszawski had 'grossly abused asylum' and was promptly repatriated to Poland.[92] The positive perception of Balts and the negative perception of Poles were constantly reinforced through local newspaper reports: Balts were piano players and carers, whereas Poles were thieves and sexual deviants.

The EVW scheme, created to deal with surplus DPs who were unwilling to repatriate, produced some positive results. In Britain the children of EVW workers often appeared in local newspapers in articles attesting to their positive integration into British society through their quick grasp of the English language and eagerness to make friends.[93] Others were not so fortunate, as some were unable to adapt to their new surroundings and instead became introverted or stuck closely to others of the same nationality.[94] Additionally, upon signing up for work and resettlement in Britain the EVWs had to sign a contract with the Ministry of Labour and National Service which determined the location and type of job in Britain. Some of the volunteer workers had believed that after a year they would be able to switch jobs and they were bitterly resentful when they realized this was not always the case.[95] Britain was not the dream location for many DPs as the threat of another European war loomed menacingly in the immediate post-war period; the majority wished to leave the continent entirely.

The EVW scheme only recruited 84,000, including Yugoslavs, Hungarians, Bulgarians, Czechs, Slovaks, and Poles, on top of the initial Balts and Ukrainians.[96] Although the scheme was created to fill positions in areas in dire need of workers, it was eventually agreed that no forced return programme would be put in place due to humanitarian concerns.[97] Consequently those who came to Britain through this scheme were expected to fully integrate into British society.[98] The initial British target for the EVW scheme was higher, with the director of the IGCR, Herbert Emerson, predicting 100,000–150,000, if not more, would come to Britain through the work schemes.[99] The number of Polish EVWs was just under 13,000 by 1951; however, the number of dependants was minimal compared to those accepted earlier, primarily under the *Balt Cygnet* scheme.[100] Yet, the main reason for the slowing-down of numbers willing to come to Britain was the increasingly tight controls on who would be accepted.

When the plan was conceived, initially married workers had been welcomed with the promise that their dependants could join them at a later date. When the housing shortage in Britain came to a crisis point however, *Westward Ho!* would only accept unattached workers. This excluded a large percentage of the readily available and eager Polish workforce in the camps of Germany.[101] Eventually restrictions to EVWs' movement around Britain, the jobs they could acquire, the acceptance of their dependants and their accommodation were relaxed, but not until 1951.[102]

By 30 June 1947, UNRRA had ceased to operate in Europe. While most recipient countries lacked the sufficient means to be self-supporting, DPs languished in the camps across Germany, Austria, and Italy. Commander Jackson's summation of UNRRA activities concluded that had the Allies 'conducted their military operations in a manner similar to their approach to world economic recovery during the past two years, the war would still be going on, if it had not already been lost'.[103]

On 1 July 1947, the Preparatory Commission of the International Refugee Organization (PCIRO) took over the operation of camps in Germany. Like UNRRA's role in the camps throughout the previous two years, the PCIRO was intended to provide care for the remaining DPs and to encourage them to repatriate. Resettlement to new countries offering work and accommodation, however, became the primary resolve. The 'Help the People to Help Themselves' ethos changed with the change of authority in the camps, with DPs' rights disregarded and the PCIRO working on the assumption that DPs were to accept the organization's priorities above all else. Yet, in reality the DPs still wielded formidable power.[104] The scale of the resettlement operation was to surpass expectations, assembling one of the largest peacetime civilian fleets with thirty-six ships under its jurisdiction at its peak.[105] Emerson conceded in an address to the PCIRO that the rate and pace of repatriation and resettlement were never predictable, and even towards the end of UNRRA's operations in early 1947 the transport situation had been precarious. Emerson lamented that 'at times it has looked as if there would be the ships and no persons to fill them, at other times that there may be too many persons and not enough ships'.[106] The uncertainty facing the PCIRO, and subsequently the IRO, was most imminently felt when few Western countries seemed willing to open their doors and accept these non-repatriables left in the camps. In a letter to the director of the Red Cross Societies the IRO's public relations officer, L M Hacking, predicted that 'the opportunities for large scale migration are slight, but it is hoped, if various schemes materialise, that perhaps a hundred thousand refugees may be enabled to settle overseas this year [1947]'.¹⁰⁷ Fortunately for some, this was indeed the case, with the two largest recruitment and resettlement schemes organized by Britain and Belgium.

As mentioned, *Operation Westward Ho!* was the largest of Britain's EVW recruitment schemes offering a chance at resettlement in Britain with the possibility of dependants joining later.¹⁰⁸ Britain conceded that 'acceptance of work in the UK should not prejudice the refugee's future resettlement opportunities'. EVWs should be allowed to return to Germany under the IRO's care to be placed in other, perhaps better-suited, work and resettlement schemes in foreign countries once their contractual obligation to Britain had been fulfilled.¹⁰⁹ The IRO rejected this premise however as it did not wish to resettle anyone for a second time. The budget for the IRO's existence had been estimated based on every person under their care being resettled once: there was no room to resettle people twice unless they had been declared unfit or unable to work. The IRO struggled to accommodate both its compassion for those who had already been victims of uncertainty and displacement, and the financial restrictions imposed on them by its member governments. This conflict was most evident when recruiting DPs and other refugees for work in the Belgian mines.

The Belgian recruitment scheme, *Operation Black Diamond*, also struggled to obtain the DP numbers they had hoped for, even though dependants were also welcomed. In 1947 the frustration about DPs and the issue of resettlement echoed in the British zone's remarks in a report on *Operation Black Diamond*, stating that 'the response to the Belgian scheme was disappointing only about 3000 persons volunteering initially' after provisions had been made for 15,000.¹¹⁰ Largely targeting Poles and Balts, *Operation Black Diamond* was one of the biggest recruitment schemes under UNRRA and the IRO. Conversely, it was the Belgian government's apparently humanitarian motives towards who they would and would not accept that ultimately led to many workers leaving Belgium by 1949.¹¹¹ Continuing the IGCR's recruitment of miners for Belgium, the IRO sought at least 15,000 from the British zone and a further 20,000 from the US zone of occupation. It was the most liberal scheme of the time. The Belgian government was not overly demanding about medical standards, and with each of the 35,000 miners expected, they also expected to receive an additional three or four dependants, making a total of 100,000–125,000 people to be established in Belgium.¹¹² Many provisions were put into place for the workers including social security benefits, assurances of fair treatment equal to their Belgian counterparts, possible future citizenship or naturalization, and, once free of their contractual obligations, they would be able to seek work in other mines, or indeed in other professions.¹¹³

On paper the scheme looked like a dream, especially to DPs bored by the monotony of the camps and eager for a new life. Yet, in practice the problems began to materialize after only a few months of the scheme's implementation. The attraction of *Operation Black Diamond* was ultimately also its downfall. Many of the DPs who were accepted were neither mentally nor physically suitable for mining, one of the hardest manual jobs. Consequently, many colliery bosses deemed them unfit for work and sent them back to IRO care. Some thought that the most difficult mining operations were being set aside specifically for these workers to dissuade them from trying to stay in Belgium indefinitely.[114] Even so, recruitment to the Belgian mines was strong and the return rate was relatively low until mid-1947. Once the PCIRO took over, the majority of former DPs became dissatisfied with the terrible living conditions in Belgium and many attempted to return to Germany, adding to the number of souls under the PCIRO's care. Apart from the strenuous work and unsatisfactory living conditions, those working in the Belgian mines soon heard of resettlement opportunities opening up elsewhere, in particular in France and the United States. Like some Poles in Britain, many were unhappy and felt duped into an unwanted profession longer than their initial contractual agreement. As Mieczysław Kalinowski noted later:

> They gave up their easy camp bread, often worked in unfair conditions on unfair contracts and only then did they find out that they could only count on working in the mines until the end of their lives. A stamp was stamped on [their IDs], 'only to work in the mine', it was forbidden to change the place of work, almost as slaves to the shafts. Every protest was met with police repression and followed by imprisonment.[115]

They wanted to return to Germany to be given the chance to resettle elsewhere, hopefully with better work and accommodation. According to Holborn, the problem of double-resettlement had wide-reaching implications for the resettlement scheme as a whole:

> If it were admitted that acceptance of a work contract with the possibility of permanent residence in Belgium, France, or the UK was not a final settlement, ending the IRO's responsibility at least as far as finding opportunities and transporting refugees to them was concerned, then the Organization might be faced with over 220,000 refugees demanding a chance of establishment overseas.[116]

As mentioned, the IRO member governments' acceptance and willingness to work with the organization had been accompanied with severe budgetary restrictions, and the idea of adding the cost of resettling an additional 220,000 people, most for a second time, was out of the question. A second chance at resettlement was only granted in limited circumstances. Many of those classified as 'resettled' in Belgium, however, found the conditions unacceptable, after being placed in an isolation camp they found themselves working their way back to Germany, with or without the IRO's help, and at the mercy of the occupation authorities. *Operation Black Diamond* was not a complete failure, however, as 15,000 DPs were still active in the Belgian mines by 1956 and many were approaching naturalization or citizenship. A large percentage of those who returned from Belgium were Poles, and so the number of Polish DPs escalated once more. This time they were mainly housed outside the camps, retaining their general and legal status as refugees but losing their eligibility for material assistance or help with further emigration.[117]

The IRO's mandate on Poles in Germany was essentially to clear the camps, repatriate all who were willing, resettle all those they could, and find suitable accommodation and care in Germany for those unable to do either. By now, not all Polish DPs under the IRO's jurisdiction were in the camps, many having found accommodation in German towns and villages. Maczków was still populated by Poles in 1947 when the PCIRO and subsequently the IRO took over, however, many were now resettling in Britain under the Polish Resettlement Act with dependants joining them as part of *Operation Pole Jump*. Yet even after countries such as Britain and Belgium had implemented large-scale EVW resettlement schemes a considerable number of DPs remained under IRO care in the British zone. Unsurprisingly, the majority were Poles, who were characterized by Emerson upon their transfer into (PC)IRO care in 1947 as possessing 'no future and little hope'.[118]

Conclusion

In the British zone, where the largest number of Polish DPs were housed, the fight to encourage repatriation was long and arduous. When Morgan was appointed the Chief of Operations to the UNRRA Mission in Germany, it became clear that the two branches of authority would become indivisible. Due to this close tie-in of authority in the British zone, repatriation attempts were often a collective push by both military officials and UNRRA workers in the camps. In reality, this mattered very little. The Polish DPs' rejection of repatriation was not from idleness or an attempt to claim DP eligibility to avoid meaningful work, but rather from a deep resentment of the new government in Poland and Britain's willingness to recognize its legitimacy. Britain had fallen prey to the rapidly intensifying Cold War. The circumstances under which most Poles found themselves in DP camps in the British zone in 1945 were not voluntary, nor did they voluntarily choose to remain in the camps throughout the summer while the British authorities and UNRRA focused on repatriating Western DPs and Soviets. By September 1945, the situation in Poland was terrifying to many of those still in the camps, whose fear of the terrible conditions and possible persecutions were heightened by the return of DPs to the British zone who had already undergone repatriation and were now voting with their feet.[119]

There was also very little compassion for the DPs in the upper echelons of UNRRA. When the second director general, Fiorello LaGuardia, heard that some eastern DPs would not return home because they did not agree with communism, he stated: 'that's no reason for refusing repatriation. I've disagreed with the government in my country for more than 20 years now – but you don't see me running away from America on that account'.[120] There seemed to be very little understanding among the British military officials, and, to a certain extent, many UNRRA workers, of what they were asking the Poles to return to. Many believed negative press about life in Poland was blown out of proportion, yet readily accepted rosy-toned newspaper articles commissioned by the Warsaw government.[121] It was no small feat to ask of Poles who had been ousted from their homes by fascists to return to it under the communists. Yet, from the authorities' point of view, the Poles were merely stalling.

The shift in emphasis from repatriation to resettlement was certainly greeted with a sigh of relief by many Polish DPs in the camps. Yet the creation of foreign worker schemes that would eventually, and reluctantly, accept Poles, and in some cases their dependants, was no easy task. For most DPs, the workers' schemes were not meant to be a long-term solution. Britain was different to some in this regard as Poles who had been accepted as part of *Operation Westward Ho!* and other EVW schemes were seen as permanent migrants, 'working their passage to British citizenship'.[122] Joining the significant numbers of ex-servicemen in Britain and their dependants brought the total Polish-born population in Britain to 162,339 by 1951.[123]

The remaining DPs underwent complex psychological changes as their eagerness to leave the camps was replaced by so-called 'apathy'. With the handover to IRO authority, concerted attempts to simultaneously reinvigorate vocational courses (to make DPs looks more attractive to potential resettlement countries) and promote resettlement through widespread propaganda (while also underpinning receiving countries' 'ban on the brain' to dissuade elite resettlement) caused consternation and exhaustion. Consequently, a state of limbo ensued.

6

Idleness bred apathy

Displaced persons left in the camps

Introduction

The pressure to repatriate Polish DPs soon fell by the wayside as UNRRA's termination approached, and a period of prolonged uncertainty took over. In the British zone, as resettlement opportunities opened up on schemes such as *Westward Ho!*, the Allies and welfare workers were confronted with a set of circumstances few had expected. Caught between drives to repatriate and drives to resettle, many of the DPs lapsed into monotonous routines. Nowakowski's protagonist, Stefan, again finds himself stuck in 'this Godforsaken Papenburg':

> He felt like a fish in an aquarium. Charitable international organizations threw crumbs in the water to keep the fish alive. That was as far as modern man went in his generosity. At first the imprisoned fish rammed the glass with its head, but soon realized that the walls were thick. Now he lay drowsily in the slime at the bottom. Buried in seaweed he waited for something, he didn't know what. Free in theory, for he had been 'liberated', Stefan was in fact a prisoner locked up every night in the All Saints barracks.[1]

Although the Allied intention was to spur repatriation attempts by banning all educational, recreational, and cultural activities in camps with more than 100 Polish DPs, it produced a disconnect with life outside the camps.[2] As UNRRA handed over to the Preparatory Commission for the International Refugee Organization, and the focus shifted from repatriation to resettlement, it became clear that vocational and educational work had to be reinvigorated in the camps.[3] Understandably, only six months after the initial ban by UNRRA of any such activities, this produced a great deal of confusion. It was quickly realized by the IRO, however, that educating the remaining Polish DPs needed to be a primary concern for two reasons. Firstly, in order to disconnect them from their pasts, and prepare them for their futures outside the camps. Secondly, to ensure the DPs looked 'desirable' to possible resettlement countries. The perceived problem among welfare workers to ready the DPs for resettlement, however, was motivation.

The term 'apathy' is used throughout this work in two ways. In earlier chapters, the British continually showed an apathetic attitude towards Poles abroad while welcoming the urban cosmopolitans in Britain, alongside ex-servicemen and their dependents. This chapter, however, focuses on the so-called 'DP apathy' as perceived by welfare workers; a severely debilitating condition for the DPs in the camps, as they saw no meaningful existence in their immediate past, present, or future and even as new opportunities were presented to them many were unable to cope. Viewed as a by-product of Americanized social welfare training that infiltrated UNRRA training centres from April 1945 onwards, the terminology soon became commonplace to recognize how prolonged suffering inhibited DPs' mental capacity to cope with ordinary situations. Yet, it was also perceived to be an inherent character trait of individuals or groups, and in particular Estonian and Polish DPs.[4] Thus, it was believed apathy could be cured through rapid alterations to the physical environment to stimulate DPs, and the (re)ignition of vocational and educational courses alongside resettlement propaganda would aid their recovery. Yet, whether 'DP apathy' really existed is also a point of contention. Rather than languidly await a future to befall them, many DPs and welfare workers make note of 'DP apathy' as a product of frustration. Some DPs, enduring the monotonous life within the camps, struggled with day-to-day tasks, but was this apathy, or rather the outward signs of mental and physical exhaustion? Many other Polish DPs actively, and continuously, voiced their protest at the enforced state of limbo; thereby defying this label.

The state of limbo was particularly acute in the British zone, as it struggled to cope with the financial consequences of caring for the remaining DPs. While eager to create the Bi-zone, or Bizonia, with the US zone and have a semblance of stability, the British authorities also realized the presence of so many Polish DPs further exacerbated east-west relations. Amid these decisions, a group of Poles in London collated information on the treatment of Polish DPs in British-occupied Germany and voiced their protest in a memorandum to draw attention to continuing unequal treatment. This memorandum will be used as a lens through which to understand the ongoing breakdown of Anglo-Polish relations due to the disconnect between treatment of Poles in Britain, and Poles abroad under British care. As a result, the issue of Polish DPs in the British zone was thrust to the forefront of policy initiatives and an urgent drive to resettle them elsewhere ensued. As this chapter shows, the creation of the Bi-zone influenced how the British pursued resettlement in their zone and used American examples pioneered by Polish-American organizations who had been operating in the US zone since 1945 to guide them.

Ultimately, this chapter illustrates how the British, in particular, viewed the DPs' mental and social well-being at a time when DPs were forced to work as a method of 'rehabilitation', but also encouraged to seek resettlement opportunities outside of Germany, all while making themselves 'desirable' to potential host countries and trying to avoid slumping into a supposed apathetic state after a prolonged period of displacement. In a Goldilocks-like predicament, this chapter also focuses on the dichotomous issue of educating Polish peasants (*chłopi*) to advance their appeal for resettlement countries, while simultaneously encouraging highly skilled Poles to downplay their abilities as no-one wanted the two extremes, but rather something in the middle.

A new 'Black Book': The London Memorandum

The bad winter of 1946 suspended most repatriation transport to Poland, and by this time the British military knew that UNRRA's operations were to be discontinued by the summer of 1947. With this in mind there would have to be a final push for repatriation. A group of Poles based in London took umbrage at increasingly negative views of Poles displayed by the British both publicly and privately and collated information of bias into a single document titled the London Memorandum. This section will therefore focus on this document, which simultaneously chastises and thanks the British for their involvement, stating 'a new "Black Book" of undeserved hardship and suffering would have to be published' to right all the wrongs done to Poland.[5] The memorandum offers an insight into the real disintegration of the special Anglo-Polish relationship, reiterates the 'brothers-in-arms' and the 'betrayed ally' stances, and warns of close ties to the Soviet Union threatening east-west relationships.

Created by the London-based 'Help the Poles in Germany' Polish Social Committee, a body representing the Polish Union (PU) in Germany, the memorandum was sent to the British Foreign Office; the director of the IGCR, Herbert Emerson; and the secretary general of the UN, Mr Lie.[6] The Secretary General Tadeusz Katelbach had previously held positions in the Polish Second Republic and was an active member of the London government-in-exile. With Britain's recognition of the Polish Provisional Government of National Unity in Warsaw, Katelbach took up administrative positions concerning welfare to help wider Polonia and became an active member of the Polish émigré circle in London. The introduction to the London memorandum reads: 'The theses of our Memorandum refer to the transitory period of the Poles' stay in Germany. Only with the settlement of the last Pole outside the boundaries of that country would they lose their validity.'[7] Although the memorandum has a clear agenda, the claims of unfair treatment within are not as sensational as might be expected and are easily corroborated with other primary documents ranging from memoranda to newspapers and memoirs. The sixty-three appendices attached to the memorandum are largely based on instances occurring in the British zone, some of which have already been discussed in earlier chapters.

The memorandum, written after the failure of *Operation Carrot*, succinctly summarizes a series of instances that could constitute unfair treatment. The Allies were readily discussing the future makeup of Germany under occupation, yet, as the memorandum states, '19 months after the end of hostilities in Europe, [the Polish refugees] are still in the same legally indefinite situation, and are still living under very precarious conditions'. The memorandum can be interpreted as a plea to the Allies, and Britain in particular, to uphold their promises to Poland in 1939 rather than turn their attention to the 'citizens of the enemy country'. Using the same rhetoric that was employed by Polish DPs in the camps, General Anders, and even the American-Polonia, the memorandum stresses the need to prioritize Polish DPs 'not only because they are nationals of an allied state, but also because they were belligerents, or at least active supporters of the Allied war effort'.[8] As the writers of this piece are so well versed in the problems of the Polish DPs in Germany, their causes and possible solutions, it is difficult not to quote the memorandum in full as it was delivered. Its purpose was to show the Allies the reasoning behind the Poles' refusal to repatriate and to reinforce the message that their presence should not be considered a 'nuisance' that the Allies wished to rid themselves of, or to bypass in favour of another, perhaps fresher, challenge.

Although the memorandum is clearly self-serving in requesting that the British prioritize the plight of Polish DPs over that of ex-enemy nationals, their arguments carried weight. After listing the reasons for Poles' refusal to repatriate, the memorandum's authors argue that many others had only chosen to repatriate as the lesser of two evils. By February 1947 the combination of impoverished camp conditions, restrictive policies, repetitive and humiliating screening procedures, increasingly negative attitudes towards Poles, and pressure on UNRRA to repatriate before the organization was wound up had led to the belief that more might repatriate, but the numbers remained embarrassingly low.

The continuous complaint that Polish DPs were lazy and unwilling to work has been voiced throughout the previous chapters by UNRRA, NGO, and military workers alike. Klemmé stated that while Jews and Balts are industrious, good people, 'the Poles and other Slavic groups are a lot like our Southern Negroes – they can lay right down by the side of work and it won't bother them in the least'.[9] Citing incidents of when Poles wished to work but lacked the opportunity, however, the London Memorandum accuses the Allies of interfering with work opportunities in order to drive towards their ultimate goal of repatriation. Indeed, even after a call for 100 per cent DP employment, an UNRRA team director states throughout a memorandum, 'Do not employ Poles. Repatriate them as they must go home'.[10] Poles were the apparent exception to the 100 per cent work rule and the memorandum blames UNRRA's repatriation programme for the lack of work opportunities, resulting in their enforced idleness. Polish DPs often complained about the lack of work causing further demoralization, which contributed to increased labelling of 'apathy' in the camps. One British officer grumbled that the Poles were rapidly deteriorating, becoming more useless by the day as they were being 'kept, housed, fed and clothed for free in idleness [. . .] refusing to make any decision about going home for as long as possible'.[11] According to this officer, idleness bred apathy, which was the result of bigger problems in the camps and among the Polish DP population.

The rest of the memorandum is carefully divided into other examples of mistreatment, claims for reparation, right to sanctuary, welfare, ID papers, and the right to self-government in the camps. Yet, the biggest criticism stems from the British authorities' differential treatment of Germans and Poles. Germans, although defeated, were afforded more freedom than Poles in the DP camps, and indeed had occasionally been given positions of authority in some Polish DP camps.[12] The accusation was that this was merely another tactic to rid the British zone of Polish DPs; the reality was the British had to rely on Germans to work in the zone on their behalf due to the severe lack of military and UNRRA personnel. As UNRRA's supply of staff came from the military, the drain on military resources for sheltering and protecting DPs was apparent and the plentiful labour of German civilians became the cheapest solution. According to a Quaker relief worker, Francesca Wilson, some were of the opinion that German workers were favoured above Poles because the Germans could be 'better servants', and 'if the cook disobeys me I can put him in the jug [solitary]. I cannot do that to a Pole'.[13]

Due to accusations of laziness, by the beginning of 1947 everyone over the age of fourteen, male and female, had to be registered to work in the German economy under German authority.[14] The British tried to make it clear that there were two options for DPs: return home, or stay in the camp earning their food through labour. At a meeting in June 1946, it was explained that no resettlement opportunities would be available for at least three years, even if the Pole in question had professional qualifications that could be of use in other countries. Instead, they were to work in Germany as manual labourers, and were told to 'forget all previous German insults, as the Germans have changed [and] are quite decent now'.[15] Regardless of this threat, repatriation numbers remained unchanged (see Figure 5.2).

Incensed by the deliberate work order thrust upon Polish DPs in the camps, the authors of the London Memorandum voiced their protest using traditional means of invoking the DPs' rights on their behalf and compiling the new 'Black Book'. Through an analysis of 300 letters of petition from Polish DPs to the American Committee for the Resettlement of Polish Displaced Persons, Katarzyna Nowak has shown how the act of letter writing and petitioning took on different forms depending on the recipient. The letters of petition, often written by ordinary Polish DPs, positioned themselves as supplicants rather than citizens in the hope of obtaining an affidavit from Poles in diaspora, already settled in the United States. According to Nowak, they thus positioned themselves as victims, 'writing upwards' to those they deemed to be in a position of power, and 'adopted the language of martyrology, patriotism, anti-communism and freedom and inscribed their own life stories into this ideological universum'.[16] In contrast, when addressing authorities, the DPs would invoke rights, demand better treatment, point out error, and make suggestions. Pieces like the London Memorandum, for instance, did not shy away from criticizing those in Britain responsible for their welfare; the recipients, who included representatives of the UN, the IGCR, and the British Foreign Office, were all perceived to be at fault for the present affairs and past injustices. Although the language observed by Nowak in the letters was repeated (martyrology, patriotism, anti-communism, and freedom), it was given a new dimension as the authors invoked the 'betrayed-ally' rhetoric and laid their futures squarely on the shoulders of British representatives.

The reaction to the London Memorandum was published in two separate articles, one at the behest of the British Army of the Rhine HQ in Germany and the other from the IGCR. Both offered the Polish DPs three options: repatriation, absorption into the present country of residence (Germany), or emigration to any country willing to accept DPs.[17] While neither article rejects the accusations, neither do they directly address them. Yet, in other pieces of inter-office communications it is clear that the two articles are direct responses to the 'Help Poles in Germany' Polish Social Committee's memorandum. In an effort to reinvigorate a collegial Anglo-Polish relationship, both articles make positive claims about Poles while simultaneously rejecting the Germans as uncivilized. Both stress the importance of foreign labour as a-much-needed diuretic for the British economy and try to dispel the negative perception of the DP as a 'dispirited supine figure who in the intervals of queueing up for his plates of stew, sits apathetically around doing nothing'.[18] Chiefly, however, the IGCR article, based on camp reports from a representative in the British zone, warns of imposing a self-fulfilling prophecy of criminality on the Polish DPs, adding that 'despair breeds dangerous offspring'.[19] The IGCR's report was much more concerned with the idea of rehabilitation and how Western governments could help prevent the spread of criminality that had already taken hold of Europe through the black market. While ignoring any direct link between previously held British perceptions of Polish DPs expressed by the British Army of the Rhine, the other article focuses more clearly on Britain's failing industry, which was short of manpower, rather than the humanitarian aspects of helping their fellow men. The two articles agree on the need to bring Polish DPs to Britain, although for very different reasons: the IGCR's reasoning was moral, and based on humanitarian principles, while the British military's was pragmatic, as the home economy needed additional labour.

In June 1947, Klemmé ended his service with UNRRA and left the British zone of Germany. He had come to dislike the British way of doing things, complaining that the British made over-complicated plans and then moved at an incredibly slow pace to achieve them. He was aggrieved at the implementation of worker registration for all DPs in the British zone in early 1947, as the penalties for not registering and the method of worker selection were, he believed, tantamount to forced labour in Germany under the Third Reich. Just as all the DPs had been forced to register for work in Germany and told that there would be penalties for refusing, another upset was brought into the lives of the DPs and another obstacle to repatriation. Britain, along with other countries, decided to take in large numbers of DPs on foreign worker schemes, and as Klemmé states, 'once the many emigration rumours got going, most of the people lost interest in employment, going home or anything else. They became interested only in getting to a new country'.[20]

A state of limbo in the camps

To persuade nations to open their minds and their doors to DPs, the IRO tentatively began referring to DPs as 'refugees' and set up resettlement centres away from the DP camps to establish their process of transition from DP to refugee. Although these changes seem small, they enjoyed a limited degree of success. The standard impression of a DP, gaunt and listless with depressing faces had become deeply marked on the British psyche from the newsreels of 1945 onwards. The IRO wished to distance the DPs from this image: they had come a long way since the end of the war, and the IRO set about proving it. Using basic informational placards, the IRO also stressed the youth of the DPs, as the majority were between twenty and forty-nine years old.[21] In contrast to the Citizens Committee for Displaced Persons (CCDP) in the United States, however, British agencies and NGOs did not downplay the ethnicity of most of the DPs but rather they emphasized it. In Germany, the overwhelming majority of DPs both in the camps and outside them under IRO care were of Polish origin. For the British zone, there was no escaping the statistics. The IRO used the DPs' Polish origin to their advantage just as the CCDP had focused on what were perceived to be the good qualities of each ethnic group; the IRO emphasized Britain's past positive experiences of Poles to create a furore of support. Despite the IRO's ongoing battle to cajole the British public into accepting more DPs (and/or refugees) from Germany, the resettlement mission quickly became stagnant. The DPs lapsed once more into the monotonous camp routine while still searching for opportunities to avoid repatriation and resettle elsewhere.

By 1948 the Polish DPs in the British zone were trapped in a déjà vu situation similar to that of winter 1945–6 when the immediate thrust of the repatriation drive had come to a halt. They felt imprisoned in a state of limbo. The clean-cut American ideal of working out the precise number of calories to nourish the body, an exact science in every practical sense, was laughable to those suspended in the camps. The DPs' freedom was limited and controlled by the removal of almost every opportunity to decide for themselves. Although the calorific amount might have been sufficient, it was antithetical to the theme of 'rehabilitation', as Józef Betari sarcastically jibed that while they might receive an adequate number of calories, telling a man how many slices of bread will fill him without feeling the aching groans of his stomach was a special kind of imprisonment.[22] Yet, the circumstances were somewhat different from those experienced under their predecessors. The IRO's preoccupation with repatriation and then with the resettlement targets pressed upon them by their contributing member governments caused rising tensions in the camp communities. It was at this time that the phrase 'DP apathy' was coined and implemented to explain the behaviours of those who lacked 'drive'. As described by Jaroszyńska-Kirchmann, DP apathy 'manifested itself in various neurotic behaviours, a rising crime rate, absenteeism from work, procrastination, and a decreasing interest in camp affairs, entertainment, and cultural events'.[23] With the separation of Polish DPs across camps in the British zone to seemingly enforce isolation during UNRRA's repatriation drive and *Operation Carrot* in 1946 it is very possible that the spirit of the Polish community was already undone. It is argued here that the shift in aim from repatriation to resettlement allowed the community to become closer again, while simultaneously pulling them apart.

The IRO's overall goal was to resettle and re-establish the Polish DPs. Yet, with their introduction it allowed for the rebuilding of communal ties once more, encouraging religious, sporting, cultural and other activities as well as a renewed focus on training DPs for work in possible receiving countries. Consequently, although the IRO's goal was to disperse the DPs, the methods they implemented in the camps, including the restoration of stimulating activities, resulted in a more peaceful and cohesive Polish camp community. On the one hand, the re-introduction of leisure pursuits was a great relief to the DPs as it allowed them to again feel like a community. On the other hand, the re-introduction of a practice terminated earlier by UNRRA was a troubling sign that a sure solution to their displacement had not yet been established. Edward Bakis, an Estonian DP and psychologist, recorded during his time spent in the camps that 'almost everybody showed at one time or another a behavior [*sic*] that had to be classified as neurotic'.[24] Even though the IRO was trying to restore a sense of community, his argument was, essentially, the damage had already been done. As one Christmas in the camps passed into two, and then three, the seemingly endless stay in 'temporary' accommodation caused an overall apathetic attitude. Additionally, the resettlement countries' restrictive conditions caused even greater frustration, which manifested as procrastination. If the Poles were to leave the IRO's care in Germany, something must change. It was not enough to re-establish the camp governing committees that had previously been dismantled, or put on concerts with talented musicians as the seats could no longer be filled. Although the DPs needed mental escapism and educational improvement through activity, most of their mental capacity was devoted to working out how and to where they would emigrate, often leaving them in a state of mental exhaustion and perceived 'psychological regression'.[25] Jacques Vernant characterized a DP as a man who 'is often unstable, embittered by misfortune and abnormally suspicious'. Consequently, as circumstances improved with their liberation from the camps and forced labour, to be followed by similar misfortune in the form of their prolonged stay in the DP camps, he claims neurosis became 'a common condition' coupled with lack of enthusiasm as the DP 'no longer has the elasticity which enables a man when fortune has dealt him a hard blow to recover his poise and carry on'.[26]

The shift in the DPs' attitude between 1945 and 1948 was remarkable. Polish DPs had spent much of 1945 and 1946 making themselves as noticeable as possible, clamouring for resettlement opportunities or at least the British authorities' recognition of their situation. Yet, 1947–8 created a shell of the former DP, and this could partially be attributed to the British preoccupation with another DP group: the Jews.[27] After the British mandate for Palestine was officially withdrawn and civil war broke out, the attention of the British, along with that of the other UN nations, turned to the problems in Palestine. Consequently, Polish DPs in the camps of Germany held much less importance to the Allies by 1948, and the overall conditions imposed on the remaining Poles ultimately meant that they were no longer able to function normally. Low food rations, compulsory registration for work with imposed penalties for non-compliance, temporary accommodation, and complete mental exhaustion as they searched for opportunities to start life anew all culminated in this apathetic attitude. Bakis argued, however, that many other aspects of this psychological state had already caused 'normality' to appear as an alien concept by late 1947, including: having lived on a limited supply of energy for years, a preoccupation with things outside the present environment, sudden changes in circumstance, the cumulative effect of constantly interrupted tasks, loss of personality, a crisis in the philosophy of living, living in an unbelievable world and a disturbed emotional balance.[28] For Polish DPs in the British zone, suspension of normality in the camps is attributed to constantly interrupted tasks and loss of personality. Yet, did the Poles themselves feel the loss of their personalities, or was this something attributed to them by psychologists such as Bakis? Nowakowski's protagonist was aware of his own anxieties, attributing it to the 'barbed wire' complex which made him act irrationally; but the habit had been formed. He also spoke of 'warblers', the type who told fortunes from coffee grounds and who had 'become eccentric' or gone 'to pieces' and acted from a broken psyche as a result of losing their pre-war stability and sense of self.[29] Yet, Nowakowski's fictionalized account shows that the DPs believed this form of neurosis existed as a result of their wartime experiences, but not that it was due to an overall 'DP apathy' endemic in the camps; this is a misattribution.[30]

Like UNRRA welfare workers, Polish DPs were tired of being moved from camp to camp at a moment's notice.[31] This was most keenly felt when UNRRA's ban on all recreational activities in camps containing 100 or more Polish DPs on 1 October 1946 came into effect. One young Polish art student named Anna recalled how she and her fellow Poles had got together to create a theatre in their camp to bring a sense of normality to their lives. Yet, she laments due to the separation orders 'our theatre never was used because, unexpectedly, an order came that we must leave this camp in a few hours and move to another one'.[32] Again, with fellow Poles and at personal cost to gather materials she created a theatre in the next camp, only to be transferred again; this repetition continued until Anna grew despondent and stopped attempting to create theatres. This became a common pattern in many of the DP camps in the British zone as UNRRA and British military staff moved Polish DPs around in an attempt to break their communal bonds and encourage repatriation. After the IRO took over, enthusiasm about this policy dissipated and the IRO tentatively began to officially encourage the strengthening of communal bonds in the camps, mostly through the implementation of vocational courses that would improve DPs' desirability to possible countries of resettlement.

At the start of their work, the welfare workers, such as Pettiss, McNeill, Close, Cooper, and Dawson, all commented on the 'loss of personality' when it came to dealing with DPs. The vast numbers they were to care for caused a blur of names and faces. As the years progressed, however, the DPs became more familiar with them, particularly if they had remained in a single camp for a long time. Close, at the end of her article for *Survey Graphic*, concludes by literally spilling her overwhelming thoughts about individual DPs onto paper with the sub-heading 'What will become of them?':

> The problem that has been haunting me ever since is not what is to become of the DP's, but what is to become of little Polish Toni who had to be kept out of the nursery because of his TB; or ten-year-old Jerzy who was beginning to develop a facial twitch; or twenty-year-old Helena, the conscientious hospital aide who wanted so badly to come to this country [US] or Canada, but had not relatives here or anywhere else.[33]

Conversely, Klemmé does not speak of the DPs' individuality but repeatedly refers to them as numbers and expresses little empathy for them. This discrepancy in terminology emphasizes the disparity between those of a welfare and those of a military background. Indeed Morgan, like Klemmé, also grouped the DPs together under an umbrella of ethnicity or nationality, leaving no room to distinguish individual DPs, even though his memoirs suggest that he was slightly more empathetic to their situation.[34]

For some welfare workers, the ties to the DPs continued even after they left the camps. Rhoda Dawson, for instance, remained in Wildflecken in the US zone for little over a year. Upon leaving in 1947, she continued to receive numerous letters from Polish DPs in the camp updating her on their circumstances since she left. One DP, Maria P., had been selected by Ludger Dionne, a Canadian minister of Parliament, to go to Canada on a resettlement scheme.[35] Dionne's scheme, infamously known as 'the Flying Virgins', recruited 100 young Polish DP women to work in textile factories in Quebec.[36] For Maria P., this was a wonderful opportunity to escape the camps. Although the contract was specifically for two years, it was being able to 'leave' and progress in some way that was at the heart of the letter. Others, left in the camps, were not so fortunate and the prolonged stay was causing frustration. In another letter to Dawson in May 1947, Barbara D., writing from Wildflecken, speaks of how aggrieved she is to be writing to her with no change in circumstances to report:

> I am personally tired with the life in the camp – you work and you have nothing for your work, not even the feeling that you are a free man able to run your home as you like or to make some decisions and arrangement for the future ... you will probably be surprised that we are so impatient, but we are really tired with this unproductive life in DP-camps.[37]

Barbara D. goes on to inquire about work opportunities in the UK and asks Dawson to help her secure her exit from the camps writing, 'if there is anything you can do for us, please, help us in giving the possibility to leave Germany and God will bless you'.[38] In another letter, the Pastor from Wildflecken Igor Tkatschuk lamented that 'the life in the camp is becoming harder and harder. In comparison to the time you were here it changed for the worse many times'.[39] Letters expressing chagrin and frustration, however, were not just coming from the DPs. When giving updates on those Dawson would remember fondly, a former colleague lists Polish DPs either reluctantly going back to Poland or opting to work in the Belgian mines, 'because they cannot bear any longer the useless life here in the camp. They also hope to find there a better job after some time'.[40] Welfare workers, many of whom believed they would cross over from UNRRA to the IRO, were becoming increasingly exacerbated with the dwindling number of staff while the DP numbers remained relatively consistent.

One former colleague from Wildflecken complained the camp is now without a nurse, and although some DPs helped to fill these roles, the gaps in staffing were becoming significant. Another reiterated that 'we do not feel any change in DP apathy since UNRRA ceased to exist', yet they still expected the DP problem to be solved within the month as staff cuts were coming.[41]

Adding to their apathetic mood, news sources were reporting that the Poles in the British zone were underfed, confirming Bakis' notion of DPs possessing only a limited supply of energy for years. Although the British zone suffered from severe food shortages in 1946, the problem had been resolved by 1948, but reports in pro-Warsaw newspapers such as *Rzeczpospolita* (Republic) were largely thought to be exaggerated to intensify the Poles' animosity towards the British and once more encourage repatriation.[42] The supply of foodstuffs was still not equal to pre-war levels, but as discussed, the British zone underwent many difficulties regarding the procurement of foodstuffs and continued rationing at home until 1954. To limit the number of news sources circulating in the Polish DP camps in the British zone, special licences were required for the continued publication and dispersion of daily, weekly, and monthly Polish newspapers, magazines, and even bulletins after 1 September 1946.[43] It was clear, however, that some were more likely to be approved by the IRO than others, primarily *Repatriant*.[44] Like the CCDP's personalization of the Polish experiences in camps, *Repatriant* frequently published letters from former DPs who had returned to Poland, thereby hoping to portray Poland in a positive and welcoming manner.

By 1948, most Poles in the British zone feared reprisals from the new Polish Provisional Government for having delayed their return to Poland once repatriation was underway. Many Poles, having heard anti-Warsaw propaganda in the camps believed that there would be repercussions for everything, but most of all for collaboration with the Allied authorities. *Repatriant*, aimed to dispel their fears by publishing letters from former DPs. One example from a former captain of the Guard Company in Germany, Captain Biginski was published in February 1948. The letter painted Poland in the most flattering light possible: plenty of food, work, and accommodation were available – there was no reason to stay in Germany any longer as all the 'Frauleins'[*sic*] had lost interest since there was 'no more chocolate and cigarettes'.[45] Biginski adds that the mothers and fathers of Polish DPs in Germany to whom he had spoken did not understand the decision to stay away from Poland, and ask him why their sons and daughters would do this, and as he says, 'I really could not answer this question'.[46] Although intended to appear as a genuine letter, it was plainly pro-Warsaw propaganda.

In the same issue of *Repatriant* another former DP claims DPs were being fed outright lies to prevent them from returning to Poland. Mr. Osipow, a former slave labourer, alleges that he was instantly over-burdened with work in his newly set-up camera repair shop in the centre of war-ravaged Warsaw. It was only then that he realized 'what liars all these people in Germany were [as] their attitude towards anything that came from Poland was negative'.[47] The conflicting messages the DPs were constantly receiving certainly affected them. *Repatriant* was widely available in the camps, endorsed by the IRO, yet it was propaganda largely emanating from officials in Poland to spread negative perceptions of the Allied countries and encourage repatriation. Arguably it was allowed to continue as one of the last pieces of propaganda literature aimed almost entirely at repatriation rather than resettlement. The IRO's March 1948 bulletin, focusing on news publications from Poland which were still available in Germany, summarized *Repatriant* as follows:

> Organ of the State Repatriation Office, semi-official weekly, dealing exclusively with repatriation and related questions. Serves the purpose of encouraging repatriation among the Poles abroad. Supplied information on recent events in [the] country's political, social, and economic life. Much of the 'Repatriant's' space is reserved for tracing of missing persons. Answers questions pertaining to the position and future of repatriates in Poland.[48]

Although *Repatriant* still circulated widely in the British zone as late as 1948, its impact is debatable as the paper's status became increasingly ambiguous and many questioned whether it was an agent for repatriation or, through its stifling bluntness, against repatriation. Opinion was certainly divided. On the one hand, many Poles were willing to take the stories it told at face value: stories of redemption, of happiness, and of freedom from uncertainty abroad. Those Poles, for the most part, repatriated. Yet there were many left in the camps by 1948 who did not believe the stories in *Repatriant* and saw them as idle gossip and crude propaganda. Instead, most Poles in the camps used *Repatriant* as a cultural reference point: seeing (and hearing) jokes in their native language, looking at pictures of cultural and religious celebrations and receiving sports news, all had an important effect on their psychological well-being. In tandem with the IRO's renewed focus on training, educating, and mentally stimulating Polish DPs in the camps, the continued dispersion of papers like *Repatriant* with culturally relevant news sections was a great boost for morale. It also served to remind the DPs that the IRO's aim was not to treat them as 'white slaves', a point sometimes made in connection to countries' resettlement selection process.[49]

Feelings of neglect and betrayal did not go unnoticed on the British home front. Shortly before the IRO take over, an article titled 'The Legacy of the Wars' was published in January 1947. Originally written by Sydney Bailey of *London's National News-Letter*, the article underwent major revisions regarding the duties of UNRRA, the future IRO, and the governing military authority towards DPs remaining in and outside camps in British-occupied Germany. The article, which was also distributed in the British zone's DP camps, stressed the need for citizens of the 'Eastern Slav States' to repatriate:

> There is no reason why displaced persons should not return home. If they were slave labourers compulsorily deported by the Germans, they will be given every opportunity to re-establish themselves. Their reluctance to go home proves that they are Fascist collaborators. We are not going to pay money from our war-devastated country to support in idleness those who were our enemies during the war. In fact, we do not see why our allies should do so either. To be frank, we thoroughly distrust your motives.[50]

Although the article reiterates the Western position rejecting forcible repatriation, it also concedes they understand communist attitudes and does not intend to fund those with 'dubious political records'.[51] The article concludes that a million DPs would remain at the end of UNRRA care – this we know. The possibility for resettlement, however, is predicted to take anywhere up to ten years to complete. Throughout discussions of what should and should not be included in the article, nobody argued, questioned, or challenged this point. By 1947 the British had already accepted that it could take another ten years to completely resettle, or if they were lucky, repatriate the DPs remaining in the British zone of occupation in Germany. It is curious that at this juncture, as UNRRA was passing its responsibilities to the yet-to-be-created IRO, that outwardly the most important task was framed as freedom from want and not repatriation or resettlement. The article declares that 'suffering and distress did not end with the signing of the armistice', and concedes that many would remain in the camps for quite some time, 'a grim prospect for those who have already been homeless for a decade'. In this context, however, freedom from want was not a reference to the provision of food, clothing, and shelter, which they already had; it meant 'determined efforts to restore a sense of purpose and self-respect to badly shattered lives'.[52] Although this meant the reinvigoration of previously suspended vocational and educational activities in the camps, it had to be carried out alongside selling life beyond the camps, as individual and productive people, as the ultimate form of 'rehabilitation'. To do this, the IRO needed to rethink how they were to sell the prospect of repatriation to the Polish DPs, while simultaneously enhancing resettlement opportunities abroad. Consequently, the IRO introduced a new type of propaganda solely aimed at promoting resettlement over repatriation.

Expanding the possibilities: The IRO and resettlement propaganda

Using various mediums, the resettlement propaganda always contained the same message: these people need *your* help. Individual personal stories of life before, during, and after the war were frequently featured alongside pictures of DP's living conditions and DPs themselves. Special issues of magazines and periodicals, such as *World Communique*, sought to juxtapose the gloominess of the DP camps with the DPs' cheery disposition in the face of their horrific conditions. The majority of articles aimed to promote the hard-working and ceaselessly optimistic attitude of DPs in Europe despite their plight, seeking to stimulate a positive perception of them abroad and encourage a broadening of resettlement opportunities.[53] According to an IRO report about newspapers published by and for DPs in October 1950, eleven Polish-language papers, periodicals, and magazines were still being printed and distributed throughout the three western zones of occupation.[54] The continuing need for multiple news sources is a testament to the endurance of the Polish community in Germany's western zones five years after the end of the war.

Schemes such as *Westward Ho!* and *Black Diamond* had some success, with DPs settling in Britain and Belgium. Yet, there remained a sizeable number in the camps. It was vital to distribute the resettlement propaganda to civilians in popular emigration countries, such as the United States, Canada, Australia, and in South America, as a favourable attitude on the part of the citizens of the destination country was considered necessary before their governments could make any decisions. Nowhere was this more important than in the United States. Echoing Commander Jackson's earlier sentiments regarding public opinion in the United States and its effect on policy decisions, it was only with the introduction of resettlement propaganda into the United States that public opinion became receptive to the idea of widening the already-established strict immigration laws. After the initial repatriation drive was over and around a million DPs of various nationalities still remained in the three western zones of occupation, President Truman issued an Executive Order on 22 December 1945 stating that DPs from the US zone could be included in the United States' pre-existing immigration quota.⁵⁵ Although this may sound generous, the hideously restrictive quotas in place from the previous 1924 Immigration Act meant that the majority of DPs in the camps, mostly of Southern and Eastern European origin, were only able to fill limited places. For instance, the Polish yearly quota was merely 5,982, a far cry from the 253,981 Poles resident in the US zone at the end of September 1945.⁵⁶

When it became clear that the number of DPs far outweighed the quota allowances, committees were set up on the DPs' behalf and created a bombardment of 'resettlement propaganda'. The CCDP led by Earl G. Harrison in 1946 wasted no time flooding every form of media with harrowing stories of DPs' lives and of their resilience, courage, strong anti-fascist and anti-communist principles, and above all their desperation to be given the chance of a new life in the land of the free, as those who were there now were given before them. Historians of US immigration policy, Loescher and Scanlan, state that the CCDP was conscious that an influx of foreigners could be perceived as a threat at any time, and 'to allay these fears, accounts of hardship and persecution were carefully balanced with descriptions of the benefits DPs would bring'.⁵⁷ Other organizations alongside the CCDP, such as the IRO and multiple NGOs, joined in blanketing the American people with resettlement propaganda to aid the DPs. In mid-1948, as the PCIRO became the IRO, placards giving brief information on the remaining DPs were displayed in public places such as universities, government buildings, offices and railway stations, and pamphlets containing the same material were distributed in office blocks and on the streets.

Information through visual representation was thought to be most beneficial, as it provided a large volume of information in a clear and concise manner: who they are, the percentage of each gender, their ages and occupations, and their citizenship and/or ethnic groups.⁵⁸ In a further effort to disentangle the 'us' versus 'them' trope, the various organizations in charge of blanketing the American media published individual success stories of DPs who had already been admitted to the country. With the Poles in particular, the CCDP focused on their strong anti-fascist, anti-communist and pro-Western attitude, often citing these 'ethnic personality traits' as the reasons behind their easy assimilation into US society. As Hilton observes, some Polish NGOs emphasized how Poles helped to build America 'by drawing attention to the four Polish men who were with Captain John Smith when he arrived in present-day Virginia' and 'played on the abbreviated DP, calling them Delayed Pilgrims'.⁵⁹ The CCDP and IRO's target audience were those who wished to help the humanitarian cause but were also fearful of the social and economic repercussions of the DP's acceptance into the United States. By mounting their campaign to humanize the DPs and recruiting many notable and respected supporters such as Eleanor Roosevelt and Marshall Field to their cause, the CCDP were well equipped for any anti-immigrant rhetoric they were likely to encounter.

The result, however, was not the drastic change in policy the CCDP and others had hoped for. The 1948 US Immigration Act did widen the net, but the figure was capped at 205,000. The number of those admitted under the 1948 Act was also deducted from future quotas, meaning that by 30 June 1951, their mortgaging of future quotas left no further openings for Poles until 1993.[60] In addition, many restrictions and conditions were imposed on DPs that seriously limited their opportunities to resettle in the United States. The two most troublesome of these were their ability to produce a legitimate birth or marriage certificate, which often had been lost or left behind when forced out of their homes, and an individual or corporate affidavit to ensure they would not become burden on public funds. These two requirements alone, aside from the rigorous questioning and medical screening, were enough to reject the majority of DPs. Owing to the nature of their displacement Poles were left particularly vulnerable. The creation of the American Committee for the Resettlement of Polish Displaced Persons and their activity in the Catholic Church, however, soon made Poles seem desirable for resettlement, at least in comparison with other DP groups wishing to settle in the United States.

Eventually the 1948 Act was amended, raising the cap to 400,000 DPs, and allowing those who had entered the US zone up until 1 January 1949 to apply for entry and residency in the United States. The campaign by the CCDP and NGOs using resettlement propaganda had some marginal success, making it possible for Polish DPs from the US zone of occupation to apply (if they had the right documents and a sworn affidavit, of course). In the British zone, no such task was undertaken by separate organizations like the CCDP. Although the British employed the use of resettlement propaganda to entice DPs to work under the EVW scheme in Britain, the IRO's contribution was largely felt over the Atlantic in its collaboration with the CCDP. Arguably, this meant that Polish DPs in the US zone felt the benefits of the resettlement propaganda much more than their counterparts in the British zone.

Initially created in September 1945 as a fortnightly review of the British Control Commission's activities in Germany, *The British Zone Review* made a comparatively feeble attempt to raise public awareness of the Polish DPs situation. From April 1948 onwards the magazine published a minimum 1,000-word article every month on IRO efforts in the British zone of Germany to influence the repatriation and resettlement of remaining DPs.[61] This was intended to show the British public what this international organization was doing to aid the DPs and what else the British could do themselves. The magazine's concentration on IRO activities was put in place to reassure the British public that plans were being implemented to assist the remaining DPs while simultaneously keeping them away from British soil. In the first instalment concentrating on the IRO, 'DPs and their Future', the author gives a brief overview of the problems facing the IRO, its valiant efforts up until that date, and measures that would alleviate the pressure of caring for the many DPs still residing in the British-occupied Germany. In short, the article is a plea to Britain to allow the resettlement of EVWs' dependants (children, the elderly, the infirm).[62] The success of the CCDP's and IRO's resettlement propaganda was strengthened by its ties to the American Committee for the Resettlement of Polish Displaced Persons which produced links between American-Polonia and Poles in Germany. In comparison to this onslaught, the efforts made on behalf of the British zone were weak. The IRO did not create any further resettlement propaganda for Poles in the British zone. Indeed, the London Memorandum, by the 'Help Poles in Germany' Polish Social Committee, was an ardent and earnest attempt to make the plight of Polish DPs clear to the upper echelons of the British military government, and organizations such as UNRRA and the IRO. While the Memorandum cannot be viewed as resettlement propaganda it spurred the creation of two articles that were certainly the beginnings of it. Ultimately the IRO's best piece of resettlement propaganda was no lengthy newsreel, monograph, or glossy magazine, but the astute use of language changing DP to 'refugee' to alter the perception of DPs in the receiving countries.

A ban on the brain: Elites, intellectuals, and the establishment of schools in Germany

As 1948 ended, a sizeable number of DPs categorized as 'intellectuals' or 'elites' still remained. They predominantly constituted those with middle-class vocations such as teachers, doctors, lawyers, and researchers as well as artists and 'cosmopolitans'. Most of these DPs were tired of not being able to emigrate due to their highly specified and indeed impressive skill-sets. Contrary to normal societal expectations, a specialist skillset was not desirable in the DP camps, it conferred no advantages and in many ways, disadvantaged the DP, especially when emigration opportunities became available. At a meeting on 2 June 1946 to discuss the employment of Polish DPs and those of other nationalities who did not wish to return home, the position of intellectuals and elites was made clear:

> In answering an enquiry about the members of the professional classes, such as physicians, engineers with university degree[s], technicians and students, it was stated that we have to make a choice: either to return to our home country or to work as miners, as the prospects of emigration to overseas countries, where we could be employed in our own professions, are nil, for a period of three years at least.[63]

This resulted in many elite or intellectual DP workers presenting themselves as unskilled or semi-skilled workers the next time a selection board came to visit the camps.[64] According to IRO statistics, by 1948 one of every thirty-one Poles in the camps were categorized as intellectuals.[65] Of course welfare workers and military officials working in the camps became suspicious of DPs presenting themselves as unskilled or skilled labourers and urged the IRO to come up with a different solution. What followed was a brief propaganda campaign encouraging resettlement countries to accept specialists. As had become common practice with the IRO, yet another brochure was produced, this time titled *The Forgotten Elite*. The brochure contained snippets about 'elite' DPs' experiences during their displacement and accused resettlement countries of putting 'a ban on the brain'.[66] Although specialists were normally highly sought after, DPs with these specialisms were often perceived as a burden on potential host countries as retraining would usually be required in a new language. Many host countries, Britain included, did not see an immediate need for specialists such as lawyers, doctors, and pianists as they had plenty of their own. What they wanted and needed were 'practical people' such as mechanics, bricklayers, and plumbers. This resulted in the retraining of many individuals at IRO vocational centres: violinists became joiners, lawyers became farmers, and so on. The IRO's target of resettling the 'forgotten elite' soon faded into the background and many found themselves retraining to secure eligibility for resettlement; others with practical skills were able to emigrate once the US immigration quota was increased and sworn affidavits were obtained.

The vocational training courses taken up by many members of 'forgotten elite' also provided much-needed training to Poles classified as unskilled, as the courses were originally intended for non-intellectuals. In the British zone the Central Inter-committee of Trade Unions formed the Vocational Training Section, which oversaw the provision of most vocational training courses, approving and starting course programme, providing materials, invigilating exams, and controlling course standards. The inadequate supply of materials, tools, and trained teaching staff, however, impeded some of the most important sectors in construction and handicrafts 'for which there was a great demand in foreign markets'.[67] Regardless, the numbers enrolling in vocational training courses increased dramatically between 1946 and 1947 with, for example, a 67 per cent increase in completed courses and a 50 per cent increase in attendance across the year.[68] The increase in interest can be attributed to a few varied factors. Firstly, the mass repatriation drive was perceived to be over by the winter of 1946/1947, and therefore those who remained were largely interested in starting a new life outside Poland. To do so they would require desirable skills to make themselves more appealing to potential resettlement countries, or indeed to German employers. Secondly, the number of vocational training options for Polish DPs in the British zone from September–October 1946 to June–July 1947 dropped considerably. This was largely due to the introduction of the 1 October 1946 ban on educational, recreational, and other cultural activities in all camps containing 100 or more Polish DPs. Yet, once UNRRA began to wind up its operations ready for the PCIRO to take over, the Vocational Training Section was allowed to re-introduce its programme in Polish DP camps.[69] The British zone was willing to advocate training and education, but only wanted manual labourers at best: intellectuals were to look elsewhere.

Alongside the need to re-educate adults and provide vocational training, there was a yearning among the DPs to create an educational system for all Polish youth in the British zone. At the end of the war, schools were immediately set up across the three western zones of occupation by the Head Office for Polish Education, headed by Dr Tadeusz Pasierbiński and supported by the Polish Red Cross in London.[70] The enthusiasm with which the buildings were erected attests to the Poles' hunger for normality, coupled with the consciousness that many children had been deprived of a simple education. A booklet published towards the end of 1948 titled *Education of Polish DPs in Western Germany* claims that 'as a rule the children, who were living in Germany for 3 to 5 years up to their 12 years of age [sic] were illiterates'.[71] The authors believed that those who had only completed one or two grades in Polish school before the start of the war were also likely to be illiterate, which included children up to fourteen years old. The task was substantial, and apart from voluntary organizations the military government in the British zone was responsible for the welfare of all DPs until UNRRA's arrival. Indeed, the military government was viewed much more favourably than UNRRA by the Polish DPs as they 'didn't interfere at all', leaving the camps to govern themselves, and as the booklet *Education of Polish DPs in Western Germany* states:

> those several months before UNRRA took up the care of the DPs were not only the period of prosperity but also of their well being. The British Authorities didn't prevent the DPs their selforganizing activity [*sic*]. . . . It can look like a paradox but that first period of Mil. Gov. activity in the DP & PWX life was the period of true democracy and liberty sensu stricto.[72]

Although lacking in materials and staff, the Polish schools in the British zone were allowed to flourish and they were all but free from accusations that they were hindering repatriation through political activity. In 1946, however, Dr Pasierbiński accepted the position of Deputy Minister of Education under the Warsaw government, and consequently Polish schools and other educational facilities could no longer claim a position of non-bias. The Polish publication *Wiadomości* reported increasing tensions at a meeting of Polish teachers in Germany, presided over by Dr Pasierbiński and held in Hannover. The speaker, Mr Wycech, a delegate from the Warsaw government, consistently implored any Polish teachers to return to Poland, as 'every Pole should take an active part in the struggle for peace and independence which now takes place in Poland'.[73] The majority of teachers teaching throughout the three western zones rejected Dr Pasierbiński as the leading authority on Polish education in Germany and agreed on the need for a new governing body. In June 1946, 48 representatives of 1180 teachers in the three western zones of occupation gathered in Maczków. They appointed Dr Szczepan Zimmer as the head of the Central Committee for Education in Germany and the Association of Polish Teachers in Emigration in Germany, both of which rejected Warsaw's authority and were loyal to the London government-in-exile.[74]

For a short time two Polish teaching factions emerged, one pro-Warsaw and the other pro-London, which co-existed until the dissolution of the pro-Warsaw faction late in the summer of 1946. Although there were many similarities between the two factions, one emphasized the beauty of Poland and its greatness as an incentive for repatriation, whereas the other focused on the preservation of all things Polish and Polishness itself to distance them from Poland's current government and ideology.[75] Yet, after the dissolution of the pro-Warsaw educational body, UNRRA refused to officially recognize the existence of the Central Committee for Education and instead looked to welfare officers of the Polish Red Cross to oversee the education of Polish DPs.

In the House of Commons on 20 November 1946, a Labour MP questioned alarming rumours that the Central Education Committee had been forced to cease its activities and the vocational school in Lübeck had been dissolved. These accusations implied that the British were all but condoning practices that would force the Polish DPs' hand and make them accept repatriation.[76] The British authorities were certainly trying to navigate through dangerous waters between the two currents of public opinion on Poles at this point. While the British public opinion was sympathetic about the situation of Polish DPs remaining in the camps, it was hostile regarding their continual need for resources as Britain faced austerity. Mr Hynd rebuffed the claim that the Central Education Committee was forced to cease activities in November 1946. Yet, only a few weeks later Dr Zimmer received a letter from the director of UNRRA Team 162 overseeing Maczków, aka Haren stating that he could 'no longer be allowed to have any administrative interest in the Haren schools, or in any other schools in the British zone'. Giving no specific reasons, the letter stated that the Red Cross education officer was to take over.[77] This soon became a cause for concern among the British military government, as they could not be seen to openly dismiss Dr Zimmer simply because he was not a representative of the ruling government in Warsaw. After further debate about flaunting United Nations' policies, Dr Zimmer's removal was suspended on the basis of 'pending inquiries'.[78] Although not outwardly hostile to the education policies developing in the British zone, particularly as they also aided local development, UNRRA's level of official involvement was questioned as its sole contribution to education was 'the restoration on an emergency basis of essential buildings for educational purposes' and did not include the supply of materials and goods, or micromanaging committees and their representatives.[79] It soon became clear, however, that the provision of a sound education was seen in the British zone as another deterrent to repatriation.[80]

With the imposed ban, education suffered the same problems as many other areas of camp life.[81] Like vocational training and cultural events, however, education was given a reprieve once the IRO took over in 1947, causing great relief among the Polish community. The British zone of occupation was perceived to be the best equipped in terms of educational facilities and freedom of teaching; indeed, unlike the French and US zones they were also able to receive funds directly from the German county's budget without interference from German administration. By 1 January 1948, there were 260 Polish schools across the three western zones of occupation in Germany, 163 of which were in the British zone.[82] The overwhelming majority of schools were kindergartens and primary schools, attesting to the age of the average Polish student in 1948 (see Table 6.1). Although the British zone had the highest number of Poles,

Table 6.1 Education of Polish DPs in British Zone of Germany, 1 January 1948

Type of School	Number of Schools	Amount of Youth	Number of Teachers	Student to Teacher Ratio
Kindergarten	68	3133	127	24:1
Primary	74	5131	304	16:1
Secondary	4	633	66	10:1
Trainings Schools	7	249	26	10:1
Training Colleges	3	176	22	8:1
Total	**163**	**9322**	**545**	**17:1**

Source: Created by Samantha K. Knapton. AN, AJ-43-1162, 'Education of Polish Refugees in West Germany', 47 [my ratios].

the ratio of teacher to pupil in the US zone was much higher. In kindergartens alone, the ratio of teacher to student was 32:1, compared with the British zone's 24:1. Yet, shortly after these figures were gathered the US and British zones joined together to create Bizonia and the Polish DPs formed larger centres, consolidating educational facilities with the intention of having stricter control over the curriculum.[83]

By the end of 1948, British officials realized that most DPs still in the camps were largely unable to be repatriated or resettled. Most had been holding out for an opportunity to resettle in countries like Canada or the United States; however, after the strict quotas were established and those without an affidavit had been rejected there was little hope of resettlement.[84] The IRO had been created to operate within a limited time scale and its termination was fast approaching. The increasing tension between East and West was escalating, and the western zones were preparing themselves for German separation. By 1949, there was an urgency to repatriate all they could and resettle the rest before time ran out and European division solidified.

Overcoming 'apathy': The development of post-war humanitarianism

Throughout UNRRA and the IRO's existence, aside from official propaganda created and distributed across zones or by governing bodies within specific zones, individual welfare workers continued to help DPs after returning home. In a series of letters sent to Rhoda Dawson throughout 1947, after she has left Wildflecken, she is repeatedly asked to find resettlement opportunities for the DPs she once cared for, such as the renowned ballet director Mieczysław Pianowski. Typical of a highly trained specialist with a particular skill set, Dawson was unable to find employment for Mr Pianowski. Nevertheless, she continually sent letters to various ballet schools throughout Britain, often attaching a brief biography and resumé, and received letters of thanks from his son, Jerzy, who was stationed at York.[85] Pianowski eventually ended up in the United States while his son settled in Britain.[86] Sometimes, however, it was also the other way round, and potential employers in England contacted Dawson asking for advice when hiring DPs. For instance, one English woman was keen to hire a DP as a maid, detailing that she did not know which 'nationality the ones you know are', but would be glad of some help.[87] In Dawson's case, the welfare work continued even after the camps, and without the aid of resettlement propaganda.

For someone who claimed at the beginning of her memoir, *The Stagnant Pool*, that she was shamed into carrying out welfare work stating, 'it was not my thing at all', Rhoda Dawson's continual efforts to exert influence over the fate of those who had fallen through the cracks of altruistic and charitable organizations indicate a new form of post-war humanitarianism had formed. One in which newly created state-driven international humanitarian organizations worked alongside long-standing charitable organizations. As Silvia Salvatici states, we cannot 'think of the post-Second World War era as a phase of marginalization for private associations, which were instead called upon to build closer relationships with national governments and develop their reporting to the new intergovernmental bodies: first UNRRA, and then the UN'.[88] Yet, the power of the individual could often be the linchpin for many DPs who had seemingly run out of options; and the individual was not necessarily wielding great power.

In 1949, the IRO changed tact and appealed directly to the already resettled DPs abroad for help. Once again, recognizing that post-war humanitarianism must take a different shape and not rely on one form of relief or another, but through a combination of international organizations and established charities, as well as the individual no matter how lowly their status. Everyone is in a position to help someone else. In a pamphlet from March 1949, titled *Help IRO to Help You*, the IRO implored those abroad to take an active role in the assurances of affidavits and places of resettlement for those left in the camps. The previously resettled DPs could help others to join them by 'contacting the IRO office in their country of residence, by making an application to the immigration authorities for an entry permit for their friends, by attempting in every possible way to find work, sponsorships and affidavits of support'.[89] The IRO repeated throughout its propaganda campaign abroad that for many, the unhappy past remains the urgent present, emphasizing the urgency of cooperation between past and present DPs to achieve a peaceable solution. For Poles, this was crucial: unlike citizens of other countries, affidavits were one of the only ways to secure their passage, especially across the Atlantic. One of the IRO's predecessors, the IGCR, had made it possible for those unable to procure a passport from their country of origin to obtain an international passport as early as 1945, this became commonly known as the London Document. Although Poland, along with other countries such as Britain and the United States, was invited to appoint experts to the commission examining the adoption and issue of an internationally recognized travel document, Poland was not one of the eighteen members who signed the London Document into existence on 15 October 1946.[90] As securing affidavits through ex-DPs had limited success, the Western powers increasingly turned back to the public to resettle the residual DPs in and outside the camps in Germany. As late as 1950, the Western Allies were calling for 'bold DP action', urging the councils of Europe to resolve the refugee problem as it was now '[threatening] the stability of Europe'.[91]

Some welfare workers continued to work within the new framework of the IRO. For example, Susan Pettiss, who found herself in the IRO's Washington office as a liaison between the IRO and voluntary agencies dealing with DPs, often 'criss-crossing the country, making speeches about the plight of DPs still needing "assurances", the magic ticket for immigration visas to our shores'.[92] Although the IRO was closing down, this did not mean that there were no DPs left to help. Indeed, reflecting on his own experiences over fifty years later regarding his time spent in Germany as a Quaker relief worker with the Friends Ambulance Unit, Grigor McClelland lamented:

> As responsibilities were transferred from the Western allies to the new democracy in West Germany, the privileged status of DPs was gradually eroded and it became increasingly urgent to help them get out of a country in which they could play no useful role. Emigration and resettlement had to be the aim when repatriation was out of the question and integration into German society was impossible. But many countries for some years offered entry and work only for able-bodied males without families, an unacceptable price for most to pay. Members of the FRS teams who had worked to the DPs' interests in Germany and had come to know them well, became convinced the emigration represented the only reasonable solution, and that, painful as it was to part, they could serve their friends' interests better by trying to open wider possibilities from the outside.[93]

The IRO's mandate was to wind up its European operations by the end of 1951 as it handed over responsibility for the remaining DPs to the newly created

Federal Republic of Germany (FRG), stating, 'all refugees and displaced persons other than those in the process of repatriation or resettlement would become the responsibility of the Federal Government, both financially and administratively'.[94] Yet even as the IRO gradually closed down, DPs were still appearing at the centres seeking help. In the British zone, it was left to people like Kanty Cooper to provide care for those who remained. Towards the end of her memoirs on Germany, Cooper recalls a young but haggard and despondent-looking DP, having escaped a Hungarian concentration camp, staggering into the IRO office for help, but as it was closing in a couple of days the IRO was no longer in a position to help him. To ensure he received some form of assistance, she enquired about his religion, and upon learning he was Catholic she rang the Catholic Voluntary Society to ask for aid. They responded immediately.[95] It was, in effect, those 'in the middle' between over-arching organizations and the DPs, that often had the biggest impact on a DPs' chances of resettlement. Indeed, although Grigor McClelland stated that 'integration into German society was impossible', efforts were made to protect the rights of DPs across the FRG under Articles 1–19 of the Basic Law of the Federal Republic. These assurances and articles were to form the basis of the eventual Homeless Foreigners Law (*heimtlose Ausländer Gesetz*), created on 25 April 1951. In discussions between the Western Allies, it was thought that if these proposed plans were to fail, establishment of a legal European Citizenship was a viable option, albeit one did not come to fruition that would have affected the Polish DPs in 1950.[96]

Conclusion

For many welfare workers in the camps, by 1947 'DP apathy' had become a rapidly spreading contaminating agent that threatened the stability of the post-war world. If the DPs refused to go home, what were the Allies to do? In reality, the application of the term 'DP apathy' to various DP groups, but in particular to Estonians and Poles, was largely the result of a myopic concentration on a singular 'problem' that required a 'solution' or 'cure'. Namely, their refusal to leave the camps. As Peter Gatrell succinctly surmised, 'the diagnosis linked displacement with alienation'.[97] Leading psychologists at the time, such as Henry Murphy and Edward Shils, linked 'DP apathy' with an almost horde mentality where DPs became nameless faces in a sea of other despondent familiars while simultaneously experiencing segregation, isolation, and dependency. They were quick, however, to point out the two extremes: a listless DP with no individuality growing evermore despondent and dependent, and the troublesome yet reluctant DP unwilling to accept repatriation or a stay in Germany, who constantly campaigned for resettlement.[98] The solution for both came back to UNRRA's motto: 'help the people to help themselves'. What that looked like, in reality, however, was zonally dependent. Increasingly, the state of limbo endured by the remaining Poles in the camps between 1947 and 1950 was alleviated only by the re-introduction of leisure, sporting, and educational activities following the IRO takeover. The pervasively apathetic mood, born more so from complete mental and physical exhaustion, however, continued to encroach on every aspect of their camp lives. Although they were relieved to be under the care of the IRO as opposed to UNRRA, the Poles continued to be sullen about their prospects, believing that the British in particular had not done enough to right the wrongs of the recent past.

In *The Last Million*, David Nasaw aptly lamented, 'the IRO turned upside down what might have been – and should have been – its primary mission'. By emphasizing the needs of the resettlement countries above the priorities of those who lingered on, displaced and exhausted, the IRO (perhaps unwittingly), 'set in motion a harsh Darwinian resettlement calculus that victimized those who had suffered most and rewarded those among the displaced persons populations who had suffered least'.[99] The mentally and physically afflicted, as well as the elderly and the young, having endured the Second World War were now thought of as 'undesirables'.

Like the founders of UNRRA, it appears that the IRO's creators were also unsure of the task that lay before them. Just as UNRRA never prescribed a concrete definition to its second 'R', the IRO could not wrestle the opposing foci of freedom from want and larger, Allied-country-friendly resettlement issues.[100] This persistent inability to adequately match rhetoric with physical action is a theme present throughout the entirety of UNRRA and the IRO's existence. In correspondence regarding 'The Legacy of Wars', a British Public Relations officer drafts a preliminary outline of the IRO's constitution hoping to clarify some details about what the takeover from UNRRA would mean. The unhappy conclusion, however, was that although 'the limitations of official assistance are laid down in a series of definitions annexed to the constitution of the IRO . . . they are of great complexity and will be very difficult to administer, partly because they are the result of political compromise'.[101] This proved to be true. Although pressure to resettle as many DPs as possible increased as the deadline of 30 June 1950 approached, there remained a sizeable number in the three western zones of Germany on 1 July 1950.[102] To avoid sudden upset to the DPs' lives, the IRO agreed to stay in Germany until the end of 1951 to oversee the handover of remaining camps and DPs to the German authorities. Even with this precaution, attempted integration into German society was to prove more complex than predicted. The British authorities left in Germany could breathe a sigh of relief as they were officially able to dust their hands of the 'sludge' that remained.

7

From displaced persons to homeless foreigners
The 'hard core' of DPs left in Germany

Introduction

The IRO's operations officially ended in Germany on 30 June 1950, although it continued to help with the transference of authority to the Federal Republic of Germany (FRG) in Bonn until the end of 1951. The IRO had been tasked with the repatriation and then the resettlement of the remaining DPs in Germany from the time of UNRRA's closure on 30 June 1947. For much of its existence, however, the IRO, like its predecessor, was hindered by its member governments and subsequently found itself bound by the same red tape UNRRA had been subjected to in previous years, albeit in a slightly more relaxed manner. The strict administrative controls on the IRO governed who was entitled to aid, how and when they received aid, and who paid the bill for this aid. In hindsight, it comes as no surprise that administrative restrictions controlled how effective an international humanitarian organization could be in the early and uncertain days of post-war Europe. The focus on DPs in Germany after the closure of the IRO and the introduction of the Homeless Foreigners Law in 1951 undoubtedly concentrated on ethnic German refugees and not 'others'. Subsequently, when control of the remaining DPs passed to the German authorities, the international community, and indeed Germany as well, seemingly ceased to care about the DPs who had repeatedly filled newspapers with headlines since May 1945.

As the IRO wound up its operations in Germany the continuous questions from welfare workers and military officials alike regarding who, how, when, and why were left largely unanswered as the FRG took over all control of the remaining 'hard core'. The once-regular attention bestowed on DPs by newspapers and other media, albeit largely negative and particularly anti-Slavic, abruptly came to an end, and as Anna Holian remarked, the 'negative interest was replaced by almost total silence'.[1]

This chapter examines the tumultuous end of the IRO, and the scramble to resettle as many DPs as possible before control was handed over to local German authorities. The success of this final push for resettlement at the end of the IRO's tenure in Germany forms the basis for exploring the options that were then available to those who would have to remain, be it inside or outside the camps. Crucially, the availability of these options put additional pressure on the British occupation authorities to find housing in a zone infamous for its acute housing shortage. Focusing on the settlement of the remaining DPs, the West German task to integrate the 'other' will be shown within the context of British-occupied Germany. Indeed, after the official handover of authority, the British attitude turned to one of almost total indifference as the lingering reminder of the war's end threatened to destabilize the teetering political balance in the new Cold War world. As seen in the previous chapter, it was often up to individual welfare workers to provide help even after their terms of service ended. Additionally, the IRO and FRG's self-professed achievable aims of resettlement were framed within the loosely defined policy of *Eingliederung* (integration) over *Einschmelzung* (assimilation). Integration is a notoriously tricky concept to define, and its shortcomings do not need to be repeated here.[2] Yet, when attempting to resettle Polish DPs in a society that was likely to reject 'newcomers', especially as they had already spent a considerable amount of time in Germany being treated as inferior, the FRG's definition of integration proved problematic.

Lastly this chapter looks at how the term 'displaced person' came to be commonly used by German authorities and citizens to refer to ethnic German expellees rather than those who had hitherto been referred to as DPs by the Allies. Even though the groups were initially distinguished, as the 1950s progressed conflation of the terms 'displaced person', *Flüchtlinge* (Refugee) and *Vertriebene* (Expellees) became more common, leading to a distinctly separate memory of DPs in the West German archives.[3] The change in focus from DPs to *Flüchtlinge* or *Vertriebene* after the IRO's departure meant that 'while the plight of German refugees remained a central issue, DPs became a footnote in Germany's migration history'.[4] Indeed, with the introduction of the Homeless Foreigners Law in 1951 the all-encompassing term for those remaining in Germany sought to minimize the remaining DPs' importance in contrast to the ethnically German *Flüchtlinge*. This would prove to have a particularly damaging effect upon the Poles remaining in the FRG.

The end of the IRO

After discussing care and rehabilitation measures to be taken by the IRO in 1949 at a Geneva conference, one representative, Ms Greene, stated that 'whatever the future of the IRO, the work could not possibly be finished by July 1950'.[5] Ms Greene was right. According to the IRO's official historian, Louise Holborn, by 30 June 1950 there remained in the British zone of Germany 100,610 persons registered with the IRO who had not been resettled or repatriated.[6] Many, often referred to as the 'hard core', were classified as in need of institutional care, with limited chances of resettlement due to their health, age or occupation.[7] Another group was termed the 'non-institutional residual', of which the largest proportion was of Poles, who made up 27 per cent of the total throughout the three western zones:

> This group of refugees receiving IRO care and maintenance had valid objections to repatriation, they were not deemed presentable for resettlement, they were not acceptable for local settlement without continuing assistance, and they were not cases requiring institutional care. Counselling Officers found no alternative but to classify them as 'potentially residual but not requiring institutional care'.[8]

In the British zone, Poles accounted for 6,099 of the 12,084 'residual cases who do not require institutional care' by 30 June 1950.[9] These figures, however, do not account for the number of Poles in Germany who were not (or were no longer) registered with the IRO, who lived outside the camps seeking to integrate without assistance, or who were afraid to register with an international organization entirely. The statistics presented here give widely differing numbers of Poles in Germany as a result of the war, depending on which classification, if any, they were given by their contemporaries. Indeed, due to discrepancies in classification, the numbers of DPs in the three western zones of Germany in other historical accounts of the era fluctuate wildly, giving estimates of between 100,000 and 300,000 DPs in the British, French and US zones by the end of 1951.[10] This work predominantly uses the IRO's official history, which puts the total at 140,011 by 31 Dec 1951, and attempts to account for any discrepancies that may arise (see Figure 7.1).[11]

The IRO's initial mandate was to repatriate as many DPs as possible within a limited time frame. Although the improbability of repatriating Poles was widely known by this juncture, attempts were still made to return them to a Poland they no longer recognized as their home. In his contemporary work on Europe's displaced persons, Malcolm J. Proudfoot argues that the United States, Britain,

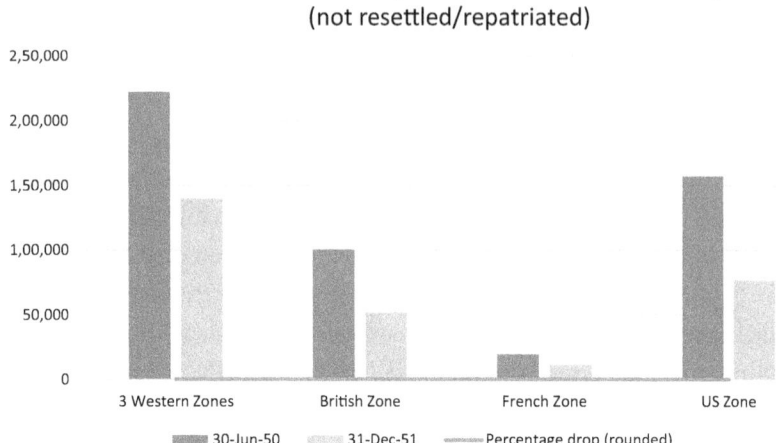

Figure 7.1 Total number of people under IRO care in Germany (not resettled/repatriated). Source: Created by Samantha K. Knapton

France, and other Western countries made 'every reasonable effort' to persuade Eastern countries, including Poland, to accept voluntary repatriation and 'the alternative of resettlement'. He further contended that the Soviet bloc did all within its power to convince the Western nations that they had the sovereign right to control their nationals, and prevention of this right was tantamount to conspiring with war criminals. Proudfoot states that when the newly formed United Nations rejected the Soviet policy of forcible repatriation 'the diplomatic language considered necessary to soften the rejection unfortunately concealed the fact that the main function of the IRO was resettlement, and confused the language of its Constitution, making its subsequent interpretation difficult.'[12] The legitimacy of focusing the IRO's efforts on resettlement rather than repatriation only became apparent a few months into the tenure of the Preparatory Commission for the IRO (or PCIRO) in Germany. Certainly, as the wording of the IRO constitution (created in 1946) demonstrates, the hierarchal placement of the organization's functions displays the level of commitment that the IRO was typically meant to devote to each task; the first and foremost being repatriation, and the last being resettlement and re-establishment with emphasis on 'temporary residence.'[13] Holborn further argues this point in the official history of the IRO: 'Repatriation, that is, return of refugees and displaced persons to their countries of origin or previous permanent residence, was repeatedly stated in the Constitution as the primary means of reducing the refugee problem.'[14] This quickly changed, however, as the situation on the ground developed further and the majority of those still remaining, especially within the camps, called for resettlement elsewhere.

Through frequent field reports, the British became aware that the rate of repatriation was slowing significantly throughout the IRO's operations in Germany. At a meeting in February 1951, it was reported that a total of only 19 people had been repatriated from the British zone of Germany in January 1951, compared to the 3,346 resettled during the same month.[15] The total number assisted by the IRO in the British zone by the later date of December 1951 was 326,738, of which only 23,168 were repatriated to their 'country of origin or former domicile' compared to 274,911 who were 'resettled in new countries'.[16] In total, just under 8 per cent of the total number assisted by the IRO in the British zone between 1 July 1947 and 31 December 1951 were repatriated. To frame this in a wider context, more people died or disappeared than were repatriated from the British zone by the end of 1951.[17]

The transition of DPs to the German authorities

As the IRO came to realize their task would not be completed within the expected time frame, they convened on several occasions to discuss the legal status of DPs remaining, particularly on German soil. The IRO conference in January 1949 produced plentiful documents on the topics of resettlement, rehabilitation, children and youth, and eligibility and protection. There was significant concern from all members in attendance that DPs were likely to be mistreated by local German authorities once the Allies relinquished control, and were similarly likely to be put at an economic and social disadvantage. Alongside those persons who still required care, the status given to remaining refugees was a concern once the IRO terminated. A memorandum in September 1949 reiterated that more secure legal measures needed to be put into place before the IRO terminated, as the British military authorities believed that 'the more urgent problem of the *Volksdeutsche* will inevitably cause the German Authorities to discriminate against DPs/refugees unless the position of the latter is specially guaranteed'.[18] This was a concern which constantly dominated discussions in the months leading up to the transfer of authority. On 19 July 1950, a couple of weeks after the official transfer date, the IRO zonal offices of the British Army of the Rhine compiled a summary of the situation in Germany, breaking it down into pre- and post-1 July 1950. The report looked at areas such as employment, housing, legal status, and public assistance, to analyse whether Germany was doing everything in its power to assure the IRO and CCG that the DPs were in capable hands. It may have been slightly premature to publish a report a mere eighteen days after the initial handover date and use it to assess the 'successes/failures' of the handover itself and the effect these findings had on the DPs when no real consequences could be discerned so early on. Consequently, the second half of the report is not wholly reliable, and largely expresses hopes about what would become of the DPs now under the care of the German authorities.

The documentation pre-1 July 1950, however, gives an interesting insight into the relationship that had developed between the IRO and CCG in the British zone between 1947 and 1951. Reminiscent of the relationship between UNRRA and the British military government, the IRO was also to take on a junior role, subordinate to the CCG.[19] The practical implications of both international organizations' subordination to the military authorities in the British zone was the implementation of a strict and militaristic hierarchy and system which eventually led Polish DPs to become even more disillusioned with British care. As a result, parallels were often drawn by DPs between the British military authorities, and the pre-war and wartime German authorities. These parallels however were by no means similarly traumatic. The problem for many Poles residing in the DP camps is that they expected sudden elation, a fevered culmination of years of suppression at the hands of the Nazis that would exhibit itself in various forms of freedom. Many dreamt of liberation centred on freedom of movement, but perhaps more importantly, freedom to access food. The inability of the British zone to provide even the minimum recommended number of calories per person was a strong indicator to Polish DPs that the total freedom they had dreamt of would not be readily obtainable in the immediate aftermath of the war. Consequently, as food supplies remained low and the regimented lifestyle in the camps continued well into the IRO's tenure in Germany many Polish DPs often saw the international organizations and the British military as one and the same.

At the same time the IRO was issuing reports on *who* remained in Germany. In March 1950, it claimed 305,407 refugees remained under its care, both inside and outside the camps, 105,174 of which were Poles. There still remained 335 camps, hospitals for DPs, and other centres. The situation seemed only marginally better since May to June 1945: they described how 'their barrack rooms – many of which house five, seven even a dozen or more persons – are poor substitutes for the homes they once had' yet they represented 'tenuous security'. They continued to disseminate propaganda to encourage countries to accept these remaining DPs and often reiterated that the DPs had governed themselves in the camps 'along the democratic lines' and were able to 'live harmoniously together in spite of the many hardships'.[20] The IRO impressed on possible receiving countries that DPs were not 'others' with strange habits, but regular people eager to be part of a democratic society. Additional sections in the IRO news bulletins were increasingly angled this way, with headings such as 'Many DPs earn their own living', 'DP camps follow community patterns', 'Educating the children' and 'They build their own Churches'. The separation of 'us' and 'them' that had existed before and throughout the Second World War, affecting the victims of war and labelling them as social outcasts were now being temporarily erased to alleviate the pressure of resettling those who remained.[21] In a booklet titled 'Is it Nothing to You?' issued by the Refugees Defence Committee in London, the authors implore ordinary citizens to understand the remaining DPs' predicament:

> For nearly four years these Irrepatriables have endured humiliation as political exiles, they have clearly stated valid reasons for not wishing to return. Yet in varying degrees pressure is still exerted on these people to change their minds – even though we all know full well what is likely to be the fate of those who elect to return after absenting themselves from their country for such a long period of time. They have constantly been denounced by Soviet Russia and her Satellites as 'Fascists' and 'Reactionaries' . . . it is therefore not difficult to imagine what will be their fate should they fall into the hands of their persecutors.[22]

In hindsight it may seem relatively obvious why so many, especially politically exiled, DPs would not wish to return to their Soviet-controlled countries. It was primarily voluntary organizations, however, that took it upon themselves to reinforce the IRO's continued use of resettlement propaganda to help clear Germany of DPs, rather than the CCG in the British zone.

In the post-IRO period, the division of responsibility for these remaining DPs was formulated in a familiar style. The IRO was made subordinate to the CCG, which asserted that 'negotiations with the German authorities would be undertaken by Displaced Persons Division, and that IRO should not take part in any discussion with the German authorities, but be consulted before and after any such meetings'.[23] The IRO begrudged these arrangements, worried about whether their interests would be satisfactorily represented, and were keen to provide care and maintenance, continuing the policy of repatriation and resettlement on 'an intensified scale' leading up to the handover. It was made very clear that discussions between CCG and the German authorities should in no way impede their efforts. The result was a significant decline in the number of refugees registered with the IRO in the British zone of occupation by more than half between 30 June 1949 and 31 December 1950.[24] After that date, however, the numbers effectively stalled as the 'hard core' was reached, and indeed some new

Table 7.1 Percentage of National Groups' Arrival Dates in Germany

Nationality	Percentage arrived in Germany at dates indicated		
	Before 1939	Between 1.9.1939 and 31.7.1945	After 1.8.1945
Poles	6	49	45
Balts	2.5	47.5	50
Yugoslavs	10.5	42	47.5
Hungarians	8	36	56
Soviet Russians	4	51	45
Czechoslovaks	15	18	67
Rumanians	6	41	53
Bulgarians	14	49	37
Stateless	28	25	47
Average	10.5	40.5	49

Source: Yale University Press. Vernant included the Länder Lower Saxony, Bremen, Hesse, Würtemberg, Bavaria, and Rhine-Palatinate. Table replicated from Vernant, *Refugee*, 146.

people began to register at the last moment before the IRO closed its offices for good.[25] Whereas some, as we have seen through Kanty Cooper's memoirs, were a little too late and had to rely on volunteer organizations for help.[26]

The exact number of DPs remaining in Germany when the IRO terminated is not wholly calculable: many were afraid to register with the IRO, some were considered ineligible, and others were simply too late. Jacobmeyer prefaces his chapter on the Homeless Foreigners Law of 1951 stating that, 'at the time of declaration, there was still no clarity regarding the make-up of the number of DPs for which the Federal Republic of Germany was to assume responsibility', setting the minimum number for all three western zones at 106,300 and the maximum at 200,000.[27] Vernant gives estimates for each nationality in *The Refugee in the Postwar World* by dividing the statistics on foreigners reported as being on West German territory on 1 January 1952 by nationality. Unsurprisingly, the Polish group dominates these statistics.[28] He then uses a sample of 61,000 nationals of East European countries and stateless persons to determine their arrival dates in percentages (see Table 7.1). Although this is only a sample based on particular *Länder*, Vernant believes that in the case of states such as Nordrhein-Westfalen the particularly large foreign-born population was overwhelmingly the result of wartime and post-war migration, arguing:

> Thus while it may be impossible to determine the exact number of refugees in Germany on 1 January 1952, it may nevertheless be concluded that the figure is nearer that which has been deduced from the German statistics (254,000

nationals of Eastern European countries and stateless persons) than that appearing in the IRO statistics (140,000 registered refugees).[29]

The number of those still registered in camps was now becoming smaller and smaller compared with those who were living in homes in German communities. When the German authorities officially took over on 1 July 1950, each Land was asked to prepare information for those who were formally under IRO care, especially those still living in the DP camps and assembly centres. In the British zone of occupation this led to miniature booklets and pamphlets being created with advice for those who wished to remain in Germany. In Nordrhein-Westfalen a small booklet titled *Hinweise für das Einleben* (Hints for Settling In) was created and circulated around the remaining DP camps and assembly centres, as well as places knowingly requisitioned for DP accommodation, such as old army barracks. The booklet opens with a small note of purpose and welcome:

> The state government of Nordrhein-Westfalen will be assuming responsibility for those foreigners in the state who fell under German jurisdiction on 1 July 1950. In order to ease their adjustment to life in Germany, we offer the following tips. We also hope that these tips will alleviate some of the technical problems that new circumstances almost always bring with them.

The booklet comprises six sections: Rights, Information, Housing, Employment, Social Insurance, and Camp Life which are further broken down into minute subsections. Primarily aimed at those who would need the information at hand, the booklet was also intended as a guide for certain sectors of the newly set-up German administrative body, staffed by the British occupation authorities. The production of pamphlets such as these allude to the German authorities' willingness and preparation to tackle the problem of the remaining DPs. The last section dedicated to the 'Suffering and Joy of Camp Life', however, offers advice and urges those residing in the camps to 'hold on' as the camps were a 'temporary and mutually unwanted emergency measure' that 'requires patience from both sides in today's difficult circumstances'.[30] One would think that this was most likely addressed to the camp inmates who had led a prolonged existence in the camps and were awaiting resettlement within German society, namely the displaced persons who had been in a state of temporary residence for so long already. Yet, the use of the terms *Flüchtlinge* (refugee) and *(Heimat-)Vertriebenen* (expellees) can be confusing, as these labels were typically applicable to Germans expelled from the East. Whereas Poles and others who had been displaced throughout and immediately after the war were commonly referred to by the

Allies' anglophone initials DP, or in some cases the German term *Verschleppte Personen*, also meaning displaced person.[31] This conflation of terms makes it hard to distinguish which group the pamphlet is addressing. There were similar problems when the DPs under the auspices of the IRO suddenly became known as *'Heimatloser Ausländer'* (homeless foreigners) overnight. As Jacobmeyer explains, the IRO's main disagreement with this new terminology was that the title implied 'homelessness', which was not congruent with the wider meaning of the IRO's clientele. Those who were truly perceived to be homeless tended to be Germans bombed out of their homes.[32] Arguably the temporary accommodation of DPs in old army barracks, ex-concentration camps and other such places was reason enough to label them homeless, as this was merely a temporary measure, although for some it became a temporary measure that lasted almost a decade.

The 'sickness in her midst': Curing the refugee problem in West Germany

After the official transfer of authority from the IRO to the German authorities in July 1950, the first concern of the IRO, which lingered in the background to aid a peaceful transition, was to secure rights for the DPs similar to the rights of German citizens. The fruition of the numerous committees, meetings, and debates regarding the rights of DPs in Germany was the Homeless Foreigners Law of 1951. Leading up to this, however, two separate surveys were conducted on Germany's three western zones to determine how well DPs and refugees were integrating into German society. Although this study focuses on the British zone of occupation, the surveys covered all three western zones and therefore both must be considered. Their purpose, conclusions, and impact will be analysed here to show how disparate and haphazard policies concerning the remaining DPs were. The first, a joint effort by the United States and FRG, commissioned a team of fourteen specialists to conduct a survey between September and December 1950. The outcome was a sizeable text analysing various facets of life and assessing how well equipped the host society and newcomers were for the task of integration. The second was a survey commissioned by the director general of the IRO, Donald Kingsley, after receiving preliminary reports from his assistant director general, Myer Cohen, in August 1950.[33] It had been commissioned after the CCG British Element raised the issue of housing as a major obstacle to peaceful integration. The IRO team consisted of only three members, with the addition of an interpreter when and where available. Both surveys conclude with largely similar assessments and advice to aid integration, yet due to one significant discrepancy they also differ considerably. Comparing the two documents and their recommendations reveals some very distinctive differences in their approaches towards housing and welfare issues as the new decade dawned. The IRO, as the last humanitarian organization to be charged with the welfare of the remaining DPs, typically embodies an international attitude that was later lost in Germany. Primarily the IRO was focusing on keeping DPs, who had been displaced during and immediately after the war, at the forefront of the German authorities' minds when discussing policies of integration. The US-German document's inability to separate the East German expellees from earlier DP groups, however, almost prophesized the context in which DPs, and particularly Polish DPs, found themselves in early 1950s Germany. Reiterating Holian's remarks, these documents show that even at an institutional level the category of DPs was being swallowed up by the all-encompassing term 'refugees'.

The major distinction between the two surveys was not where the teams conducted their research or the length of time spent in each zone, but rather who the surveys focused on. The IRO survey provoked by British concerns was titled *A Survey of Conditions of Displaced Persons Transferred to the German Economy*, whereas the US-German report was called *The Integration of Refugees in German Life*. The former targeted those known as DPs, and the latter used the all-encompassing term 'refugees' which includes not only DPs but also ethnic German expellees, and refugees fleeing the Soviet zone and Berlin. This led to some discrepancies in the reports' conclusions regarding what could be done to help these groups of people integrate. Although all were expected to follow the policy of *Eingliederung* (integration) there were undoubtedly great differences in how this would be achieved between the groups.

Kingsley's initial summary stated that during the four-month handover period favourable reports about the actual turnover of authority were received. Yet, 'the conditions in which the refugees concerned now find themselves vary considerably not only between the three Zones of Western Germany but also in the different Länder within each Zone'.[34] This concern about the DPs' basic needs not being met also affected possible resettlement opportunities, and the IRO were worried that sub-standard accommodation and welfare could lead to deteriorating health and thus prevent the DPs from being accepted onto possible resettlement schemes. The proposed solution was the *Survey of Conditions* to be conducted in all three western zones focusing solely on DPs. A team was immediately put together, and the survey was conducted in the same month as Kingsley's report. The short turn-around meant, however, that the committee could only visit a select few installations to report on their conditions.³⁵ The generalized findings stated that 'the material condition of the displaced persons in Germany since the turnover from IRO to the German authorities is somewhat worse than it was during IRO operations'.³⁶ Although the report's author, Mr Grigg, conceded that differing weather conditions could impact DPs' living standards, he was more concerned by the various and uneven unemployment benefits available in the British zone. Of the handful of families questioned, he spoke with at least two who were paid insufficiently, but concluded that even the correct amount is barely sufficient (although equal to their German counterparts). There was a dire need of clothing, which was only given out on an emergency basis; however, what constituted an emergency was not defined, and consequently the team found no one lucky enough to receive such a parcel. Overall, conditions in the British zone were given a somewhat contradictory appraisal as Grigg concludes that 'the camps on the whole were about the same as they had been under IRO with some deficiencies and apparent worsening of physical accommodation. In our opinion, the German authorities had been either unable or unwilling to maintain the camps in the same degree of repair as CCG'.³⁷ The duality of this summation in the report leads to the unhappy conclusion that the standards of living for those transferred to German authority were deteriorating, particularly it seems in Lower Saxony. As the report was written only four to five months after the official handover date, and during the IRO's continuing period of assistance, it levels accusations of either unwillingness or, more likely, inability to keep up with the demands of those remaining in the three western zones.

The US-German report, which was much lengthier (eighty-six pages and another entire book of appendices), concludes that the 'refugee problem and the problems of Germany are inseparable', blaming the newly formed government's lack of central organization as one of the main reasons for the poor conditions. The concluding notes detail a scornful appraisal of West Germany and German industry, accusing those who had sought to boost the economy of being 'too self-seeking' and doing so at the expense of 'the needy', underhandedly stating that 'this attitude seems to be handed down from the past'. The US-German report invoked the basic tenets of democracy to underscore all that Germany had done wrong to its people. At the same time, it emphasized the importance of the rich helping the poor for the greater good, as so many other Western democracies were thought to have done. Ultimately, the report stated that West Germany would not be able to develop as a nation 'until the sickness in her midst – the Refugee problem – has been successfully cured'.³⁸

The conclusions were similar: those left in Germany without adequate housing, employment or social insurance needed attention. Of course, the two reports were addressing different groups of people integrating into German society, and therefore the extent of the recommendations varied. The IRO's recommendations were simple: provide adequate housing by moving DPs out of the camps but ensuring they are not moved somewhere of a lower standard; and most importantly, ensure they are treated as fellow citizens in all ways. In a follow-up report in March 1951, they stated that providing private accommodation had proved 'extremely difficult; i[n] many areas . . . impossible'. In the case of Nordrhein-Westfalen, however, they detailed significant improvements, commending the British Land Commissioner and the German Land authorities for their joint efforts seeking to provide houses for a total of '1,000 refugee families comprising of 4,500 persons'. This was predicted to cost a total of 12.5 million DM, which was 'to be borne by the Land Government'. Of course, this full plan had not come to fruition by March 1951, but within this short time 140 houses had already been built thanks to construction taking place 'on a 24-hour 7-day week basis'.[39]

The US-German recommendations, on the other hand, were not so straightforward, and provided further insight into potential future problems should the existing problems of housing and employment be exacerbated. There were notable fears about increased friction between the host population and the incoming migrants, many of whom were unemployed or employed in unsuitable work not relevant to their skill-sets. An even greater percentage was 'living under crowded, unhealthy conditions – in camps, in ruins, in old cellars, or billeted with the local population', and if this were to continue, 'the good will on the part of the home population may weaken under the constant friction'.[40] To avoid further resentment developing between the various groups, the plan was to invest a staggering 12.5 billion DM to carry out the suggested 'Plan for Integration of Refugees', which would include the construction of over 1 million new homes, 100,000 farm settlements, loans to industry, investment in youth, and various other schemes over a six-year period. The plan gives a very detailed account of Germany's assets, foreign debt, and borrowing options (an estimated 7 billion DM would come from foreign loans), for the greater purpose of the sound economic, and hopefully social, integration of the refugees. The US-German document makes it clear, however, that the refugees to be helped would be those who were still able to be resettled elsewhere (part of the funding was allocated to this venture), or able and willing to work in Germany's industries (coal, steel, production of tools, and other big industries).

There is little mention of those who could not work or be resettled; in other words, the majority.

The US-German document appears wistful, constantly implying worldwide responsibility for the refugee problem in West Germany and regularly giving out 'advice' imbued with a morally didactic tone. The last paragraph of the conclusion is repetitive in this sense, almost to the point of being patronizing, written as if West Germany were once a rotten child, and it was up to the 'civilized world' to halt the 'drag on human progress that may retard European and world recovery'.[41] In comparison to the IRO's document, the US-German document is significantly more thorough and rigorous about the estimated number of housing units needed (2.5 million), the overall estimated costs (12.5 billion DM), and the pitfalls of being unable to provide either. Yet, as set out at the beginning, it focuses strongly on unifying all types of incoming migrants under one umbrella term: 'refugees'.

A large part of these reports' outcomes may have been dependent on the conditions of the British home front. The British faced a spectacularly different situation than the United States and the FRG in 1951. The US economy was booming and the FRG was significantly on the rise, leading to increasing interest in enabling those on the lower rungs of the social ladder to achieve better living standards. Yet, Britain's economy was worse than it had been before the war, with rationing heavily enforced (until 1954).[42] The Marshall Plan had given aid to both Britain and West Germany, yet West Germany's economy certainly benefited to a greater extent, as it was able to use it to bolster industry. In Britain, the majority of Marshall aid went into relieving its debts.[43] As the United Nation's World Economic Report for 1950–1 attests, Germany's economy was expanding rapidly due to the sharp increase in industrial production (up 21 per cent from 1949 to 1950). Yet, as its relative share in Western European industrial production increased, that of the UK fell.[44] Although these factors are rarely mentioned in reports about housing the remaining DPs and/or refugees in Germany, they will certainly have played a significant role in each country's ability to adequately assess care, housing, and rehabilitation needs. Even though the UK had ostensibly relinquished control of the remaining DPs to the German authorities, they were still responsible for providing adequate housing within their zone; a problem that was symptomatic of the British zone in Germany for many years to come.

As the IRO's authority in Germany declined, increasing east-west tensions caused a notable shift in policies towards remaining DPs. Simultaneously, social tensions escalated, leading to complaints about crowded living conditions and deteriorating relations between hosts and migrants. For example, Stefan Schröder's study of the district and city of Münster focuses on local newspapers reporting tensions between social groups in 1950 that linked remaining DPs with housing problems and criminality. In a brief collection of the papers from '*Münstersche Zeitung*' and '*Westfälische Nachrichten*' between March and August 1950, some words are constantly repeated: *Polen* (Poles), *Schläger* (thugs), *Einbrecher* (burglars), *Aufruhr* (revolt/turmoil), *Sittlichkeitsdelikte* (sexual offences), and *Räuber* (robbers), alongside terms such as *Arbeitslosenziffer* (unemployment figures), *Eingliederung* (integration) and *Wohnungslisten* (apartment lists). Schröder notes that until 1950 the majority of local Germans rarely had contact with DPs and received the majority of their information about them from daily newspapers.[45] If the locals were receiving a negative impression from these sources, a certain amount of hostility would be expected. Anna Holian found that when Germans did choose to engage with DPs, their negative perceptions were often based on two interrelated themes: 'criminality and the illegitimacy of DP claims to German assistance'.[46] DP criminality was often attributed to numerous causes ranging from necessity (petty thievery), to opportunism, to 'genuine' personality traits.[47] Although there were criminal elements among the DPs, Jacobmeyer states that the statistics were frequently inflated in German reports. Newspapers often gave way to stereotyping DP groups with anti-Semitic (black-market activities) or anti-Slavic (robbery, assault, murder, and sexual crimes) stories about criminality, echoing the British press' own depictions of Poles discussed earlier.[48] This typecasting was also reinforced by the Allied military, akin to the British military labelling Polish DPs a troublesome 'nuisance' in 1945. Those who replaced the initial liberators tended to see the DPs as 'layabouts and lawbreakers', further reinforcing the negative stereotypes.[49]

In Britain itself, there was little to no discussion of the DPs who remained in Germany after the Homeless Foreigners Law was passed on 25 April 1951. Between April 1951 and April 1953, much of the discussion about DPs in the House of Commons focused on those who were already in Britain and what changes were to be made regarding their rights, work, health, and housing. Britain had already refused to absorb further DPs after the European Voluntary Worker schemes and various operations, such as *Westward Ho!* and *Pole Jump*, had concluded years earlier. The only DPs that had been allowed in since these larger schemes had ended were those lucky enough to be admitted under the Distressed Relatives Scheme, which had only accepted 4,108 between 1945 and 1952.[50] Indeed, between April 1951 and 1953, only five instances of displaced persons still resident in Germany were being discussed in the House of Commons.[51] It is interesting to note that four of the five instances were Q&As about who was now in charge of, or rather responsible for, those remaining in the British zone. The response was often a repetition from earlier instances, explaining that legal protection was provided by the United Nations High Commissioner for Refugees (UNHCR), but overall responsibility for all other matters was now placed upon the German authorities. The tone of these responses was infused with a remarkable sense of tiredness to the plight of DPs abroad.

In newspapers during the same period very few mentions of DPs appear in relation to their status in Germany. As Table 7.2 indicates, of a combined 114 mentions in *The Daily Mail*, *The Telegraph* and *The Times*, only 13 were directly related to DPs still residing in Germany and their 'situation'. Of these thirteen, five of these were specifically referred to Eastern Germans, or *Vertriebene* (expellees), rather than DPs.[52]

A further breakdown in social relations was discerned, with reports of extensive housing being built mainly for refugees and not for local Germans. Only half of the 2.5 million housing units were for refugees, yet they were given priority and were the first to receive the new social housing. Of course, the exact number of DPs needing care, accommodation, and help during this transitional period is hard to estimate, although reports confess that the majority were now living outside the camps as they often bemoaned the impossibility of keeping 'track' of various groups. Yet most did not stray far from their previous places of residence (e.g. the camps), and continued to live in small enclaves often organized along ethno-national lines regardless of resettlement plans put into place to distribute them throughout various German states more evenly.[53] This is not surprising, given the particular DP camp communities that evolved as a result of all they had collectively endured since arriving in Germany. The creation of these enclaves and their continuation after the dissolution of the camps was in

Table 7.2 Number of Times 'Displaced Persons' Mentioned between 25 April 1951 and 25 April 1953

Newspaper	DPs in Germany	DPs in the UK	Other DP issues	Total
The Daily Mail	2	1	3	6
The Telegraph	3	6	28	37
The Times	8	18	45	71

Source: Created by Samantha K. Knapton.

itself an act of resistance, as they did not permit the endlessly 'temporary' nature of their woeful existence to govern their identities. Hilton suggests that Polish DPs 'consciously and consistently rebuilt their lives based on their conception of cultural nationalism', which continued outside the camps and throughout their attempt to settle into German society.[54] Indeed, it is argued here that due to the number of Polish DPs living outside the camps throughout UNRRA and the IRO's tenure in Germany, especially with the influence of Polish towns such as Maczków, the collective Polish DP camp identity explored in Chapters 2 and 3 had developed similar foundations outside the camps as well.

As early as 1946, Czesław Łuczak found that up to an estimated 25 per cent of Polish DPs in the British zone of Germany were living outside the camps, many inhabiting whole streets.[55] As the overall numbers had dwindled, especially towards the end of the IRO's service in Germany, the number of Poles residing within largely Polish communities in Germany as a result of the DP camps being systematically closed increased. This move from the DP camps to residences within the German community was part of the German authorities' proposed plans for *Eingliederung*, or integration, as proposed by surveys such as those conducted by the IRO and the combined US-FRG initiative. Conversely, the German authorities' inability to provide suitable housing was not the sole reason for the decline in living standards. As the bulk of the IRO's personnel dispersed and the British military brought in further soldiers to enforce the occupation of the north-west corner of the FRG, the British began to requisition barrack-type installations, most of which had previously been occupied by DPs. This led to the unhappy situation of pushing these DPs into increasingly dilapidated buildings, seemingly deemed unfit for the British occupation authorities.[56] Of course, according to the US-German report the intention was to house those pushed from '*kaserne*' installations into new and better social housing created for them by the government. In reality, there was no way to keep up with the demand for housing.

A large part of the appendices belonging to the US-German report analyses the social problems arising between the host society and the groups of 'newcomers'. One recurring problem is apparent, 'strong family ties exist among the Refugees … ties to the new communities and to the state, however, are very loose'.[57] Yet no real recommendations were made other than marriage between the two groups, and frequently the 'recommendations' shifted from integration to assimilation. The recommendations for those still living in shared camp accommodation were about creating recreational activities, reminiscent of the initial programmes conducted by UNRRA as early as 1945 to give families plots of land to grow vegetables, create playground spaces for children, and instigate vocational job training at various levels. In short, they had come full circle back to the principle of helping the people to help themselves.

A disappointing caesura: Germany's 'Homeless' Foreigners Law

The Homeless Foreigners Law was signed into existence on 25 April 1951 and from this point onwards, the remaining DPs were officially the responsibility of the FRG.[58] The passing of this law was somewhat uneventful. Yet German attitudes toward the remaining DPs, however, is telling of the manner in which they considered their responsibility to those who had been made homeless by German aggression. The cost for the DPs' upkeep in Germany was almost entirely covered by the Germans themselves which only proved to heighten animosity towards the remaining DPs in the 1950s as many Germans viewed them as an 'undesirable mass of foreigners burdening a country already struggling with its "own" refugee problem'.[59] It is within this context that most remaining DPs found themselves as their plight was not considered worthy of attention, particularly in comparison to that of ethnic Germans. Although, as DPs, they had access to bigger food rations and priority housing the reality was very different, and anti-Slav tendencies still pervaded German society at all levels, causing friction between various groups, in particular among ethnic minority groups. Westphalian Poles, for example, who had largely settled in Germany at the end of the nineteenth century, found this new group of Polish DPs a source of unwanted attention as their presence highlighted their 'otherness' and caused relationships with the German community to become strained.[60]

The primary function of the Homeless Foreigners Law was to afford the same rights to the remaining DPs as those of ordinary German citizens. Yet, although the law protected this vulnerable group's civil, social, and economic rights it did not afford them political rights. Neither were they provided with any special path to German citizenship that would take their status into consideration, and they were ineligible for the financial assistance that was specifically available to German refugees.[61] Thus they existed in a limbo-like state as a group of seemingly semi-permanent guests. As the IRO was propelled into full liquidation, little else could be done for the remaining Polish DPs in the British zone. Kanty Cooper, a British Quaker relief-turned-IRO worker, describes how 'frantically we tried to tie up loose ends' to ensure the maximum number of DPs were given every opportunity before being handed over to the German authorities, but the lack of adequate staff, transport, and money seriously hindered any last-minute efforts. Cooper, one of the last members of IRO staff operating within the British zone, recalled how desperately worried she was about the DPs they were leaving behind and lamented that 'they would become a German responsibility, and as the Germans were overwhelmed with refugees of their own from the Eastern Zone, they would, naturally, regard the DPs as an extra, less urgent, burden'.[62] It did not take long for reports to be submitted to the CCG accusing the German authorities of discrimination against the remaining DPs. On 5 June 1951, IRO staff operating from the British zone reported findings of discrimination towards DPs to an Allied High Commission liaison officer. The discriminatory practices were varied, ranging from ineffectual handling of compensation for Nazi persecution to comparatively increased taxes levied against DPs and lack of adequate concessions for public transport. The report details numerous instances of alleged discrimination, the recurring theme being that DPs were being charged more for utilities, taxes, and transport, than their German refugee counterparts. A reply to the report stated that no such discrimination could be discerned, and that each case had been investigated and they were satisfied with their findings; further clarification was lacking.

Yet, the report makes a point that had been reiterated several times in British zone correspondence: that DPs have 'had for some years free maintenance at the expense of the German economy and the protection of the Occupation Powers'. In other words, they had been cared for long enough and it was time for them to live without aid.[63] The report displays a mindset that quickly becomes reminiscent of the earlier articulation of Polish DPs as a troublesome 'nuisance'. Furthering this argument, the report goes on to state:

> Fluchtlingsausweis [sic] 'A' holders and Heimatlose Auslander [sic] are both privileged categories of persons, but it does not follow that their privileges should be the same or that one category should be accorded the privileges of the other in addition to its own. Moreover, our objective and that of the German Federal Authorities is that the residual Displaced Persons should be assimilated into the German indigenous population; the implication of this being that they should substantially receive the same treatment as a normal German national not that they should be equated to any abnormal privileged category such as the holders of Fluchtlingsausweis 'A'.[64]

By this definition the British authorities are declaring those persons with a Flüchtlingsausweis 'A' pass, for example, ethnic Germans (Vertriebene), to belong to a more privileged category than others, for example, *Heimatlose Ausländer*, or DPs. This view is evocative of a mentality pervading the British occupation of North-west Germany which perceived people relying on international aid as an annoyance. The DPs, a sizeable group that had shrunk to a mere fraction of what it was in May 1945, still existed. This was the thorn in British authorities' side; they had helped some of these DPs for six years and were now ready to relinquish responsibility for them to the German authorities. Those in possession of a *Flüchtlingsausweis* 'A' pass were the newer, needier category. The troublesome 'nuisance' label was not applied as a blanket term to all remaining DPs, as they were a problem of the past and the German refugees were now the main problem as their displacement took precedence. Kanty Cooper's prediction was becoming a reality.

From the outset the British authorities and Germans had shown little sympathy towards DPs, and in particular Polish DPs. Now, they were further burdening British-occupied Germany and causing collective contempt among their administrators. Professor Dr Ulrich Scheuner, a constitutional lawyer in the FRG, viewed DPs as 'practically permanent guests [and] if they stay – a kind of immigrant'. He equated the experiences of expelled Germans, or *Vertriebene*, with those of DPs and argued that suitable 'life-adjustments' by Slavic groups could only be accepted in Germany with some reservations. He emphasized that Germany could no longer be held responsible for DPs' wanderings after the war, which was the fault of those who had opposed Tehran, Yalta, and Potsdam – in other words, Polish DPs loyal to the government in exile. Scheuner's views became increasingly prominent as the shift in focus from DPs to German refugees went hand-in-hand with the IRO's liquidation. Scheuner had accepted that some DPs would inevitably become 'permanent guests', and thereby de-facto immigrants, but did not accept that all were equally deserving of this status. Still critical of Scheuner's stance, Jacobmeyer claims that views such as these were often expressed because of an increasing departure from legal argumentation in favour of politicized polemic.[65] As the decade wore on, the increase in political activity grew in tandem with the rising Cold War tensions. The observance of DPs as a category that would require special consideration, and not in a positive manner, was indicative of how German society started to navigate its own interactions with those it had wronged in the recent past. The Homeless Foreigners Law, however, made sure legal security was afforded to those who needed it most: legally they were protected, although in reality discrimination was prevalent.

By October 1951, the statistical yearbook for West Germany records 38,808 remaining Poles classed as 'foreigners' across the British zone who were now living within the German economy.[66] By October 1952, this number had dropped to 31,836; however, this reduction of 6,972 is thought to have been largely a by-product of the high concentration of elderly and/or infirm, rather than a consequence of further repatriation or resettlement. It is questionable, however, whether these statistics included those not covered by the Homeless Foreigners Law and therefore not deemed '*Ausländer*', these were often excluded (sometimes willingly) from the earlier IRO statistics or had arrived in earlier migrations to the north-west corner of Germany. As we have seen in the case of the Westfalen Poles or *Ruhrpolen*, due to the brief time classified as Germans through their place on the Nazi *Volksliste* they were then unable to register as Poles after the war, and constituted a significant contingent of Poles in the British zone of Germany that is unaccounted for in the above statistics. Although there remained a visible Polish community in the British zone of Germany, it was a community that was split by its own internalized sense of national identity, which would have a lasting effect on the make-up of diasporic Polish communities thereafter.

Conclusion

The resettlement of Poles in the British zone of occupation under German authority was an uneasy task that was handled with little consideration for the former DPs themselves. These Polish DPs, many of whom identified very strongly with their own notion of Polish nationality, or Polishness, were now essentially to become stateless refugees, relying on their former oppressors to treat them with dignity and equality. Malcolm J. Proudfoot summarized the inherent problem of the end of the IRO's work in his seminal work on Europe's refugees:

> The Western nations have therefore, to all intents and purposes, chosen to ignore the continuing European refugee problem. At the close of the IRO operations the High Commissioner's Office for Refugees, with no United Nations support for the individual care and maintenance of individual refugees, has been required to rely on voluntary contributions to assist approximately 400,000 European refugees of whom about one-third, at the end of 1951, were still living in camps awaiting resettlement or re-establishment.[67]

It was only with the adoption of the United Nation's Convention Relating to the Status of Stateless Persons in September 1954 that de-facto stateless persons, those who no longer had the protection or assistance of their country (either by choice or revocation), became fully protected.[68] It is obvious from British inter-office memoranda during 1951 and 1952, however, that the handover of all responsibilities to the Germans was a welcome relief. The British had, by this point, been caring for the DPs for six or seven years and were glad to resume their duties outside the realm of humanitarianism. Indeed, the press release about the liquidation of the IRO in March 1952 gives a very matter-of-fact summary of the British relinquishing all matters to the German authorities with little mention of *how* integration into German society was playing out.[69] Sometimes the lack of material is just as telling. As we have seen from Stefan Schröder's case study of Münster, when regional newspapers chose to report on DPs, often referring to them as aliens, they wrote of them negatively and in connection with criminality. When newspapers reported on ethnic German refugees at the same time, it was in a positive way, pleading that these were now the people in need and that German society should forget the others. Similarly, British newspaper discussions of Polish DPs were virtually non-existent as efforts concentrated on those who had already arrived in Britain rather than those who remained in Germany.

While the IRO's closure was inevitable, it did not make it any easier for those who remained in Germany with little option but to try and 'integrate' into German society. It was not until the emergence in 1958 of 'World Refugee Year' (WRY) that public attention in Britain was once more drawn to the plight of DPs at home and abroad. Originally awoken by the Hungarian uprising in 1956, WRY shone a spotlight on those who had been displaced after the Second World War and their continuing displacement. Practically, it achieved very little for former Polish DPs, who were now ascribed the title of *Heimatlose Ausländer*. Even with the UN's support in an attempt to 'swell the coffers of NGOs', Peter Gatrell contends that WRY was primarily 'driven by a strong sense of Western guilt and a willingness to atone for failing to prevent the creation of the "hard core"' in the first place.[70] As discussions in the House of Commons, British newspapers, and inter-office memorandums reveal, little was left to be discussed regarding the original DPs and their status in Germany; they were a German responsibility now. The negativity displayed in newspapers, and elsewhere throughout society was now replaced by near total silence.

Conclusion

In an attempt to reconcile the different aspects of displacement directly resulting from the war, the Federal Ministry for Expellees, Refugees, and War Victims commissioned a booklet of short essays titled *After Ten Years: A European Problem, Still No Solution*, about the fates of those displaced since 1945.[1] The book, an English counterpart to a far weightier German edition, gathered individual essays from various sources including German politicians, historians, political scientists, and federal workers on how those displaced by war were faring. Although the booklet's introduction makes numerous references to both 'expellees' and 'refugees', the book's focus is very clearly on German expellees from the East. Why then does it use both terms as though they are distinctly different categories? One would think this alludes to the booklet discussing the fate of the UN-defined 'Displaced Persons' under the title of 'refugees'. Yet we find, in a very factual two-page summary of 'Problems of Non-German Refugees' written by a member of UNHCR, that no attempt has been made to seriously cover the plight of DPs. Indeed, a section of the two pages is even boxed off for a Professor of Economics to talk about how the expellee problem has not yet been solved.

The booklet's tone is set from the beginning in the first section, written by Konrad Adenauer, the FRG's much-vaunted Federal Chancellor. Although the first paragraph discussed both expellees and refugees, attention quickly and solely turns towards expellees for the remainder of the piece, closely accompanied by maps showing Allied territories with 'one-fourth missing' (e.g. north-east France and America, or southwest Britain or Russia). The difference between these two pages and the remaining fifty is extreme, as the ethnic German stories are often accompanied by not just emotive pictures and personal testimonies but also graphs and tables showing the number of expellees and areas of both expulsion and absorption. A large section is even devoted to buildings and artworks lost to the East alongside portraits of 'Great Sons of our Country' who were 'born in the Eastern parts of our country, in districts that are today "administered" by Poles, Russians, and Czechs'.[2] Little to no attempt is made to address the problems of those once classed as DPs. The histories, lives, and voices of DPs in the new Germany were at once silenced and replaced by a much more pressing matter: the expellees. The DPs had not been seen as a German issue; they were an Allied issue, an UNRRA issue, an IRO issue, and now under German control, they were no longer an issue. The British had been more than willing to pass on the administration of DPs remaining in Germany to the German authorities, although given the overall sense of tiredness among the British in Germany by 1951 this is no surprise.

The place of Polish DPs in the post-war literature has received some attention in recent years, with many studies focusing on comparisons with other groups, on the layered meanings of new exile communities evolving from this displacement, and on how the Poles who arrived in various countries adapted to their situation.[3] This work, however, has focused on how they were influenced by those whom they saw as protectors from the start: the British. Held up as a model of democracy and viewed favourably by the majority of Polish DPs from all backgrounds, the inability of the British to live up to preconceived notions of them as protectors and friends caused a deepening divide in Anglo-Polish relations.

As the UN no longer deemed it necessary for an international agency to provide full care and maintenance for European refugees, it was thought sufficient to only provide 'international protection' for specified categories of refugees, *but not for individuals*. In Malcolm J. Proudfoot's estimation, this was a 'grave error' which 'disregarded the proven necessity of the kind of work done by Dr Nansen and the League of Nations, the work of the IGCR, of UNRRA, and that of the IRO'. Indeed, a refugee requires protection even if they find themselves in a friendly country with adequate welfare provisions, as they remain 'in the legal state of an orphan without a guardian'.[4] Was Germany classed as a refugee-friendly country by 1951? The British certainly seemed to think it would fit the bill; however, the individual Polish DPs, having endured a variety of wartime abuses, may not have shared this view. There is no doubt that many Polish DPs held on to their own concepts of Polishness within their individual DP camp communities, yet after the handover to German authorities and removal from the camps, it becomes difficult to estimate whether the ties that bound them in the DP camps continued outside of it. Adding to the pressure of dispersal was the German imperative to follow a policy of *Eingliederung* (integration), blurring the boundaries with *Einschmelzung* (assimilation).

The extent to which the British shaped and influenced Polish DPs in post-war Germany is discussed throughout this work, both offering insights into the history of Poles in Germany, and contributing to German migration historiography more widely. It has bridged and developed research in a number of areas including Anglo-Polish relations, population movement, humanitarianism and relief, militarism, forced labour, minority history and, more widely, integration. In doing so, it has demonstrated how humanitarian organizations and military authorities' co-construction of aid operations in the immediate post-war era was heavily influenced by those 'in the middle'. With its analysis of how military officials, welfare workers, relief workers, liaison officers, and camp directors reacted to policies from above, this work has shown that the official discourse was rarely the reality. Many of those 'in the middle' implemented policies based on the circumstances of individual DP camps, often guided by the compositions of particular DP groups and their social, ethnic, and educational backgrounds. In the latter years, many welfare workers were influenced by bonds they had established with DPs in their care and frequently ignored official policy in favour of practical action.

In UNRRA, the military, and other agencies, those who had regular contact with the DPs had the ability to break or maintain relationships with the people they were there to help and consequently influence their decisions. The British treated the Polish DPs in their zone as a troublesome 'nuisance'; many did not have the patience to deal with their apparently impossible demands and reacted in a high-handed and unsympathetic manner to this 'paradoxical people' who, although devoted to their homeland, were unwilling to return home.[5] Yet, the British authorities who greeted the Polish DPs in April and May 1945 were not prepared for them to remain in their zone of occupation indefinitely. Similarly, Polish DPs who ended up in the British zone were not prepared for the very threads of Polish political, ideological, and geographical fabric to be unravelled in the first few short months following the end of the Second World War. They were still less prepared for their former ally to be complicit agents of this unravelling.

Through investigating the conflicting nature of international humanitarian agencies and numerous British authorities, led chiefly by military-minded officials, this work has also analysed the conditions in which Polish DPs found themselves by September 1945, and questioned whether this was congruent with the claim that they had the weakest basis for refusing to return. It has found that it was zonally dependent, as opportunities to resettle for Ukrainian and Baltic DPs were much more likely to appear when coming from the British zone than the US zone. Conversely, the number of people, charities, and religious groups in the United States willing to sign affidavits on behalf of Polish DPs were greater than those willing to sign for the more 'eastern' DPs, who were thought to have already possessed communist tendencies. Instead of focusing on typical and isolated narratives, this work has interwoven elements of post-war humanitarianism to provide deeper contextualization in order to understand why many Polish DPs rejected Poland in 1945, and thereafter.

The case of Polish DPs in the British zone is unique, as the multifarious elements of the Anglo-Polish relationship between 1918 and 1945 obscured the humanitarian principles embodied by UNRRA and the welfare workers in the camps. The attitude of British personnel, particularly those in military positions, is telling of the wider issues in Anglo-Polish relations in the post-war world. Britain had fallen from its position as a global superpower and needed to choose its allies carefully. This included cutting ties with the Polish government-in-exile in London in favour of the new Soviet-commissioned government in Warsaw.[6] The Poles in the camps, however, were of a completely different composition to those in London. They were predominantly peasants from rural areas of Poland who had been used as forced labourers during the Third Reich, and they did not understand the British refusal to acknowledge their government in London.[7] The government that they had dreamed would return to its rightful place once Nazism was eradicated was *their* government, an ideological embodiment of *their* Poland, *their* people, and *their* nation. Indeed, as the memorandum at the beginning of this book emphasizes, the characterization of Polish DPs as a 'nuisance' was often thought to stem from a lack of understanding on both sides. The apathetic British attitude to the Poles in Germany and the exhaustion (often attributed as so-called DP apathy) that took hold in the DP camps once the focus on repatriation turned to resettlement were equally unwelcome in the post-war world. The situation in the British zone was certainly more complex than that in the US zone, where ties to Polish exile communities in the United States were strong and they advocated better treatment, signed affidavits that secured their passage to the United States, and once the immigration quota was lifted, paved the way to a brighter future.

Wherever possible, the voices of Polish DPs have been presented throughout, emphasizing the experiences of those who endured the harshest conditions of the post-war world. What it meant to be Polish in 1945, where they perceived Poland to be, how they characterized Polishness, and the inclusivity of this selective community have all been explored. The focus on the creation and retainment of Polishness in the camps during this period of stasis has uniquely framed the conception of not only what it meant to be Polish to the Poles in 1945 but also how this was perceived and received by those in charge. The Poles in the camps were predominantly peasant Poles, the product of a nation which had fought for its independence for over 123 years. Their nationalism was already pronounced before war broke out in 1939, and after six years of oppression under communism and/or Nazism these proud Polish people were further aggrieved to find that their allies did not recognize their ideals but rather ignored them in favour of placating a new ally. The communities found in the camps were the product of pre-war nationalism reinforced by independence and wartime suffering, consolidated by their rejection of overbearing and oppressive ideologies. After surviving the war, they found communism at home threatening to suppress their Polish identity once more. Their rejection could not have been more vehement.

Building on Anderson's concept of 'imagined communities' this work has shown the criteria by which a Pole was considered part of or excluded from a community. It has shown that this not only depended on the geographical context that the Polish DP communities found themselves in, but also on who was governing these communities. In comparison, the Polish DPs in the US zone similarly built communities, yet they lacked ostracism from a larger community. They were eventually able to attach themselves to a large and already-established Polish exile community in the United States. The Poles in the British zone, however, were given no such hope of joining a large exile community in Britain. None existed. Indeed, the fragmentary remnants of a Polish exile community in Britain were numerically insignificant in comparison to the United States and were largely the result of cosmopolitan and polyglot exiles from the nineteenth century keen on continuing the exiled narrative, which did not match with that of those waiting in the camps. Those who had recently been resettled in Britain were largely Polish soldiers and their dependants, the only group to be afforded a privileged position. The majority of those left in the camps were infirm, elderly, young or seen as 'undesirable' for political or vocational reasons. Consequently, they were also unable to fully take part in the Polish DP community in the British zone as the community's organizational structure was based upon pre-existing social structures inherited from pre-war Poland. Thus, for example, a Pole who had been a middle manager in pre-1939 Poland became an important figure in a British DP camp, as they were predominantly surrounded by peasant Poles; unable to interact with or establish a place in the new social hierarchy of the DP camps, those who had been irrevocably weakened by war were ill-fated. By simultaneously examining who constituted a Pole in the eyes of both the Polish DPs themselves and the British military officials, government ministers, welfare workers and all the others present or involved in the running of the DP camps, this work has enlarged the criteria by which nations, ethnicities, states, and even the abstract notion of 'a people' were considered and defined. It has also revealed a British proclivity for treating people of other nations as subjects to be 'democratized' or 'anglicized' in the missionary zeal which carried its imperialist past into the camps.

Somewhere in the middle, UNRRA was placed between the British military government and the Polish DPs vying for official recognition as equals. UNRRA's 'goodie-goodie' position, however, was seen by many military officials as a product of the American New Dealism which many found to be an intolerable form of mollycoddling and was an often additional and unwelcome reminder of the gendered division of labour among the military government officials and UNRRA welfare workers in the camps.[8] Yet, when Ernest Bevin addressed the House of Commons in January 1948, he stated 'What sort of Europe we should have had without UNRRA, I really do not know: It is too horrible to contemplate'. Bevin's speech concentrates solely on stemming 'the horrible disease we had following the 1914–18 war which most have forgotten', a claim that was not entirely true.[9] As Jessica Reinisch shows in *The Perils of Peace*, the lasting legacy of the Great War's influenza epidemic was never far from the public conscience in Germany, even though early Allied preparations were insufficient.[10] UNRRA's medical officers were alert to the plethora of problems that can occur when mass movements of people among rubble and ruin are forced to gather in small spaces. In contradiction to Bevin's claim, however, stemming epidemics was not the sole legacy of UNRRA's triumphs.

UNRRA was the first instance of international humanitarianism following an era of total war. It was equally ill-fated: largely perceived by its contemporaries to be a failure due to administrative issues, UNRRA did succeed in feeding, clothing, and sheltering millions of people across Europe at a huge financial cost to the United States and Britain in particular. Its efforts were not in vain: they not only protected the war's most vulnerable from famine and disease but also helped millions to return home. Yet it was UNRRA's middlemen, the welfare workers, who had the biggest impact on the DPs themselves. Their position was used to convey the sense of desperation felt by many Polish DPs in the post-war period to the military authorities and in turn to the British government. On the one hand, using the 'top-down' and 'bottom-up' perspectives allows for rich and specific views of particular events. When analysing the place and purpose of those in the middle, however, the reasons for 'top-down' decisions becomes apparent while simultaneously revealing the reactions of those from the 'bottom-up'. It would be foolish to say that this has provided a complete view of events and policy implementations in the camps; however, it does provide a fuller picture. Any attempt at a complex history of DPs certainly benefits from encapsulating various viewpoints and contextualizing them as this book has done.

Central to all was the issue of repatriation, and it was problematic from the beginning, with no easy answers. Although this work recognizes from the outset that many did willingly repatriate to Poland, the crux of this book's thesis is the thorough evaluation of factors preventing other ordinary DPs from wanting to repatriate to Poland. It is thus a case study of how the co-construction of aid operations in the immediate post-war period hinged on cooperation between respective militaries and humanitarian organizations, yet it is also a particular case study of the issues that arose with the Poles in the British zone, which were not replicated in other zones or other groups. This has been shown by foregrounding the administrative mechanisms, policies, and procedures that governed Polish DPs' experiences rather than the experiences of individual DPs. This group had been largely cast aside and labelled an embarrassment long before the repatriation policies' intensity increased in the British zone. The relationship between British authorities and Polish DPs can only be understood after investigating each sides' perception of the 'other'. This work has contextualized the Anglo-Polish relationship and the reasons for its rapid deterioration shortly after the end of the Second World War and until the 1950s. Such an explanation is wanting in other histories of the British zone in Germany. Although many attempts have been made to present the viewpoints of DP groups and the British military, there is often a lack of contextualization that leaves the reader to question policy implementation, DP reactions, and, quite frequently, where, how and even if UNRRA figured into decisions about DPs at all.[11]

Above all, liberation did not bring with it the freedom and camaraderie the Polish DPs had hoped for in the immediate aftermath of war. Instead, it produced confusion and was the catalyst for the Polish 'betrayed ally' rhetoric readily propagated by those living in exile for years after 1945.[12] The elation felt upon liberation was quickly dampened by British officials' lacklustre and irritated attitude towards Polish DPs, many of whom had expected to be greeted as 'brothers in arms'. Although this was a romanticized version of what might await them in the DP camps of Germany after the war, the Polish DPs continued to hold onto the belief that their British allies would treat them as equals, until the introduction of screening in 1946. Their disillusionment turned the mood from joy and gaiety to sadness and dejection in a matter of months. Many Poles counted their lives in exile from the moment of their displacement rather than from the end of the war when they were officially displaced. Consequently, as four

Christmases turned into seven or eight without seeing 'home', the blame shifted ever more squarely to those who were trying to push them into an uncertain future outside Poland, outside Britain, and outside the camps. Those who had willingly repatriated to Poland, taking the good word of UNRRA and others, were sometimes also left disappointed. As Rhoda Dawson returned to Britain, and eagerly searched for the next chapter in her life, the old chapter remained open. DPs she had cared for in the camps were still at a loose end. Some, having repatriated to Poland, were writing to her about their experiences. In a letter sent in February 1947, Wanda S. wrote to Dawson after being repatriated and settling in Poznań. She described her life back in Poland: 'My homeland is not so, such me imagining. I have of this day the job notwithstanding [sic].'[13] Wanda had repatriated on 23 August 1946, at the height of *Operation Carrot*. Upon returning to Poland, however, she found that work was sparse and to make ends meet she took care of her uncle's household while her elderly, ill father worked in an apothecary. Wanda, like many others, returned to rebuild Poland. What she found upon arriving, alongside the ruins of war, was further uncertainty and longed for happier times, requesting that Dawson would send her a photograph of 'American-Polish Victory day at 8.V. [May]' to 'remind me many a time these amiables moments [sic].'[14] How many other Polish DPs, upon returning to Poland in the immediate post-war years, were disillusioned with their lot upon arrival is hard to estimate.[15]

The attitudes of those charged with ensuring that the remainder of Poles were handed over to the German authorities correctly is telling of the British authorities' reluctance to deal with the 'Polish problem' any longer. By 1951, the DP issue had become frustrating for everyone involved. Following the dissolution of the IRO and the creation of the FRG's infrastructure to care for the newly labelled 'homeless foreigners', this work has shown how willingly the British rid themselves of this unexpectedly prolonged burden. Contextualizing Britain's place in 1951 within Europe, and indeed the world, however, the picture of the 'once great nation' crumbling largely under financial pressures in the new global market creates a better understanding of its unwillingness to continue to care for DPs. To plead for continued care would be negligent of the broader problems facing the British. Indeed, as welfare workers like Cooper and Dawson became increasingly anxious about the handover to the German authorities their predictions became a reality, the DPs passed from a chorus of 'nuisance' and 'embarrassment' to silence, as they were almost entirely ignored.

This book's contribution to the history of post-war displacement offers a unique insight into the experiences of Polish DPs in the British zone of occupation between 1945 and 1951. It has explicitly analysed the implementation of multiple organizations' policies on Polish DPs. Those eager for the post-war Anglo-Polish fraternal relationship to flourish were left questioning where it had gone wrong. Unravelling the British and Polish expectations of the post-war world – ideologically, geographically, and in a spirit of communality – the notion of a troublesome 'nuisance' on one side and a 'betrayed ally' on the other have been juxtaposed and found to be in equal measure depressing and frustrating. The spirit with which UNRRA took on the DPs in post-war Germany was hindered by the jaded and lacklustre attitude of British personnel, the highly emotive and understandably disheartened Polish DPs, and the uncomfortable reality that UNRRA was staffed by less-than-suitable candidates from the outset: 'do-gooders, crooks and crackpots', as Morgan reminisces.[16] By contrasting international humanitarian organizations' policies on all groups in all zones, and specifically those enforced in the British zone directed at Poles, this work has shown how the conflicting forces of humanitarianism and militarism deeply affected a community already devastated by war and influenced their decisions to repatriate, resettle or stay in the camps: a lesson which also still applies to contemporary refugees.

Notes

Introduction

1 The National Archives (hereafter TNA), Foreign Office (FO) 1052/273, 'Polish Displaced Persons (DPs): Policy (1945)' – Memorandum on Poles, Allied Liaison Branch, British Army of the Rhine (BAOR) HQ 17/09/45.
2 Alan Moorehead, *Eclipse* (London: Hamish Hamilton, 1946), 212.
3 Kenneth G. Brooks, 'The Re-establishment of Displaced Peoples', in *When Hostilities Cease: Papers of Relief and Reconstruction Prepared for the Fabian Society*, ed. Julian Huxley, H. J. Laski, and W. Arnold-Forster (London: Victor Gollancz, 1943), 99.
4 Peter Gatrell, *The Making of the Modern Refugee* (New York: Oxford University Press, 2013), 3. Malcolm J. Proudfoot, *European Refugees, 1939–1952. A Study in Forced Population Movement* (Evanston: Northwest University Press, 1956).
5 Proudfoot, *European Refugees*, 21, 158.
6 Anna D. Jaroszyńska-Kirchmann, *The Exile Mission: The Polish Political Diaspora and Polish Americans, 1939–1956* (Athens: Ohio University Press, 2004), 60; Proudfoot, *European Refugees*, 238–9.
7 Proudfoot, *European Refugees*, 260.
8 Jan Rydel, '*Polska okupacja' w północno-zachodnich Niemczech 1945–1948: Nieznany rozdział stosunków polsko-niemieckich* (Kraków: Fundacja Centrum Dokumentacji Czynu Niepodległościowego Księgarnia Akademicka, 2000).
9 George Woodbridge (ed.), *U.N.R.R.A. The History of the United Nations Relief and Rehabilitation Administration*, Vols. I–III (New York: Columbia University Press, 1950), Vol. III, 426; The resettlement of Poles between 1945 and 1947 in the British zone was minimal and the figures are complex as some went to Belgium and returned, whereas many were obstructed from resettlement schemes as countries preferred Balts or Ukrainians. Equally frustrating, however, the British also tried to reserve Polish agricultural workers in the zone to help rebuild Germany and sustain Germans and DPs alike. See, Archives Nationales, Paris (hereafter AN), AJ-43-47, 'Polish Nationals: Repatriation', letter from Updyke to Dow (IGCR), 13 November 1946.
10 See, Samantha K. Knapton and Katherine Rossy (eds), *Relief and Rehabilitation for a Postwar World: Humanitarian Intervention and the UNRRA* (Bloomsbury Academic, 2023).
11 Daniel S. Cheever and Henry Field Haviland, Jr., *Organizing for Peace: International Organization in World Affairs* (London: Stevens & Sons Limited, 1957), 227.

12 General Sir Frederick Morgan, *Peace and War: A Soldier's Life* (London: Hodder & Stoughton, 1961), 222.
13 Pamela Ballinger, 'Impossible Returns, Enduring Legacies: Recent Historiography of Displacement and the Reconstruction of Europe after World War II', *Contemporary European History* 22 (2013): 127–38, 128. For works on the Twentieth Century and the place of post-war history in the historiography, see: Eric Hobsbawm, *The Age of Extremes: The Short Twentieth Century, 1914–1991* (London: Abacus, 1995); Mark Mazower, *Dark Continent: Europe's Twentieth Century* (London: Penguin Books, 1999); and Tony Judt, *Postwar: A History of Europe since 1945* (London: Pimlico, 2007).
14 Most notably, Peter Gatrell, *The Unsettling of Europe: How Migration Reshaped a Continent* (New York: Basic Books, 2019). Additionally: Matthew Frank and Jessica Reinisch (eds), *Refugees in Europe, 1919–1959: A Forty Year Crisis?* (London: Bloomsbury Academic, 2017); Becky Taylor, *Refugees in Twentieth Century Britain: A History* (Cambridge: Cambridge University Press, 2021); Jessica Reinisch, *Perils of Peace: The Public Health Crisis in Occupied Germany* (Oxford: Oxford University Press, 2013); Gatrell, *The Making of the Modern Refugee*. For a further discussion on the place of refugee history in today's debates, see: Lauren Banko, Katarzyna Nowak, and Peter Gatrell, 'What is Refugee History, Now?', *Journal of Global History* 17, no. 1 (2021): 1–19; Peter Gatrell, 'Refugees – What's Wrong with History?', *Journal of Refugee Studies* 30 (1 June 2017): 170–89; Silvia Salvatici, *A History of Humanitarianism, 1755 – 1989: In the Name of Others* (Manchester: Manchester University Press, 2019).
15 Woodbridge, *U.N.R.R.A*; Louise Holborn, *The International Refugee Organization: A Specialized Agency of the United Nations: Its History and Work, 1946–1952* (Oxford: Oxford University Press, 1952). Other histories produced close to the period remain foundational works and as influential as the official histories: Jacques Vernant, *The Refugee in the Post-War World* (London: George Allen & Unwin Ltd, 1953); Proudfoot, *European Refugees*; Eugene M. Kulischer, *Europe on the Move, War and Population Changes, 1917–1947* (New York: Columbia University Press, 1948); Joseph B. Schechtman, *European Population Transfers 1939–1945* (New York: Oxford University Press, 1946).
16 Wolfgang Jacobmeyer, *Vom Zwangsarbeiter zum Heimatlosen Ausländer. Die Displaced Persons in Westdeutschland, 1945–1951* (Göttingen: Vandenhoeck & Ruprecht, 1985); Michael Marrus, *The Unwanted: European Refugees in the Twentieth Century* (Oxford: Oxford University Press, 1985); Mark Wyman, *DPs: Europe's Displaced Persons, 1945–1951* (New York: Cornell University Press, 1989).
17 For the compiling of oral history interviews, letters, memoirs, and other material culture on former forced labourers, see: Alexander von Plato, Almut Leh and Christoph Thonfeld (eds), *Hitler's Slaves: Life Stories of Forced Labourers in Nazi-Occupied Europe* (Oxford: Berghahn, 2010).

18 For particularly notable works on Polish DPs, see: Czesław Łuczak, *Polacy w Okupowanych Niemczech 1945–1949* (Poznań: Pracownia Serwisu Oprogramowania, 1993); Jaroszyńska-Kirchmann, *The Exile Mission*; Rydel, *'Polska okupacja'*; Janusz Wróbel, *Na rozdrożu historii. Repatriacja obywateli polskich z Zachodu w latach 1945–1949* (Łódź: IPN, 2009). For notable works on other DP groups, see: Angelika Königseder and Juliane Wetzel (eds), *Lebensmut im Wartesaal: die jüdischen DPs (Displaced Persons) im Nachkriegsdeutschland* (Frankfurt a. M.: Fischer Taschenbuch Verlag, 1994); Zeev W. Mankowitz, *Life Between Memory and Hope: The Survivors of the Holocaust in Occupied Germany* (Cambridge: Cambridge University Press, 2002); Lubomyr Y. Luciuk, *Searching for Place: Ukrainian Displaced Persons, Canada and the Migration of Memory* (Toronto: Toronto University Press, 2000); Andrew Ezergailis, *The Latvian Legion: Heroes, Nazis or Victims* (Riga: The Historical Institute of Latvia, 1997). For histories on areas, see: Stefan Schröder, *Displaced Persons im Landkreis und in der Stadt Münster 1945–1951* (Münster: Aschendorff, 2005); Andreas Lembeck and Klaus Wessels, *Befreit aber nicht in Freiheit: Displaced Persons im Emsland, 1945–1951* (Bremen: Temmen, 1997); Mechtild Brand, *Verschelppt und Entwurzelt: Zwangsarbeit zwischen Soest, Werl, Wickede und Möhental* (Essen: Klartext, 2010).

19 A few notable works: Ben Shephard, *The Long Road Home: The Aftermath of the Second World War* (London: Bodley Head, 2010); Gerard D. Cohen, *In War's Wake: Europe's Displaced Persons in the Postwar Order* (New York: Oxford University Press, 2012); Tara Zahra, *The Lost Children: Reconstructing Europe's Families after World War II* (New York: Harvard University Press, 2011).

20 For works relating predominantly to the US zone, see: Anna Holian, *Between National Socialism and Soviet Communism: Displaced Persons in Postwar Germany* (Ann Arbor: University of Michigan Press, 2011); Adam Seipp, *Strangers in a Wild Place: Refugees, Americans, and a German Town, 1945–1952* (Bloomington: Indiana University Press, 2013). See also, Anna Holian, 'A Missing Narrative: Displaced Persons in the History of Postwar West Germany', in *Migration, Memory, and Diversity: Germany from 1945 to Present*, ed. Cornelia Wilhelm (Oxford: Berghahn, 2017), 32–55.

21 For works on the British zone, see: Francis Graham-Dixon, *The Allied Occupation of Germany: The Refugee Crisis, Denazification, and the Path to Reconstruction* (London: I. B. Taurus, 2013); Arieh J. Kochavi, 'British Policy on Non-Repatriable Displaced Persons in Germany and Austria, 1945–1947', *European History Quarterly* 21 (1991): 365–82. For works on the French zone, see: Laure Humbert, *Reinventing French Aid: The Politics of Humanitarian Relief in French-Occupied Germany, 1945–1952* (Cambridge: Cambridge University Press, 2021); Laure Humbert, 'French Politics of Relief and International Aid: France, UNRRA and the Rescue of European Displaced Persons in Postwar Germany, 1945–7', *Journal of Contemporary History* 41, no. 3 (2016): 606–34; Julia Maspero, 'Les autorités

françaises d'occupation face au problème des personnes déplacées en Allemagne et en Autriche, 1945-1949', *Revue d'Allemagne* 40 (2008): 485-501; Julia Maspero, 'La question des personnes déplacées polonaises dans les zones françaises d'occupation en Allemagne et Autriche: un aspect méconnu des relations franco-polonaises (1945-1949)', *Relations internationals* 138 (2009): 59-74.

22 Margaret McNeill, *By the Rivers of Babylon* (London: The Bannisdale Press, 1950), 93.
23 See Woodbridge, *U.N.R.R.A.*, Vol. II, 486.
24 For a nuanced and developed insight into how British colonial practises followed officials into DP camps, see: Jochen Lingelbach, *On the Edges of Whiteness: Polish Refugees in British Colonial Africa During and After the Second World War* (Oxford: Berghahn Books, 2020). See also, David Phillips, *Educating the Germans: People and Policy in the British Zone of Germany, 1945-1949* (London: Bloomsbury Academic, 2018), 49.
25 Halik Kochanski, *The Eagle Unbowed: Poland and the Poles in the Second World War* (Cambridge, MA: Harvard University Press, 2012), xxv.

Chapter 1

1 There were an estimated 7 million under SHAEF care in the three western zones, and an equal amount in the Soviet zone of occupation. See, Proudfoot, *European Refugees*, 158-61.
2 Harold J. Laski, 'The Machinery of International Relief', in *When Hostilities Cease*, 30-42; Eugene M. Kulischer, *The Displacement of Population in Europe* (Montreal: The International Labour Office, 1943), 163; US President Franklin Delano Roosevelt quoted in 'Long Range Plan for Refugee Care', *The New York Times*, 18 October 1939, 17.
3 Great Britain. United Nations Information Organization, *Helping the People to Help Themselves: UNRRA – The Story of the United Nations Relief and Rehabilitation Administration* (London: His Majesty's Stationery Office, 1944), 2.
4 It is worth noting that the Soviet zone of occupation had not reached an agreement with UNRRA, and therefore the Soviet DPs were re-labelled as 'repatriates' as they could not fall under the official categorization of a United Nations Displaced Person. For simplicity's sake, however, they will be referred to as Soviet DPs throughout. See, Proudfoot, *European Refugees*, 230; Woodbridge, *U.N.R.R.A.*, Vol. II, 257-320; William Arnold-Forster, 'U.N.R.R.A.'s Work for Displaced Persons in Germany', *International Affairs* (Royal Institute of International Affairs 1944-) 22, no. 1 (1946): 1-13.
5 See Gatrell, *The Unsettling of Europe*, 35-50.

6 'Foreign Relations of the United States: Diplomatic Papers, 1945. European Advisory Commission, Austria, Germany. Vol III'. Accessed 10 October 2021. http://images.library.wisc.edu/FRUS/EFacs/1945v03/reference/frus.frus1945v03.i0005.pdf.
7 Northern Prussia including Brandenburg, Pomerania and Saxony. See D. G. Williamson, *Germany from Defeat to Partition: 1945–1963* (Essex: Pearson, 2001), 3.
8 The Americans were also allocated the 'northern port of Bremen through which their occupying army would be supplied'. – See, Williamson, *Germany*, 3; Württemberg-Baden was created by the US occupation forces in 1945, the capital was Stuttgart, it was later changed to Baden-Württemberg in 1952 after it was merged with Württemberg-Hohenzollern and Baden. It remains Baden-Württemberg today.
9 David Phillips, 'The Rekindling of Cultural and Intellectual Life in the Universities of Occupied Germany with Particular Reference to the British Zone', in *Kulturpolitik im besetzten Deutschland, 1945–1949*, ed. Gabriele Clemens (Stuttgart: Franz Steiner Verlag, 1994), 102.
10 See, 'United States–Great Britain–Soviet Union: Report of Tripartite Conference of Berlin', *The American Journal of International Law* 39 (1945): 256.
11 The number is not canonical, some refer to 'decentralization' over democratization as one of the four, whereas some say there were three and some say there were five. See, Alan Bullock, *Ernest Bevin: A Biography* (London: Politico's Publishing, 2001); John Ramsden, *Don't Mention the War: The British and the Germans since 1890* (London: Little, Brown and Company, 2006); Nicholas Pronay and Keith Wilson, *The Political Re-education of Germany and Her Allies after World War II* (Lanham: Rowman & Littlefield, 1985), Richard Bessel, *Germany 1945: From War to Peace* (London: Simon & Schuster, 2009); Frederick Taylor, *Exorcising Hitler: The Occupation and Denazification of Germany* (London: Bloomsbury, 2011).
12 'Report of Tripartite Conference', 248.
13 Volker Gransow and Konrad H. Jarausch (eds), *Uniting Germany: Documents and Debates, 1944–1993* (Oxford: Berghahn, 1994), 6.
14 Letter of Pastor Paul Piekert to Schönrig of Niedersalzbrunn in Sebastian Siebel-Achenbach, *Lower Silesia from Nazi Germany to Communist Poland, 1942–1949* (London: Macmillan Press, 1994), 127.
15 Douglas, *Orderly and Humane*, 66.
16 Ibid., 200.
17 Ibid.
18 Institut für Besatzungsfragen, *Das DP-Problem: Eine Studie über die ausländischen Flüchtlinge in Deutschland* (Tübingen: Verlag J. C. B. Mohr, 1950), 17–19.
19 Proudfoot, *European Refugees*, 238–9; 243.
20 Besatzungsfragen, *Das DP-Problem*, 17.
21 Wyman, *DPs*, 87.
22 Ibid., 93; Zahra, *The Lost Children*.

23 Nicholas Stargardt, *Witnesses of War: Children's Lives Under the Nazis* (New York: Alfred A. Knopf, 2006), 351.
24 AN, AJ-43-596/7, 'Summary Statement on unaccompanied children in Germany, March 24, 1947'; AN, AJ-43-598-9, 'unaccompanied children in Austria and Germany, April 29, 1948'; AJ-43-169, 'Statistics on unaccompanied children, 5 April 1951'.
25 For more on IRO policies towards unaccompanied and disabled children, see Ruth Balint, *Destination Elsewhere: Displaced Persons and their Quest to Leave Postwar Europe* (New York: Cornell University Press, 2021).
26 For more on Unaccompanied Children, see: Zahra, *The Lost Children*; Katherine Rossy, 'The Plot Against Children: France, Britain, and the United Nations in Postwar Germany, 1945-1949', PhD diss., Queen Mary University of London, London, UK, 2017; Stargardt, *Witnesses of War*.
27 Proudfoot, *European Refugees*, 238-9.
28 Ulrich Herbert, *A History of Foreign Labour in Germany, 1880 – 1980: Seasonal Workers/Forced Labourers/Guest Workers* (Ann Arbor: The University of Michigan Press, 1990), 156.
29 Proudfoot, *European Refugees*, 211.
30 Wyman, *DPs*, 65.
31 John Danylyszyn, 'Prisoners of Peace: British Policy towards Displaced Persons and Political Refugees within Occupied Germany, 1945-1951', PhD diss., London School of Economics, London, UK, 2001, 3.
32 Herbert, *A History of Foreign Labour*, 156.
33 Besatzungsfragen, *Das DP-Problem*, 15-16.
34 For more on Ruhrpolen and the presence of Poles in the post-1945 period, see: Samantha K. Knapton, 'Resettling, Repatriating and "Rehabilitating" Polish Displaced Persons in British-occupied Germany', in *A Transnational History of Refugees in Europe: Forced Migrants in the Age of the Two World Wars*, ed. Bastiaan Willems and Michał Palacz (Bloomsbury Academic, 2022), 199-214.
35 For more on the Warsaw Uprising and Home Army, see Norman Davies, *Rising '44: The Battle for Warsaw* (London: Penguin Books, 2004); Kochanski, *The Eagle Unbowed*.
36 See Ian D. Turner, 'Denazification in the British Zone', in *Reconstruction in Post-War Germany: British Occupation Policy and the Western Zones, 1945-1955*, ed. Ian D. Turner (Oxford: Berg, 1989), 245.
37 Justus Fürstenau, *Entnazifizierung: Ein Kaptiel deutscher Nachkriegspolitik* (Berlin: Luchterhand, 1969), 192.
38 See Werner Sollors, '"Everybody Gets Fragebogend Sooner or Later": The Denazification Questionnaire as Cultural Text', *German Life and Letters* 71 (April 2018): 139-53.
39 Taylor, *Exorcising Hitler*, 307-12.

40　See Taylor, *Exorcising Hitler*; Sollors, 'Everybody Gets Fragebogend'.
41　For further discussion, see Chapters 3 and 6.
42　See Phillips, *Educating the Germans*.
43　For further discussion, see Chapter 5.
44　Andrew. H. Beattie, *Allied Internment Camps in Occupied Germany: Extrajudicial Detention in the Name of Denazification, 1945–50* (Cambridge: Cambridge University Press, 2020), 126.
45　(Translation by author) – see Lutz Niethammer, *Entnazifizierung in Bayern: Säuberung und Rehabilitierung unter amerikanischer Besatzung* (Frankfurt a. M: Fischer, 1972), 13.
46　John H. Herz, 'The Fiasco of Denazification in Germany', *Political Science Quarterly* 63 (December 1948): 569.
47　United Kingdom, *House of Commons Debate*, 20 August 1940, vol. 364, cc1161-3 – 'War Situation' – Prime Minister (Mr Churchill) to the House.
48　In Morgan's private papers he often writes unfavourably of Field Marshall Montgomery, or 'Monty', calling him 'a nuisance of a man' that lives in 'splendid isolation' far away from the DP camps; see Imperial War Museum, London, UK (hereafter IWM), 02/49/01, Lt. Gen. Sir F. Morgan, *'Diary as Director of Operations for UNRRA mission in Germany 01.09.1945 – 27.08.1946'*.
49　Colonel Wilson quoted in Reinisch, *Perils of Peace*, 40.
50　Robert W. Carden, 'Before Bizonia: Britain's Economic Dilemma in Germany, 1945–46', *The Journal of Contemporary History* 14 (July 1979): 537.
51　Save Europe Now (SEN) was a campaign organized to promote providing relief for German citizens, the meeting in question was between Prime Minister Clement Attlee, and a delegation of SEN including Sir William Beveridge and Victor Gollancz. See John E. Farquharson, '"Emotional but Influential": Victor Gollancz, Richard Stokes and the British Zone of Germany, 1945–9', *Journal of Contemporary History* 22 (July 1987): 502–3.
52　Barbara Marshall, 'German Attitudes to British Military Government 1945–47', *Journal of Contemporary History* 15 (October 1980): 655–84.
53　AN, AJ-43-1162, 'Education of Polish Refugees in West Germany' – SHAEF Guide to the Care of Displaced Persons in Germany, Revised May 1945, 38.
54　TNA, CAB 129/9/42, 'Memorandum: Food Situation in British Zone of Germany' – Annex. Appreciation of the Effects of a Further Reduction or Cessation of Imports of Food Grains into the British Zone of Germany, Section V. point 20. 5/5/1946.
55　TNA, CAB 129/9/42, 'Memorandum: Food Situation in British Zone', Section IV. Point 13.
56　BMJ, 'Starvation in Germany', *The British Medical Journal* 2 (November 1946): 821; Victor Gollancz's letter to *The Times* (30 October 1946); see Victor Gollancz, *In Darkest Germany* (London: Victor Gollancz, 1947), 24.
57　Danylyszyn, 'Prisoners of Peace', 107.

58 Ibid., 111–12.
59 TNA, Medical Research Council (FD), 1/148, 'Nutritional Surveys in Germany: Report by MRC observers on behalf of FO', letter from Meiklejohn to Klatt, 12 November 1947.
60 Jacobmeyer, *Vom Zwangsarbeiter*, 211.
61 See Shephard, *The Long Road Home*, 281.
62 For examples of letters to the PW/DP division in the British zone about maltreatment of Poles regarding black market goods, see TNA, Foreign Office (FO) 1006/580, 'Repatriation of Poles', 1946–7.
63 Jaroszyńska-Kirchmann, *The Exile Mission*, 70; see also, TNA, FO 945/689, 'Polish Displaced Persons in Germany, 1945–1947' – Complaints to Mr. Hynd MP as Minister of Germany and Austria from various Polish DP camps.
64 Referred to Poles living in this country (Germany) as a 'plagą społeczną' (social scourge) in Łuczak, *Polacy w Okupowanych Niemczech*, 49; for British reports about Polish elements at fault, see TNA, FO 1052/273, 'Polish Displaced Persons (DPs): policy (1945)' – Memorandum on Poles, Allied Liaison Branch, British Army of the Rhine (BAOR) HQ 17/09/45.
65 IWM, Morgan, *'Diary as Director'*, Wednesday 19 June 1946.
66 Marshall, 'German Attitudes', 665.
67 Sir Arthur Salter (MP for Oxford University from 1937 to 1950) paraphrased in 'Feed Europe Before We Get More', *The Derby Evening Telegraph*, 26 October 1945, 8; for the full debate, see United Kingdom, *Hansard Parliamentary Debates*, 5 ser., vol. 414 (1945).
68 'Bread Rations', *The Gloucestershire Echo*, 28 June 1946, 3.
69 55611-07039 CCG(BE) Intelligence Review 23 January 1946. German Views of their Economic Situation in Marshall, 'German Attitudes', 668.
70 Reinisch, *Perils of Peace*, 39.
71 Emile Brontë quoted by Lord Beveridge in 'Outlook in Germany II', *The Times* (London, England) 30 August 1946, 5.
72 UNRRA had promised the military 450 complete teams in February 1945 as they were eager to please; however, due to lack of sufficient personnel the actual numbers were much fewer. IWM, Morgan, *'Diary as Director'*, letter from Hansi Pollak to Morgan, 5 November 1947.
73 Marrus, *The Unwanted*, 321.
74 Jessica Reinisch, '"Old Wine in New Bottles?": UNRRA and the mid-century world of refugees', in *Refugees in Europe, 1919–1959: A Forty Years' Crisis?*, ed. Matthew Frank and Jessica Reinisch (London: Bloomsbury, 2017), 161.
75 TNA, FO 371/51095, 'Operations of UNRRA: Assistance for Displaced Persons in Liberated Territory' – Cabinet Committee on the Reception and Accommodation of Refugees, 13 June 1945.
76 Danylyszyn, 'Prisoners of Peace', 123.
77 Łuczak, *Polacy w Okupowanych Niemczech*, 13.

Chapter 2

1. An example of *Katechizm polskiego* dziecka recited by heart. Accessed 20 May 2022. https://www.youtube.com/watch?v=HPmwV1QaXPs.
2. For the full text written in first person, see: Biblioteka Narodowa (BN), BP 1901–1939 vol. 2 pos. 11465, Władysław Bełza, *Katechizm Polskiego Dziecka* (1901, Lwów); Władysław Bełza (1900) in Brian Porter-Szűcs, *Faith and Fatherland: Catholicism, Modernity, and Poland* (Oxford: Oxford University Press, 2011), 3.
3. Richard English and Joseph Morrison Skelly, 'Ideas Matter', in *Ideas Matter: Essays in Honour of Conor Cruise O'Brien*, ed. Richard English and Joseph Morrison Skelly (London: University Press of America Inc., 2000), 9–38.
4. Emilio Gentile, 'The Sacralisation of Politics: Definitions, Interpretations and Reflections on the Question of Secular Religion and Totalitarianism', *Totalitarian Movements and Political Religions* 1 (2007): 21. DOI: 10.1080/14690760008406923; Conor Cruise O'Brien quoted in English and Skelley, 'Ideas Matter', 17.
5. See, Timothy Snyder, *Bloodlands: Europe Between Hitler and Stalin* (London: Vintage, 2010).
6. IWM, 95/26/1, Rhoda Dawson, Typescript, '*The Stagnant Pool: Work Among Displaced Persons in Germany, 1945–1947*' [c. 1992]. Additional Materials boxed with typescript '*The Stagnant Pool*', Letter to Dawson in Polish with the title 'Victory Day' (no date given). Translation by author.
7. See Benedict Anderson, *Imagined Communities: Reflection on the Origin and Spread of Nationalism* (London: Verso, 1991).
8. Although many Poles had repatriated by late 1946, those who stayed in the British zone's DP camps were often classified as recalcitrant, and later whittled down to the 'hard core'. See Woodbridge, *U.N.R.R.A.*, Vol. III, Table 13, 426.
9. Lloyd Gorge quoted in Norman Davies, 'Lloyd George and Poland, 1919–20', *Journal of Contemporary History* 6 (1971): 132; Lloyd George quoted in Norman Davies, *God's Playground: A History of Poland in Two Volumes. Volume II. 1795 to Present* (Oxford: Oxford University Press, 2005), 393.
10. E. H. Carr and Lloyd George quoted in Davies, *God's Playground Vol. II*, 393.
11. See Peter D. Stachura, *Poland, 1918–1945: An Interpretive and Documentary History of the Second Republic* (London: Routledge, 2004), 47; Davies, *God's Playground Vol II*.
12. The censuses were conducted using different criteria; for example the second focused on 'mother tongue'. See: *Pierwszy powszechny spis Rzeczypospolitej Polskiej z dnia 30 września 1921 roku* (Warsaw: Główny Urząd Statystyczny, 1927); *Drugi powszechny spis ludności z dnia 9 XII 1931 roku* (Warsaw: Główny Urząd Statystyczny, 1932). There were also smaller ethnocultural groups, including Lithuanians and Czechs. See: Henryk Zieliński, *Historia Polski, 1914–1939* (Wrocław: Ossonlineum, 1985), 124–6; Davies, *God's Playground Vol. II*, 404–7.

13 Anita Prażmowska, *Poland: A Modern History* (London: I. B. Taurus, 2010), 102; Morgane Labbé, 'National Indifference, Statistics and the Constructivist Paradigm. The Case of the Tutejsi ('The People from Here') in Interwar Polish Censuses', in *National Indifference and the History of Nationalism in Modern Europe*, ed. Maarten Van Ginderachter and Jon Fox (London: Routledge, 2019), 161–2.

14 Quoted by R. A. Rothstein, 'The Linguist as Dissenter: Jan Baudouin de Courtenay', in *For Wiktor Weintraub: Essays in Polish Literature, Language and History*, ed. Victor Erlich (The Hague: Mouton, 1975), 399.

15 Timothy Snyder, *The Reconstruction of Nations: Poland, Ukraine, Lithuania, Belarus, 1569–1999* (New Haven: Yale University Press, 2003), 52–73.

16 Davies, *God's Playground Vol. II*, 403–7.

17 See Brian Porter, *When Nationalism Began to Hate: Imagining Modern Politics in Nineteenth-Century Poland* (Oxford: Oxford University Press, 2000), 103–34.

18 Jaroszyńska-Kirchmann, *The Exile Mission*, 1.

19 See Knapton, 'Resettling, Repatriating and Rehabilitating'.

20 E. Renan, 'What Is a Nation?', text of a conference delivered at the Sorbonne on 11 March 1882, in E. Renan, *Qu'est-ce qu-une nation?* (Paris: Presses Pocket, 1992 – Trans. E. Rundell). Accessed 10 October 2021, http://ucparis.fr/files/9313/6549/9943/What_is_a_Nation.pdf.

21 IWM, 95/26/1, Rhoda Dawson, 'The Stagnant Pool', 145a.

22 A trilogy on the Second Great Emigration is often used as a reference point: Andrzej Friszke, *Życie polityczne emigracji*, Paweł Machcewicz, *Emigracja w polityc/e międzynarodowej*, Rafał Habielski, *Życie społeczne i kulturalne emigracji* (Warsaw: Biblioteka Więzi, 1999).

23 Snyder, *The Reconstruction of Nations*, 2.

24 AN, AJ-43-607/8, 'Polish Repatriation, 1947–1948': *Robotnik* article by Dr. Kazimierz Libera titled *Under the Rodło Symbol (part 2)*, 6 January 1948.

25 Tara Zahra, 'Travel Agents on Trial: Policing Mobility in East Central Europe, 1889–1989', *Past & Present* 223 (May 2014): 181–5.

26 Davies, *God's Playground Vol. II*, 411.

27 Katherine Lebow, 'The Conscience of the Skin: Interwar Polish Autobiography and Social Rights', *Humanity: An International Journal of Human Rights, Humanitarianism, and Development* 3 (Winter, 2012): 298.

28 Ibid., 302; Jerzy Sulimski quote from Jerzy Sulimski, *Kraków w procesie przemian: Współczesne przeobraz.enia zbiorowości wielkomiejskiej* (Kraków: Wydawnictwo Literackie, 1976), 155.

29 Lebow, 'The Conscience of the Skin', 312.

30 According to Pogonowski, the six wars were between Poland and: Ukraine, Germany (over Poznań), Germany (over Silesia), Lithuania, Czechoslovakia, and the Soviet Union. I. C. Pogonowski, *Poland, A Historical Atlas* (New York: Hippocrene Books, 1987); Davies, *God's Playground. Vol II*, 394.

31 For more on the Polish-Soviet war, see: Piotr S. Wandycz, *Soviet-Polish Relations, 1917–1921* (Harvard University Press, reprint: 2014); Norman Davies, *White Eagle, Red Star: The Polish-Soviet War 1919–1920 and 'The Miracle on the Vistula'* (London: Pimlico, 2003).
32 Davies, *White Eagle, Red Star*, 21.
33 Lord D'Abernon, *The Eighteenth Decisive Battle of the World: Warsaw, 1920* (London: Hodder & Stoughton Ltd, 1931), 9.
34 TNA, FO 688/21/14 – 'Attitude of Poles to Russia 1927', Letter titled Memorandum on the Russian situation to Sir. Max-Muller from A. G. Marshall, 27 November 1927.
35 David Dilks, *The Diaries of Sir Alexander Cadogan, O.M., 1938–1945* (London: Cassell, 1971), 168.
36 'Prime Minister Neville Chamberlain's Broadcast to the Nation', 3 September 1939. BBC transcript, Accessed 10 October 2021: http://www.bbc.co.uk/archive/ww2outbreak/7957.shtml?page=txt.
37 TNA, Cabinet Papers (CAB) 65/1/19, War Cabinet meeting 18 September 1939, The Military situation in Poland.
38 Kochanski, *The Eagle Unbowed*, 96; Jan T. Gross, *Polish Society under German Occupation: The Generalgouvernement, 1939–1944* (New York: Princeton University Press, 1979).
39 See Jaroszyńska-Kirchmann, *The Exile Mission*, 16–18.
40 Martin Broszat, *Nationalsozialistische Polenpolitik, 1939–1945* (Stuttgart: Deutsche Verlags-Anstalt, 1961), 9–25.
41 See Alexander B. Rossino, *Hitler Strikes Poland: Blitzkrieg, Ideology, and Atrocity* (Kansas: University of Kansas Press, 2003).
42 Piotr Filipowski and Katarzyna Madroń-Mitzner, '"You Can't Say it Out Loud, and You Can't Forget": Polish Experiences of Slave and Forced Labour for the "Third Reich"', in *Hitler's Slaves*, ed. von Plato et al., 71–85; Robert Lewis Koehl, *RKFDV: German Resettlement and Population Policy, 1939–1945* (Cambridge, MA: Harvard University Press, 1957).
43 See Czesław Madajczyk, *Polityke III Rzeszy w okupowanej Polsce: okupacja Polski, 1939–1945, Vol. I* (Daleszyn: Państwowe Wydawn, Naukowe, 1970); Ulrich Herbert, *Hitler's Foreign Workers: Enforced Foreign Labour in Germany under the Third Reich* (Cambridge: Cambridge University Press, 1997), 61–82; Gross, *Polish Society under German Occupation*, 73–94.
44 The Upper Silesia Plebiscite, as accorded by the Treaty of Versailles, was held in 1921 to determine whether the area should remain part of Germany or become part of the newly formed Polish state. The period leading up to it was rife with violence. The outcome was the industrially strong eastern portion of Upper Silesia was declared Polish (and became an autonomous region, Silesia Voivodship) and the west remained German even though the majority win was German. For more

information, see Hugo Service, *Germans to Poles: Communism, Nationalism and Ethnic Cleansing after the Second World War* (Cambridge: Cambridge University Press, 2013), 153–4.
45. See Theodore R. Weeks, 'Population Politics in Vilnius 1944–1947: A Case Study of Socialist-Sponsored Ethnic Cleansing', *Post-Soviet Affairs* 23 (2007): 80; Service, *Germans to Poles*, 312.
46. Snyder, *The Reconstruction of Nations*, 94.
47. Czesław Łuczak (ed.), *Documenta Occupationis Teutonicae IX – Położenie Polskich Robotników Przymusowych w Rzeszy, 1939–1945* (Poznań: Instytut Zachodni, 1975).
48. Polish Ministry of Information, *German New Order in Poland* (London: 1942) 181.
49. Kochanski, *The Eagle Unbowed*, 100–1.
50. Sophie Hodorowicz Knab, *Wearing the Letter P: Polish Women as Forced Laborers in Nazi Germany, 1939–1945* (New York: Hippocrene, 2016), 103–6.
51. Ibid., 111.
52. IWM, 95/26/1, Dawson, 'The Stagnant Pool', Letter to Dawson in Polish with the title 'Victory Day' (no date given).
53. For a more graphic description, see Davies, *God's Playground Vol. II*, 448–50.
54. Tadeusz Piotrowski, *The Polish Deportees of World War II: Recollections of Removal to the Soviet Union and Dispersal Throughout the World* (London: McFarland, 2004), 4–5.
55. Polish Institute and Sikorski Museum (hereafter PISM), *Polskie Siły Zbrojne w drugiej wojnie światowej* (London: Institute of General Sikorski, 1950), 226–30.
56. Jaroszyńska-Kirchmann, *The Exile Mission*, 21.
57. This comparison between work selection and slave markets makes an uncomfortable reappearance in Chapter 5 when discussing applications to Western countries for foreign workers or resettlement schemes in the DP camps. See Filipowski and Madroń-Mitzner, 'You Can't Say It Out Loud, and You Can't Forget', 75.
58. Madajczyk, *Polityke III Rzeszy*, 483.
59. Tomasz Szarota, 'Poland under German Occupation, 1939–1941', in *From Peace to War: Germany, Soviet Russia, and the World, 1939–1941*, ed. Bernt Wegner (Oxford: Berghahn, 1997), 50.
60. See Herbert, *Hitler's Foreign Workers*, 61–82.
61. Filipowski and Madoń-Mitzner, '"You Can't Say It Out Loud"', 80.
62. Herbert, *Hitler's Foreign Workers*, 329–37.
63. AN, AJ-43-60, 'British Zone in Germany: Agreements between the UNRRA Intergovernmental Committee and the Military Authorities, Correspondence, August 1945–February 1947' – The London Memorandum from the 'Help Poles in Germany' Polish Social Committee to H. Emerson, Feb. 1947. 2. See also Herbert, *Hitler's Foreign Workers*, 329–37.
64. See: Alexandra Richie, *Warsaw 1944: Hitler, Himmler, and the Warsaw Uprising* (New York: Picador, 2019); Davies, *Rising '44: The Battle for Warsaw*.

65 See Davies, *God's Playground Vol II.*, 474–8.
66 IWM, 95/26/1, Dawson, '*The Stagnant Pool*', Letter to Dawson in Polish with the title 'Victory Day' (no date given).
67 Hodorowicz Knab, *Wearing the Letter P*, 239.
68 Adam Zagajewski, *Two Cities: On Exile, History, and the Imagination*, trans. Lillian Vallee (Canada: Harper Collins, 1995), 14.
69 Matthew Frank, 'Reconstructing the Nation-State: Population Transfer in Central and Eastern Europe, 1944–8', in *The Disentanglement of Populations: Migration, Expulsion and Displacement in postwar Europe, 1944–49*, ed. Jessica Reinisch and Elizabeth White (London: Palgrave Macmillan, 2011), 27–47.
70 TNA, CAB 65/45/7, War Cabinet meeting 25 January 1944, Poland.
71 Kochanski, *The Eagle Unbowed*, 435.
72 TNA, CAB 65/45/7, 25 January 1944. p. 1, point a.
73 Anita Prażmowska, *Britain and Poland, 1939–1943: The Betrayed Ally* (Cambridge: Cambridge University Press, 1995), 195.
74 Keith Sword, Norman Davies, and Jan Ciechanowski, *The Formation of Polish Community in Great Britain 1939–1950* (London: The University of London School of Slavonic and East European Studies, 1989), 150–6.
75 United Kingdom, *House of Commons Oral Answer*, 21 February 1945, vol. 408, c794 – 'Atlantic Charter', Mr. Petherick to the Prime Minister. For the principles of the Atlantic Charter. Accessed 10 October 2021: https://www.nato.int/cps/en/natohq/official_texts_16912.htm. For more on the perceived role of the United Kingdom & United States in the appointment of the Polish Provisional Government of National Unity, see Marek Kazimierz Kamiński, *W obliczu sowieckiego ekspansjonizmu: Polityka Stanów Zjednoczonych I Wielkiej Brytanii wobec Polski i Czechosłowacji 1945–1948* (Warsaw: Instytut Historii PAN, 2005), 11–71.
76 For an insight into the considerations of those serving with the Polish army, and based in the UK, see Irena Protassewicz (edited by Hubert Zawadzki with Meg Knott and translated by Hubert Zawadzki), *A Polish Woman's Experiences in World War II: Conflict, Deportation and Exile* (London: Bloomsbury Academic, 2019), part III.
77 Władysław Anders, *An Army in Exile: The Story of the Second Polish Corps* (Nashville: Battery Press, 1981), 250–1.
78 Speech of General Anders, PISM, quoted in Jolanta Chwastyk-Kowalczyk, *Katyń, dipisi, PKPR na łamach polskich czasopism wychodźczych* (Kielce: Wydawnictwo Uniwersytetu Humanistyczno-Przyrodniczego, 2011), 108. Translation by K. Nowak.
79 Keith Sword, '"Their Prospects Will Not be Bright": British Responses to the Problem of the Polish "Recalcitrants" 1946–49', *Journal of Contemporary History* 21 (July 1986): 367.

80 Porter, *When Nationalism Began to Hate*, 15–42.
81 Mickiewicz quoted in Davies, *God's Playground Vol. II*, 12.
82 Tadeusz Piotrowski, *Poland's Holocaust: Ethnic Strife, Collaboration with Occupying Forces and Genocide in the Second Republic, 1918–1947* (North Carolina: McFarland, 1998).
83 Catherine Gousseff, 'Evacuation versus Repatriation: The Polish-Ukrainian Population Exchange, 1944–6', in *The Disentanglement of Populations*, 91–111: 92.
84 Grigor McClelland, *Embers of War: Letters from a Quaker Relief Worker in War-Torn Germany* (London: British Academic Press, 1997), 27.
85 Julian Ursyn Niemcewicz, 'Wygnańcy', 12 May 1841 in *Przegląd Poznański*, 163.
86 See: 'Let Them Be Displaced', *The Daily Mirror*, 20 July 1948, 2; 'Britain and UNRRA', *The Times*, 10 August 1946; 'Very Displaced Persons', *Britannia and Eve*, 1 June 1946, 13.
87 Morgan, *Peace and War*, 222.
88 Katarzyna Nowak, *Kingdom of Barracks: Polish Displaced Persons in Allied-occupied Germany and Austria, 1945–1952* (McGill-Queen's University Press, forthcoming).

Chapter 3

1 IWM, 95/26/1, Dawson, '*The Stagnant Pool*', 16–17.
2 Proudfoot, *European Refugees*, 238–9.
3 Rydel, '*Polska okupacja*', 64.
4 TNA, War Office (WO), 171/8048, '701. Det. Relief Detachment, May–December, 1945' – Appendix G2 of War Diary.
5 R S Lawson Private Collection (RSL) – Liselotte Becker, 'Diary of One Year Working for 220 (R) Det Mil Gov', 7.
6 Rydel, '*Polska okupacja*', 73: TNA, WO 205/27, 'Organization and Administration of Polish Forces in the British Zone: 1 September 1943 – 30 June 1945'.
7 TNA, FO 1049/104, 'Poles in the British Zone: vol. I. 1945 Mar–July', Telegram 2354 from Sir. A. Clark Kerr.
8 TNA, FO 371/66145, 'Placing of Poles in Employment and Provision of Accommodation', 1947. R. M. Hankey, discussing employment of Poles in UK.
9 Łuczak, *Polacy w Okupowanych*, 44–5.
10 GL Collection – Reports on Maczków and photographs of weddings, June 1945.
11 TNA, FO 1049/104, 'Poles in the British Zone'; notes on the present situation of HAREN V66 now renamed 'Maczkow' by the Poles.
12 GL Collection, 'Agenda report for Polish DPs in and around Haren/ Maczków', 13 June 1945.

13 Jaroszyńska-Kirchmann, *The Exile Mission*, 77–80.
14 Anderson, *Imagined Communities*, 6–7.
15 George Orwell, '1945: Notes on Nationalism', *Collected Essays* (London: Secker & Warburg, 1961), 287.
16 Rydel, *'Polska okupacja'*, 68–9.
17 IWM, 95/26/1, Dawson, *'The Stagnant Pool'*, Letter to Dawson in Polish with the title 'Victory Day' (no date given).
18 Łuczak, *Polacy w Okupowanych*, 90–2, 104.
19 Asocials included gypsies, Roma, physically and mentally disabled persons, convicts, prostitutes, homosexuals and 'sex offenders' – see IWM, 16528, *Memoir of a Polish Officer and a Gentleman*, Private Papers of Adam W Kruczkiewicz, 212.
20 Table 6 'Uczniowie Gimnazjum i Liceum w Maczkowie' in Rydel, *'Polska okupacja'*, 171.
21 See Jaroszyńska-Kirchmann, *The Exile Mission*, 85–7; Łuczak, *Polacy w Okupowanych*, 109.
22 Rydel, *'Polska okupacja'*, 306–7.
23 RSL, 'A Brief History of Wentorf Displaced Persons Camp', Preamble.
24 RSL, 'A Brief History of Wentorf Displaced Persons Camp', Law and Order, 8.
25 Jerzy Niemokowski, *Zmartwychwstania Zabitych* (Hanower: Wydawnictwo Polskiego Związku Wychodźctwa [sic] Przemusowego w Hanowerze, 1946), 32.
26 RSL, 'A Brief History of Wentorf Displaced Persons Camp', Conclusion, 15.
27 More on this in Chapter 5. See also Samantha K. Knapton, '"There is No Such Thing as an Unrepatriable Pole": Polish Displaced Persons in the British Zone of Occupation in Germany', *European History Quarterly* 50, no 4 (2020): 689–710, 697–9.
28 RSL, 'Diary of Year One working for 220 (R) Det Mil Gov', *Liselotte Becker* (1946–7), 29 May 1945, 4.
29 RSL, 'The Second Year With for 220 (R) Det Mil Gov', *Liselotte Becker* (1946–7), 14 August 1946, 7.
30 Susan Pettiss and Lynne Taylor, *After the Shooting Stopped: The Story of an UNRRA Welfare Worker in Germany, 1945–47* (Bloomington: Trafford Publishing, 2004), 53–4; Dawson, *'Stagnant Pool'*, 42.
31 Kathryn Hulme, *The Wild Place* (London: Pan Books, 1959), 16.
32 McNeill, *By the Rivers of Babylon*, 10.
33 Pettiss and Taylor, *After the Shooting Stopped*, 51–61.
34 Dawson, *'Stagnant Pool'*, Rosenheim, 28–9; for a description of how UNRRA used pictures of DPs, see Salvatici, *A History of Humanitarianism*, 128.
35 Ibid., 29.
36 Kathryn Close, 'The Want to Be People', *Survey Graphic*, 35 (November, 1946): 392.
37 See Arnold-Forster quoted in Shephard, *The Long Road Home*, 269; Edward Bakis, 'The So-Called DP-Apathy in Germany's DP Camps', *Transactions of the Kansas*

Academy of Science (1903–) 55 (March 1952): 81–2; Dawson, 'Stagnant Pool', 8; Pettiss and Taylor, *After the Shooting Stopped*, 82; Hulme, *The Wild Place*, 16.

38 Kathryn Hulme referred to the president of the Polish Committee in Wildflecken as Tak Schön due to the frequency with which he would use this Polish-German expression of understanding; see Hulme, *The Wild Place*, 24.

39 Pettiss and Taylor, *After the Shooting Stopped*, 82.

40 Close, 'They Want to Be People', 421 (emphasis in original).

41 McNeill, *By the Rivers of Babylon*, 37.

42 IWM, Dawson, 'Stagnant Pool', 6.

43 Marvin Klemmé, *The Inside Story of UNRRA: An Experience in Internationalism; A First-hand Report on the Displaced People of Europe* (New York: Lifetime Editions, 1949), ix–x.

44 For more on Polish education in Germany and illiteracy rates, see Chapter 6.

45 See, PISM, KOL 131/3, *Protokóły z posiedzeń zarządu Miejskiego*, 12 June 1946; Rydel, 'Polska Okupacja', 306–7.

46 IWM, Dawson, 'Stagnant Pool', 26–7. Translation by author (emphasis in original).

47 Hulme, *The Wild Place*, 40.

48 IWM, Dawson, 'Stagnant Pool', 98, 147.

49 IWM, Dawson, Additional Materials boxed with typescript 'The Stagnant Pool', Various Letters to/from publishers and Quakers' Friends Society in London.

Chapter 4

1 TNA, HM Treasury (T) 188/255, 'UNRRA: Discussions with US State Department' – Outline of Post-war Relief Problem, July 1942.

2 'Allies Attack Hitler's Murder of Jews', *The Gloucestershire Echo*, 17 December 1942, 1; 'Persecution of Jews', *The Daily Mail*, 18 December 1942, 4; '11 Allies Condemn Nazi War on Jews', *The New York Times* 18 December 1942, 1.

3 United Nations Information Organization, *Help the People to Help Themselves: The Story of the United Nations Relief and Rehabilitation Administration* (London: HM Stationery Office, 1944), 4.

4 Ibid., 21.

5 UNRRA, 'Psychological Problems of Displaced Persons', June 1945, JRU Cooperation with other relief organizations, Wiener Library (WL), London, UK, 1.

6 See Laura J. Hilton, 'Prisoners of Peace: Rebuilding Community, Identity and Nationality in Displaced Persons Camps in Germany, 1945–1952', PhD diss., The Ohio State University, Ohio, US, 2001; Holian, *Between National Socialism and Soviet Communism*; Seipp, *Strangers in the Wild Place*.

7 See Louise Holborn, 'The League of Nations and the Refugee Problem', *Annals of the American Academy of Political and Social Science* 203 (May 1939): 124–35.
8 In 1938 President Roosevelt called the Evian conference to discuss the problem of racial, religious, and political refugees from central Europe. The IGCR was the fruit of this conference and its mandate primarily focused on helping those fleeing Nazi persecution. However, the IGCR largely existed on paper until 1943 as no meetings were held between 1938 and 1943 and no action was taken. See Tommie Sjöberg, *The Powers and the Persecuted: The Refugee Problem and the Intergovernmental Committee on Refugees* (Lund: Lund University Press, 1991), 127–30.
9 'Early Refugee Aid Termed Unlikely', *The New York Times*, 19 April 1943, 4.
10 Although this led to the creation of an organization to help refugees, some could not bear the disgrace that the Allies now knew of Nazi intentions towards Jews and were powerless to stop it. As a protest to the seeming indifference of the world to the fate of the Jews, Szmul Zygielbojm (an active member of the National Council of the Polish government in exile) committed suicide on 12 May 1943. See Isabelle Tombs, '"Morturi vos salutant": Szmul Zygielbojm's Suicide in May 1943 and the International Socialist Community in London', *Holocaust Genocide Studies* 14 (Fall 2000): 242–65.
11 See AN, AJ 43-23 – "Minutes on Fourth Plenary Session of IGCR, 15–17 August 1943".
12 Sjöberg, *The Powers and the Persecuted*, 153.
13 AN, AJ-43-14 – 'U.N.R.R.A., August 1944 – January 1947' – Memorandum 25 June 1945.
14 Cheever and Haviland, Jr., *Organizing for Peace*, 227.
15 TNA, T 188/256 – 'UNRRA: four-power discussions' – From Washington to Foreign Office, F.A.O. Viscount Halifax, 11 December, 42.
16 Herbert. H. Lehman (January 1944–March 1946); Fiorella LaGuardia (April 1946–December 1946); Maj. Gen. Lowell Howard Rooks (January 1947–September 1948). UNRRA operations in Europe ceased 30 June 1947; however, operations in the Far East continued till September 1948. See Anon, 'Farewell to U.N.R.R.A', *Social Service Review* 21 (September 1947): 398–401.
17 Expansion to 7 Great Powers was a topic of considerable debate during UNRRA's creation, with other major suppliers such as Canada lobbying to join the Great Powers; however, the decision to remain at 4 eventually triumphed. See TNA, FO 370/1716 – 'Paper on the origins of UNRRA. Code 402 file 541' – UNRRA Background and Formation, 1–55 – Rosemary Miller, 27 January, 48.
18 UN, *Help the People to Help Themselves*, 8.
19 See Samantha K. Knapton, 'UNRRA: "You Never Really Rehabilitate Anyone": Problems of Rehabilitation in Definition and Practice', in *Relief and Rehabilitation for a Postwar World: Humanitarian Intervention and the UNRRA*, ed. Knapton and Rossy (Bloomsbury Academic, 2023).

20 Indeed, even the way the British conducted their denazification process among the Germans was found to be part of the 'incurable British colonizing instinct' – see Phillips, *Educating the Germans*, 49.
21 Bessel, *Germany 1945*, 281–9.
22 Dean Acheson cited in Gerard D. Cohen, 'Between Relief and Politics: Refugee Humanitarianism in Occupied Germany 1945–1946', *Journal of Contemporary History*, 43, Relief in the Aftermath of War (July, 2008), 442.
23 TNA, FO 371/41164 – 'Ministry of Information guidance regarding aims of relief and rehabilitation publicity overseas. Code 850 File 168' – 1944; TNA, FO 371/62823 – 'Final Report on the Work of UNRRA. Code 50 File 4934' – Commander Jackson's 'Life and Death of UNRRA' – Robert Jackson, 15 September 1947; 'Relief Problems', *The Western Morning News*, 14 December 1944, 2; 'Why Europe is Hungry', *The Hull Daily Mail*, 10 February 1945, 3.
24 TNA, FO 371/62823 – 'Life and Death of UNRRA' – Jackson, 15 September 1947.
25 Proudfoot, *European Refugees*, 107–10.
26 Wyman, *DPs*, 40; Quoted in Wyman, U.S. Army, *Displaced Persons*, Occupation Forces in Europe Series, 1945–1946, Training Packet 53 (Frankfurt am Main, Germany: U.S. Army, n.d.), 9–10.
27 UNRRA had two primary training centres in France; Granville and Jullouville – see Francesca Wilson, *Aftermath: France, Germany, Austria, Yugoslavia, 1945 and 1946* (London: Hazell, Watson and Viney, Ltd., 1947), 18–19.
28 Soest Stadtarchiv (SoA), D1793 "Statistiken über die in Westfalen wohnhaften Flüchtlinge" – punkte 3 und 4 in 'Der Stadtverwaltung Soest betreffend Mitarbeit der deutschen Kommunen an Vorbereitungen für ein Friedensstatut' – 1 March 1947.
29 Reinisch, *Perils of Peace*, 291; One of UNRRA's major goals was to prevent the spread of epidemic disease, including sexually transmitted disease, to re-establish normalcy. See SHAEF, *Technical Manual for Public Health Officers* (prepared on 22 November 1944, rev. 2 February 1945). Accessed 10 October 2021: https://collections.nlm.nih.gov/ext/dw/30620010R/PDF/30620010R.pdf; Wilfrid Harding, 'Reorganization of the Health Services in the British Zone of Germany', *The Lancet* 254/6576 (10 September 1949): 482–5.
30 Katarzyna Nowak, 'A Gloomy Carnival of Freedom: Sex, Gender, and Emotions among Polish Displaced Persons in the Aftermath of World War II', *Aspasia* 13 (2019): 113–34, 115.
31 For more general reference on the concept of the body as a thing of power, see Bryan. S. Turner, *The Body and Society: Explorations in Social Theory* (London: SAGE Publishing, 2008).
32 See Sharif Gemie, Fiona Reid, Laure Humbert, and Louise Ingram, *Outcast Europe: Refugees and Relief Workers in an Era of Total War 1936–1948* (London: Continuum International Publishing Group, 2012), 220.

33 McNeill, *By the Rivers of Babylon*, 93.
34 Braunschweig in Lower Saxony was also referred to as Brunswick.
35 SHAEF disbanded in July 1945, after which military care in DP camps was carried out by the military occupation authorities of that particular zone.
36 See Laure Humbert for similar issues in the French occupation zone – although responsibilities were divided between the military and UNRRA, as well as the PDR officers (French Prisoners, Deportees and Refugees Organization): Humbert, *Reinventing French Aid*, 100.
37 AN, AJ-43-1162, 'Education of Polish Refugees in West Germany' – SHAEF Guide to the Care of Displaced Persons in Germany, G5 Division, revised ed. May 1945; see also Proudfoot, *European Refugees*, 162–3.
38 TNA, WO 219/580 – 'UNRRA: Relations with the Military and Assumption of Responsibility for Relief and Rehabilitation' – 3 March 1945.
39 Rydel, *"Polska Okupacja"*, 235–7.
40 Shephard, *The Long Road Home*, 59.
41 Proudfoot, *European Refugees*, 135.
42 IWM, 02/49/01, Lt. Gen. Sir F. Morgan, *'Diary as Director'*, Private correspondence letter to Morgan from Hansi Pollak, 05.11.47.
43 See Reinisch, 'Old Wine in New Bottles?', 160–1.
44 Salvatici, '"Fighters without Guns": Humanitarianism and Military Action in the Aftermath of the Second World War', *European Review of History: Revue européenne d'histoire* 25, no. 6 (2017): 957–76, 964–5.
45 IWM, 95/26/1, Dawson, *'The Stagnant Pool'*, 16 (emphasis in original).
46 See Shephard, *The Long Road Home*, 143; for an alternative, see Reinisch, 'We Shall Build Anew a Powerful Nation', 453.
47 Salvatici, 'Fighters without Guns', 967.
48 Proudfoot, *European Refugees*, 230–6.
49 Marrus, *The Unwanted*, 321–2; Nowak, 'A Gloomy Carnival of Freedom', 130.
50 The two other companies are listed as Josef Bertram and a *Zuckerfabrik* in Soest; see: E. Meyer, *List of German Firms that Used Prisoners from Concentration Camps for Slave Labor: ITS Archives*. Accessed via Wiener Library. See also http://www.dpcamps.org/slavecamplist.pdf.
51 SoA, D1620 'Besatzungsamt Verfügungen: Entschädigungsforderungen an die Militärregierung; Requisitionsrecht des Landes Nordrhein-Westfalen'.
52 Esterwegen camp was a former forced labour camp that became one of the Neugamme satellite camps in Emsland before it was liberated by the British army. See T. B., 'Relief Work with Displaced Persons in Germany', *The World Today* 1 (September 1945): 138.
53 RSL Collection, 'A Brief History of Wentorf Displaced Persons Camp'.
54 Wacław Sterner, *Gefangeni i dipisi* (Warszawa: Czytelnik, 1979), 171–2, 148.
55 Ibid., 189–90.

56 For more on repatriation policies, see Chapter 5.
57 Kanty Cooper, *The Uprooted: Agony and Triumph among the Debris of War* (London: Quartet Books, 1979), 119.
58 Morgan, *Peace and War*, 220-2.
59 Shephard, *The Long Road Home*, 154; IWM, Morgan, 'Diary as Director'.
60 Proudfoot, *European Refugees*, 299.
61 Ibid., 105.
62 Salvatici, 'Fighters without Guns', 968.
63 Lingelbach, *On the Edges of Whiteness*, 133.
64 Ibid., 132-8.
65 IWM, Morgan, 'Diary as Director', entry Sunday 23 March 1946.
66 Morgan quoted in Shephard, *The Long Road Home*, 158.
67 For more on Eugenics in Britain, the United States and elsewhere, see Michael S. Teitelbaum and Jay M. Winter, *The Fear of Population Decline* (London: Academic Press Inc, 1985), 45-58.
68 TNA, FO 1006/580, 'Repatriation of Poles, 1946-7', UNRRA report 105/4/RD, Travemünde 21 October 1946 (original emphasis).
69 TNA, FO 1006/580, 'Repatriation of Poles, 1946-7', Krysz report of Travemünde.
70 TNA, FO 1006/580, 'Repatriation of Poles, 1946-7', BAOR replies to Polish Repatriation at BAOR.
71 Similar sentiments were also shared upon receiving the Harrison Report which investigated the living conditions of Jewish DPs in post-war Germany. See Earl G. Harrison, *The Plight of the Displaced Jews in Europe: A Report to President Truman* (New York: American Jewish Joint Distribution Committee, 1945).
72 IWM, Morgan, 'Diary as Director', entry Thursday 11 October 1945.
73 See '"Well Fed" Jews from Poland', *The Times*, 3 January 1946, 3.
74 See 'I Am Still Waiting', *The Daily Mail*, 5 January 1946, 1; 'OUR OWN CORRESPONDENT. Support for General Morgan' *The Times*, 5 January 1946, 4; 'OUR OWN CORRESPONDENT. General Morgan in New York' *The Times*, 28 January 1946, 4.
75 See 'General Morgan's UNRRA Post', *The Times* (London: England), 30 January 1946: 4. *The Times Digital Archive*. Wednesday, 16 November 2015.
76 See Reinisch, '"We Shall Rebuild Anew A Powerful Nation"'; Pettiss and Taylor, *After the Shooting Stopped*; Gemie et al., *Outcast Europe*; Morgan, *Peace and War*; '600 UNRRA sackings: 'In Black Market'', *The Daily Mail*, 30 November 1945, 1.
77 Morgan, *Peace and War*, 256-62.
78 'U.N.R.R.A. Bound Up with Red Tape: Britain to Give Another £75 Million', *Dundee Courier and Advertiser*, 17 November 1945.
79 Morgan, *Peace and War*, 222-9.
80 "Rehabilitation is not merely helping people. It is better than that. It is helping the people to help themselves." See Francis B. Sayre cited in The National Planning

Association, 'UNRRA: Gateway to Recovery', *Planning Pamphlets* 30–1 (1944): 16.
81 See UN, *Help the People to Help Themselves*.
82 Laura J. Hilton, 'Who Was "Worthy"? How Empathy Drove Policy Decisions about the Uprooted in Occupied Germany, 1945–1948', *Holocaust and Genocide Studies* 32 (April 2018): 15.
83 Sterner, *Gefangeni*, 189–90.
84 IWM, Dawson, 'Stagnant Pool', 6–16.
85 Jones, 'Report re Euskirchen Camp', UNRRA Team 8, to G-5 HQ 15th Army Group, 15 June 1945, UNRRA Archives, Germany Mission, British Zone (Lemgo) Central Registry, Narrative and Special Reports cited in Wyman's, *DPs*, 42.
86 Woodbridge, *U.N.R.R.A.*, Vol. 1, 251–2; although sometimes it is listed as one welfare officer and one assistant officer, see AN, AJ-43-1162 – 'Education of Polish Refugees in West Germany' – SHAEF Guide. May 1945 – UNRRA Team for Assembly Centre of 3,000 Displaced Persons.
87 Particularly refers to soldiers, visiting politicians and journalists; see Jessica Reinisch, 'Auntie UNRRA at the Crossroads', *Past and Present*, 218, no. Supplement 8 (2013): 86.
88 See Pettiss and Taylor, *After the Shooting Stopped*; Wilson, *Aftermath*; McClelland, *Embers of War*; Klemmé, *The Inside Story of UNRRA*; IWM, Dawson, 'Stagnant Pool'; Hulme, *The Wild Place*.
89 S. Salvatici, '"Help the People to Help Themselves": UNRRA Relief Workers and European Displaced Persons', *Journal of Refugee Studies* 25 (June 2012): 446.
90 Ibid., 446–7.
91 Ralf Hodge quoted in Salvatici, 'Fighters without Guns', 967.
92 IWM, Dawson, 'Stagnant Pool', 237–8.
93 IWM, Dawson, *Preface*, 6.
94 Dawson was sent to Rosenheim, Föhrenwald, Pasing, Wildflecken and various transports to Poland to accompany those willing to repatriate – see IWM, Dawson, 'Stagnant Pool'.
95 Peter J. Conradi, *Iris Murdoch: A Life* (London: Harper Collins, 2002), 206–7.
96 TNA, FO 371/62823 – 'Life and Death of UNRRA' – Jackson, 15 September 1947, 16.
97 See TNA, FO 1013/2102, 'Repatriation of Poles, 1945–1947' – Notes by the Corps Commander on the Organization and Accommodation of DPs; AN, AJ-43-1162, 'Education of Polish Refugees in West Germany': Booklet, Ch. 2 How the Polish School in Western Germany was set up, 13; Wyman, *DPs*, 161.
98 Holian, *Between National Socialism and Soviet Communism*, 54.
99 For more on the trajectory of migration policies for Polish and Jewish DPs in British-occupied Germany, see Imogen Bayley 'Fighting for a Future: Postwar Migration Policy and the Displaced of the British Zone, 1945–1951', PhD diss., Central European University, Vienna, Austria, 2020.

100 For a deeper discussion of how the British approached the issue of repatriation, see Chapter 5.
101 IWM, Dawson, 'Stagnant Pool', 269–70.
102 Ibid., 76.
103 This screening procedure was introduced due to UNRRA passing Resolution 92 in March 1946 which called for the complete registration of all DPs in centres and full occupation history – see Woodbridge, *U.N.R.R.A.,* Vol. III, 156.
104 COBSRA consisted of forty British organizations, eleven of which sent teams to Europe: The British Red Cross Society and Order of St. John of Jerusalem; The Friends Relief Service; The Friends Ambulance Unit; The Young Women's Christian Association; The Save the Children Fund; The Salvation Army; The Catholic Committee for Relief Abroad; The Jewish Committee for Relief Abroad; The International Voluntary Service for Peace; The Boy Scouts Association; The Guide International Service – see TNA FO 936/698 – Council for British Societies of Relief Abroad – Yearly Report (1947).
105 See Chapter 5, and Cohen, *In War's Wake*, 34–5.
106 Klemmé, *The Inside Story*, 247.
107 Ibid., 114–16.
108 Łuczak, *Documenta Occupationis Teutonicae IX*, xv.

Chapter 5

1 IWM, Dawson, 'Stagnant Pool', 229.
2 Laura J. Hilton, 'Pawns on a Chessboard? Polish DPs and Repatriation from the US Zone of Occupation of Germany, 1945–1949', *Beyond Camps and Forced Labour*. Secolo Verlag (2005): 90; Knapton, 'There is No Such Thing as an Unrepatriable Pole', 692.
3 After the term 'rehabilitation' had been added to what was meant to be a relief organizations policy, the US ambassador in London, John. G. Winant, requested a definition of rehabilitation within the context of post-war planning. Acheson surmised that 'A good question it was, but never answered' in Dean Acheson, *Present at the Creation: My Years in the State Department* (New York: W. W. Norton, 1969), 69.
4 The acronym of UNRRA's name has been mentioned in the majority of texts concerning the early works of UNRRA as an organization in Europe; however, for specific use of the phrase by a Red Cross worker, see Shephard, *The Long Road Home*, 143.
5 For more on the UNRRA's inability to define 'rehabilitation', see Knapton and Rossy, *Relief and Rehabilitation for a Postwar World*.

6 Polish DPs accounted for 68 per cent of the total DP population in the three western zones of Germany by 30 September 1945. Proudfoot, *European Refugees*, 238–9.
7 Morgan, *'Diary as Director'*, Wednesday 10 September 1945, 7.
8 IWM, Dawson, *'Stagnant Pool'* Jullouville UNRRA training notes, May–July 1945.
9 AN, AJ-43-77, 'SHAEF Situation Reports and DP matters' – Stateless Persons in Germany Policy, 12 June 1945.
10 TNA, FO 1049/106, 'Poles in the British Zone: Vol. III, 1 August 1945 – 31 October 1945' – PolPress, London. 17 July 1945.
11 TNA, FO 1049/106, 'Poles in the British Zone' – From Foreign Office to Warsaw, 26 August 1945.
12 TNA, FO 945/689, 'Polish Displaced Persons in Germany, 1945–1947' – Extract from note handed to the Chancellor by Ms Rathbone, M. P.: – Repatriation of Poles: The New Measures, Dec. 1945; TNA, FO 1049/622, 'Repatriation of Poles, 1946–1947'. From Troopers to Bercomb, subj. Poles: Repatriation – additional handwritten notations, 2 January 1946.
13 For further discussion of these three points and the effects they had on repatriation, see Knapton, 'There is No Such Thing as an Unrepatriable Pole'.
14 TNA, FO 1049/622, 'Repatriation of Poles, 1946–1947' – Foreign Office to Berlin, Telegram No. 1009 of 4 July 1946.
15 TNA, FO 1049/622, 'Repatriation of Poles, 1946–1947' – Steel (Berlin) to Foreign Office, Telegram No. 832 of 10 July 1946.
16 McNeill, *By the Rivers of Babylon*, 37.
17 Morgan, *Peace and War*, 234.
18 Gemie et al., *Outcast Europe*, 174.
19 Humbert, *Reinventing French Aid*, 31–2.
20 See Francesca Wilson, *Advice to Relief Workers Based on Personal Experience in the Field* (London: John Murray and Relief Service, 1945), 25; 110.
21 Hilary Footitt and Simona Tobia, *Wartalk: Foreign Languages and the British War Effort in Europe, 1940–1947* (London: Palgrave Macmillan, 2013), 146.
22 Sterner, *Gefangeni*, 212.
23 AJ-43-1162, 'Education of Polish Refugees' – SHAEF Guide to the Care of Displaced Persons in Germany, G5 Division, revised ed. May 1945.
24 Proudfoot, *European Refugees*, 180.
25 HathiTrust's Digital Library in partnership with academic and research institutions – Point 2. c. of Resolution 92. Accessed 10 October 2021: https://babel.hathitrust.org/cgi/pt?id=mdp.39015074829428;view=1up;seq=31
26 Cohen, *In War's Wake*, 39.
27 Cohen, 'Between Relief and Politics', 445.
28 Jacobmeyer, *Vom Zwangsarbeiter*, 106–7; British zone refused to give DP status to anyone showing up after 30 June 1946, the American zone, the date was 1 August

1945, later extended to 21 April 1947 to allow for persecuted races, for example, Jews – see Wyman, *DPs*, 58.
29 Cohen, 'Between Relief and Politics', 446.
30 IWM, Morgan, '*Diary as Director*', entry Friday 2 August 1946.
31 Gitta Sereny, *The German Trauma: Experiences and Reflections, 1938-2001* (London: Penguin Books, 2001), 26.
32 United Nations Archives: A. C. Dunn to C. J. Taylor, 22 July 1946 in Shephard, *The Long Road Home*, 214–16.
33 This refers to the Allies' preference of Baltic DPs over practically every other group. Although it was known that many of them came to Germany in the early years of the war out of their own free will, their DP status was granted on the basis that during 1944 they were conscripted for labour. See Sereny, *The German Trauma*, 25–52.
34 IWM, Dawson, '*Stagnant Pool*', 70.
35 Ibid., 170–1.
36 Proudfoot, *European Refugees*, 115; AN, AJ-43-14 – 'U.N.R.R.A., August 1944 – January 1947' – UNRRA Cable – Re: Date of Displacement of Displaced Persons, orig. London #7689 20/12/45 – forwarded copy 05/01/46; see Knapton 'Resettling, Repatriating and 'Rehabilitating''.
37 Cohen, *In War's Wake*, 37; Woodbridge, *U.N.R.R.A.* Vol. II, 486.
38 For more on problems between the Warsaw and London Polish liaison officers, see Knapton, 'There is No Such Thing as an Unrepatriable Pole', 700–1.
39 Woodbridge, *U.N.R.R.A.*, Vol. II, 486.
40 See Proudfoot, *European Refugees*, 220–3.
41 Tadeusz Nowakowski, *Camp of All Saints*, trans. Norbert Guterman (New York: St. Martin's Press, 1962), 6–7.
42 Ibid., 14.
43 Nowak, 'A Gloomy Carnival of Freedom', 115.
44 Ibid., 114.
45 IWM, Dawson, '*Stagnant Pool*', Letter to Dawson in Polish with the title 'Victory Day' (no date given).
46 IWM, Kruczkiewicz, *Memoir of a Polish Officer*, 212.
47 IWM, Dawson, '*Stagnant Pool*', Letter to Dawson in Polish with the title 'Victory Day' (no date given).
48 Cohen, 'Between Relief and Politics', 446.
49 IWM, Morgan, '*Diary as Director*', Saturday 10 August 1946; For the amounts and types of food on offer in the bulk parcels, see AN, AJ-43-47, 'Polish Nationals: Repatriation', from US Forces HQ to ALL, re: Polish Repatriation Program, pt. 9, 11 October 1946.
50 IWM, Morgan, '*Diary as Director*', Friday 2 August 1946.
51 Proudfoot, *European Refugees*, 284.

52 Hulme, *The Wild Place*, 114–5.
53 TNA, FO 945/689, 'Polish Displaced Persons in Germany, 1945–1947' – *What Every Citizen Should Know*. For figures, see Figure 6.
54 AN, AJ-43-60, 'British Zone in Germany: Agreements between the UNRRA Intergovernmental Committee and the Military Authorities, Correspondence, August 1945–February 1947' – The London Memorandum from the 'Help Poles in Germany' Polish Social Committee to H. Emerson, February 1947. Appendix 49.
55 For more detail on Operation Carrot and reactions to the restrictive 1 October 1946 order, see Knapton, 'There is No Such Thing as an Unrepatriable Pole'.
56 McNeill, *By the Rivers of Babylon*, 18 (original emphasis).
57 GL Collection – UNRRA report on 'Psychological Problems of Displaced Persons', June 1945.
58 Charles Rozmarek quoted in, Kochanski, *The Eagle Unbowed*, 566.
59 Sjöberg, *The Powers and the Persecuted*, 206.
60 TNA, FO 1049/468 – 'UNRRA' – Memorandum on the 5th U.N.R.R.A. Council Session – 5 August 1946.
61 TNA, FO 371/62823 – 'Final Report on the Work of UNRRA. Code 50 File 4934' – Commander Jackson's 'Life and Death of UNRRA' – Robert Jackson, 15 September 1947; Commander Robert Jackson, a high-achieving Australian naval officer, was asked by UNRRA's first director general, Herbert Lehman, to overhaul UNRRA's administrative apparatus in February 1945 as it was realized the current structure was too burdensome and inefficient to work.
62 See TNA, FO 371/62823 – Jackson. Point 8b (viii).
63 For more on resettlement to Australia, see Balint, *Destination Elsewhere*.
64 See Johannes-Dieter Steinert, 'British Post-War Migration Policy and Displaced Persons in Europe', in *The Disentanglement of Populations*, ed. Reinisch and White, 233.
65 Humbert, *Reinventing French Aid*, 69.
66 Teitelbaum and Winter, *The Fear of Population Decline*, 47.
67 Royal Commission on Population, *Report*, 124.
68 By 1949, Britain was also setting up schemes for German girls as well; see Kreisarchiv Höxter (hereafter HX), B1 703 – *Freiwilligenwerbung für deutsche Frauen zur Arbeitsaufnahme in Großbritannien*, published by the British Ministry of Labour and National Service (1949).
69 Holborn, *The International Refugee Organization*, 391.
70 See Jaroszyńska-Kirchmann, *The Exile Mission*, 107; Kathy Burrell, *Polish Migration to the UK in the 'New' European Union: After 2004* (Surrey: Ashgate Publishing, 2009).
71 Kathleen Paul, *Whitewashing Britain: Race and Citizenship in the Postwar Era* (New York: Cornell University Press, 1997), 79.
72 See TNA, FO 371/62823 – Jackson. Point 5; TNA, FO 1049/468 – 5th UNRRA Council. Paragraph 2 & 3; Salvatici, 'Help the People', 445.

73 Acheson, *Present at the Creation*, 201.
74 Philip Marfleet, *Refugees in a Global Era* (London: Palgrave Macmillan, 2006), 142.
75 From 1949 they set up schemes for German women; see HX, B1 703 – *Freiwilligenwerbung für deutsche Frauen* and *Ausbildungsgelegenheiten für deutsche Frauen als staatlich anerkannte Krankenschwestern in Großbritannien* (British Ministry of Labour and National Service, 1949).
76 Cooper, *The Uprooted*, 126–7.
77 Sword, Davies and Ciechanowski, *The Formation of the Polish Community*, 245–55.
78 Roman Królikowski, 'Operation Polejump', in *Zeszyty Historyczne* (Paris: Instytut Literacki, 1968), 150–88; Lingelbach, *On the Edges of Whiteness*, 47–8; Jaroszyńska-Kirchmann, *The Exile Mission*, 107; Holborn, *The International Refugee Organization*, 389–93.
79 Sword, Davies and Ciechanowski, *The Formation of the Polish Community*, 338.
80 Timeline created by author.
81 They were termed Baltic Cygnets due to their more than average beauty, being women predominantly between 21–40 who were picked and scrupulously examined before selection. See John Allen Tannahill, *European Volunteer Workers in Britain* (Manchester: Manchester University Press, 1958), 21.
82 Ibid., 22; see also Shephard, *The Long Road Home*, 323–45.
83 McNeill, *By the Rivers of Babylon*, 204–5.
84 Ibid., 205.
85 Sword, Davies and Ciechanowski, *The Formation of the Polish Community*, 338.
86 Tannahill, *European*, 20; see Steinert, 'British Post-War Migration Policy', 232.
87 'Foreigners Find Derby a Friendly Place', *The Derby Evening Telegraph*, 16 August 1949, 7.
88 Baltic EVWs were often viewed as cultured, and regularly given better jobs. For an example, see 'Larissa Plays Piano Again', *Market Harborough Advertiser and Midland Mail*, 06 February 1948, 1.
89 Farmhands were to be paid the same amount for idleness as they were for farm work as the EVW scheme made it a pre-requisite to pay the labourers a steady, and uninterrupted, wage. See 'E.V.W. Faults' *Aberdeen Press and Journal*, 14 February 1949, 2.
90 For local bias in the case of hiring Poles, 'Object to Poles', *The Western Morning News*, 13 June 1947, 3.
91 'Plucky Student Praised', *Aberdeen the Press and Journal*, 13 October 1948, 6.
92 'Polish Worker Sentenced to Six Months: Grossly Abused Asylum: To be Deported', *The Berwick Advertiser*, 28 October 1948, 6.
93 This article specifically refers to Latvia, Estonian and Ukrainian children, 'E.V.W. Children Make Friends at Driffield', *The Hull Daily Mail*, 21 April 1948, 3.

94 For a discussion on how well EVWs, and other foreign workers, integrated in British, as well as American and Canadian societies, see Shephard, *The Long Road Home*, 390.
95 Holborn, *The International Refugee Organization*, 391–2.
96 Ibid., 391.
97 For an overview of the EVW schemes, see Diana Kay and Robert Miles, *Refugees or Migrant Workers? European Volunteer Workers in Britain, 1946–1951* (London: Routledge, 1992); Tannahill, *European*; Linda McDowell, 'Workers, Migrants, Aliens or Citizens? State Constructions and Discourses of Identity among post-war European Labour Migrants in Britain', *Political Geography* 22 (November 2003): 863–86.
98 See handbook for EVWs – *To Help You Settle in Britain*, prepared by the Central Office of Information for the Ministry of Labour and National Service (Revised, July 1948).
99 AN, AJ-43-74, 'Information: Press Communications' – Statement by Sir Herbert Emerson on the Possibilities of Resettlement of Refugees. Given on 8 May 1947 at the Second Part of the Preparatory Commission of the International Refugee Organization Held in Lausanne, 2.
100 Only eighty-eight Polish dependants were recorded compared to 2,558 from Baltic states. See, Holborn, *The International Refugee Organization*, 432.
101 Holborn, *The International Refugee Organization*, 392; McNeill, *By the Rivers of Babylon*, 199–205.
102 AN, AJ-43-209, 'Outgoing Information: New York, News Reports (not correspondence)' – IRO News Report, Vol. 1, No. 7 (28 August 1950); subtitle: 'England Eases Work Regulations for DPs', Front page.
103 TNA, FO 371/62823 – Jackson. Point 8 b (vi).
104 Gemie et al., *Outcast Europe*, 251; TNA, FO 945-570, 'Proposed Scheme: "Help Polish Displaced Persons to Help Themselves", 1947'.
105 AN, AJ-43-210, 'Public Information: Correspondence Concerning IRO Pamphlets': IRO: What it is . . . What it does . . . How it Works . . . , 4.
106 AN, AJ-43-74, 'Information: Press Communications' – Statement by Sir Herbert Emerson on the Possibilities of Resettlement of Refugees, 8 May 1947, 5.
107 AN, AJ-43-74, 'Information: Press Communications' – Letter from L. M. Hacking to E. Winsall, Esq., 20 January 1947.
108 AN, AJ-43-793, 'The British Zone' – List of various schemes being prepared for DPs and Refugees, 1947.
109 Holborn, *The International Refugee Organization*, 392.
110 AN, AJ-43-793, 'The British Zone' – List of various schemes being prepared for DPs and Refugees, 1947.
111 Gatrell, *The Making of the Modern Refugee*, 110.
112 Holborn, *The International Refugee Organization*, 377–82.

113 AN, AJ-43-411, 'Repatriation of Refugees, 1947–1950'.
114 Cohen, *In War's Wake*, 105.
115 Instytut Józefa Piłsudskiego Ameryce (hereafter PIA) Mieczysław Kalinowski, 'Powracający z Belgii lub Holandii. Nowi uchodźcy', *Nasza Emigracja*, 10.2.1951, (folder 464/024) 2.
116 Holborn, *The International Refugee Organization*, 380.
117 Ibid., 379–82.
118 AN, AJ-43-74, 'Information: Press Communications' – Statement by Sir Herbert Emerson on the Possibilities of Resettlement of Refugees, 8 May 1947, 7.
119 TNA, FO 1049/622, 'Repatriation of Poles, 1946–1947' – To Mil. Gov. Det. From UNRRA Team 128, Information DP Travel, 18 December 1945.
120 Fiorello LaGuardia on anti-repatriation among Poles and Yugoslavs, quoted in Wyman, *DPs*, 70.
121 For examples, see AN, AJ-43-47, 'Repatriation', *PolPress* London 17 July 1945; AN, AJ-43-607/8, 'Polish Repatriation, 1947–1948', Issues of *Repatriant* 15 November 1947–10 January 1948.
122 United Kingdom, *House of Commons Debate*, 11 November 1948, vol. 457, cc1721-2 – 'Foreign Workers', Mr Joyson-Hicks to Mr Isaacs (Minister of Labour).
123 For more information on the Polish Resettlement Act, Poles in Britain, and *Operation Pole Jump*, see Colin Holmes, *John Bull's Island: Immigration and British Society, 1871–1971* (New York: Routledge, 2016); Sword, Davies and Ciechanowski, *The Formation of the Polish Community*; Jaroszyńska-Kirchmann, *The Exile Mission*, 107; Holborn, *The International Refugee Organization*, 389–93.

Chapter 6

1 Nowakowski, *Camp of All Saints*, 12.
2 AN, AJ-43-60, 'British Zone in Germany: Agreements between the UNRRA Intergovernmental Committee and the Military Authorities, Correspondence, August 1945–February 1947' – The London Memorandum from the 'Help Poles in Germany' Polish Social Committee to H. Emerson, February 1947, Appendix 49.
3 PCIRO was created as a 'stop-gap' until the IRO was truly ready to take over the full DP operation – consequently the PCIRO operated with very limited funds in the camps until August 1948 and relied heavily on volunteer organizations to provide necessities such as clothing. For simplicity's sake, I will refer to both PCIRO and IRO as the IRO.
4 See also Humbert, *Reinventing French Aid*, 62–3, 70.
5 AJ-43-60, 'British Zone in Germany: Agreements between the UNRRA Intergovernmental Committee and the Military Authorities, Correspondence, August 1945–February 1947' – The London Memorandum, 12.

6 Polish title: *Społeczny Komitet Pomocy Obywatelom Polskim w Niemczech*.
7 AJ-43-60, 'British Zone in Germany: Agreements between the UNRRA Intergovernmental Committee and the Military Authorities, Correspondence, August 1945–February 1947' – The London Memorandum: Annex.
8 AJ-43-60, 'British Zone in Germany' – The London Memorandum, 1.
9 Klemmé, *The Inside Story*, 265.
10 AJ-43-60, 'British Zone in Germany – The London Memorandum', Appendix 14.
11 TNA, FO 1032-821, 'Polish Displaced Persons: Vol II'.
12 As Atina Grossmann has discussed, Germans were also given 'subordinate' positions helping new mothers as their nannies or sometimes as cleaners. See, Atina Grossmann, *Jews, Germans, and Allies: Close Encounters in Occupied Germany* (Princeton: Princeton University Press, 2007), 208–17.
13 Wilson, *Aftermath*, 119.
14 Klemmé, *The Inside Story*, 271.
15 AJ-43-60, 'British Zone in Germany – The London Memorandum', Appendix 18.
16 Katarzyna Nowak, '"To Reach the Lands of Freedom": Petitions of Polish Displaced Persons to American Poles, Moral Screening and the Role of Diaspora in Refugee Resettlement', *Cultural and Social History* 16, no. 5 (2019): 637.
17 AJ-43-60, 'British Zone in Germany – Copy for Public Relations Article', 27 February 1947 & Displaced Persons in Occupied Europe, 13 March 1947.
18 AJ-43-60, 'British Zone in Germany – Displaced Persons in Occupied Europe', 13 March 1947, 1.
19 Ibid., points 12–13.
20 Klemmé, *The Inside Story*, 275–9.
21 AN, AJ-43-411, 'Repatriation of Refugees, 1947–1950', Placards Selection, Chart A., 'Who are the Refugees? – Public information chart for the United States about DPs in Europe (1948).
22 Józef Betari, 'Witaminy, gulasz i UNRRA', in *Repatriacja na Księżyc* (Słowo Polskie: Dachau-Allach, 1945), 28–9.
23 Jaroszyńska-Kirchmann, *The Exile Mission*, 69–70.
24 Bakis' research was primarily conducted among Baltic DPs, his peers; however, he argues that his findings are applicable to all DP groups in the camps that have suffered prolonged durations in what was meant to be temporary accommodation. See Bakis, 'The So-Called DP-Apathy in Germany's DP Camps', 62.
25 Edward A. Shils, 'Social and Psychological Aspects of Displacement and Repatriation', *Journal of Social Issues* 2 (August 1946): 3–18; Bakis, 'The So-Called DP-Apathy', 64.
26 Vernant, *The Refugee in the Post-War World*, 17.
27 Gerard D. Cohen, 'The Politics of Recognition: Jewish Refugees in Relief Policies and Human Rights Debates, 1945–1950', *Immigrants and Minorities* 24, no. 2 (2006): 125–43.

28 For a full discussion of these points, see Bakis, 'The So-Called DP-Apathy'.
29 Nowakowski, *Camp of All Saints*, 13–14.
30 Banko, Nowak, and Gatrell, 'What is Refugee History, Now?', 12.
31 PIA, Documents of Shame (folder 387/024).
32 'A cutting from a school-teacher's paper', Arnold-Forster papers quoted in Shephard, *The Long Road Home*, 268.
33 Close, 'They Want to Be People', 421.
34 See Morgan, *Peace and War*, 218–62.
35 Rhoda Dawson private collection, St. Paul's Girl's School (hereafter, RD collection). Letter from Maria P. to Rhoda, 03 January 1947.
36 Vincent E. Slatt, 'Nowhere to Go: Displaced Persons in Post-V-E-Day Germany', *The Historian* 64, no. 2 (Winter 2002): 275–93, 287.
37 RD Collection. Letter from Barbara D. to Rhoda, 10 May 1947.
38 Ibid. (Barbara letter).
39 RD Collection. Letter from Pastor Igor Tkatschuk to Rhoda, 30 August 1947.
40 RD Collection. Letter from Anonymous to Rhoda, 02 June 1947.
41 RD Collection. Letter from Anonymous (in French) to Rhoda, 02 February 1948; Letter from Alvin Martin to Rhoda 17 August 1947.
42 *Rzeczpospolita* was a newspaper of the Polish Committee of National Liberation, pro-Soviet and anti-government-in-exile. AN, AJ-43-607/8, 'Polish Repatriation, 1947–1948': Rzeczpospolita, 12 January 1948 – 'Tragic Position of Poles in Germany'.
43 Some of those allowed to continue after 1 September 1946 included general publications such as *Jutro Pracy* (Working Tomorrow), *Wczoraj i Jutro* (Yesterday and Tomorrow), *Kronika Dnia* (Daily Chronicle), and *Wiadomości* (News), as well as publications for more specific audiences such as the youth magazine *Młody Polak* (Young Pole) and the armed forces *Dziennik Żołnierza* (Soldier's Daily); see Jaroszyńska-Kirchmann, *The Exile Mission*, 90–2.
44 AN, AJ-43-607/8, 'Polish Repatriation, 1947–1948': Informational Material Bulletin No. 4, News Publications from Poland – Name & Stated Aims.
45 AN, AJ-43-607/8, 'Polish Repatriation, 1947–1948': PCIRO, Warsaw, 08 March 1948 – Summaries in English of Current Polish Repatriation Press II, Repatriant No. 6 (106) 07 February 1948 – 1 'To Former Members of Guard Companies in Germany' by Cpt. Biginski.
46 Ibid.
47 AN, AJ-43-607/8, 'Polish Repatriation, 1947–1948': PCIRO, Warsaw, 08 March 1948 – Summaries in English of Current Polish Repatriation Press II, Repatriant No. 6 (106) 07 February 1948 – 3 'How do Repatriates Live?', Mr. Osipow.
48 AN, AJ-43-607/8, 'Polish Repatriation, 1947–1948': Informational Material Bulletin No. 4, News Publications from Poland – Name & Stated Aims.
49 See AN, AJ-43-608, 'Polish Repatriation, 1947–1948': Władysław Wolski, 'Do Rodaków na Obczyźnie' in *Repatriant* (December 1947), original – białymi

50 niewolnikami; JK, 'The Emigration Bread is Bitter' in *Życie Warszawy* (December 1947), Dr K. Libera, 'Under the Rodło symbol: Remembrance of Poles in Germany' (Part IV) in *Robotnik* (January 1948).
50 AN, AJ-43-74, 'Information: Press Communications': *The Legacy of the Wars*, received 11 January 1947, 2–3.
51 Ibid., 3.
52 Ibid., 1–7.
53 AN, AJ-43-210, 'Public Information: Correspondence Concerning IRO Pamphlets': World Communique – 'The Seek a Country: February 1949'.
54 AN, AJ-43-210, 'Public Information: Correspondence Concerning IRO Pamphlets': Technical Instruction No. DP. 4., Amendment No. 2., 13 October 1950.
55 Also stipulating that potential emigrants had to have come to the US zone on or before 22 December 1945 to be eligible.
56 See, *Statistical Abstract of the United States* (Washington, DC: Government Printing Office, 1929), 100. Accessed 10 October 2021: https://www.census.gov/library/publications/1929/compendia/statab/51ed.html
57 Gil Loescher and John A. Scanlan, *Calculated Kindness: Refugees and America's Half-Open Door, 1945 to Present* (London: Collier Macmillan, 1986), 11.
58 AN, AJ-43-411, 'Repatriation of Refugees, 1947–1950', Placards Selection, Chart A., 'Who are the Refugees? – Public information chart for the United States about DPs in Europe (1948).
59 Hilton, 'Prisoners of Peace', 429.
60 Ibid., 426–7, see footnote 65; Vernant, *The Refugee in the Postwar World*, 483.
61 AJ-43-210, 'Public Information. Correspondence Concerning IRO Pamphlets': IRO Information office telegram, subject: 'Article in the British Zone Review'.
62 AJ-43-210, 'Public Information: Correspondence Concerning IRO Pamphlets': Draft from the Office of Public Information, the British Zone Review – 'DPs and their Future – I'.
63 AN, AJ-43-60, 'British Zone in Germany' – The London Memorandum Appendix 18.
64 See Vernant, *The Refugee in the Post-War World*, 589.
65 This number is taken across all three western zones of occupation; see AN, AJ-43-646, 'Resettlements of Specialists and Students in Various Countries, 1947–1951': Polish specialists in DP camps; The International Refugee Organization, *Occupational Skills of Refugees* (Geneva, Switzerland: International Refugee Organization, 1948).
66 The International Refugee Organization, *The Forgotten Elite: The Story of Refugee Specialists* (Geneva, Switzerland: International Refugee Organization, 1950).
67 AN, AJ-43-1162, 'Education of Polish Refugees in West Germany': Booklet, Ch. 2 How the Polish School in Western Germany was set up, 53.
68 Ibid.

69 AN, AJ-43-407/8, 'Repatriation to Poland, 1947–1950' – Conference of IRO and Voluntary Organizations, Geneva, January 18–21, 1949, Section on Care and Rehabilitation, 19–34; AN, AJ-43-1162, 'Education of Polish Refugees in West Germany': Booklet, Report of Vocational Training, 52–66.
70 Tadeusz Pasierbiński was previously a secondary school inspector in Poland before the outbreak of war in 1939. See Władysław Kowalczyk, *Szkolnictwo polskie w Niemczech, 1945–1948* (Warsaw: PZDS, 1961), 46–7.
71 AN, AJ-43-1162, 'Education of Polish Refugees in West Germany': Booklet, Ch. 2 How the Polish School in Western Germany was set up, 12.
72 Ibid., 13.
73 TNA, FO 1052/269, 'Administration Policy for Displaced Persons (DPs) – *Wiadomości*, 96:4, Polish Teachers in Germany (translation), 09 March 1946.
74 See AN, AJ-43-60, 'British Zone in Germany – The London Memorandum. Appendix 38; Jaroszyńska-Kirchmann, *The Exile Mission*, 86.
75 For more on the differences between the two factions, see Jaroszyńska-Kirchmann, *The Exile Mission*, 86.
76 United Kingdom, *House of Commons Written Answer*, 20 November 1946, vol. 430, c114w – 'Displaced Poles: Educational Activities', Mr. Stokes (Labour MP) to Mr. J. Hynd (Duchy of Lancaster).
77 AN, AJ-43-60, 'British Zone in Germany – The London Memorandum from the 'Help Poles in Germany', Appendix 38.
78 United Kingdom, *House of Commons Sitting*, 12 February 1947, vol. 433, c354 – 'Education (Displaced Poles)', Vice-Admiral Taylor to Mr. Hynd (Duchy of Lancaster).
79 AN, AJ-43-14 – 'U.N.R.R.A., Aug. 1944–January 1947' – To H. Emerson, Memo Re: UNRRA Policy with Regard to the Restoration of Essential Educational Facilities and Services, 06 August 1945.
80 For more information on setting up and disrupting the educational system (including universities) in both the US and British zones, see Anna D. Jaroszyńska-Kirchmann, 'The Mobilization of American Polonia for the Cause of the Displaced Persons', *Polish American Studies* 58, no. 1 (Spring, 2001): 29–62; Bayley, 'Fighting for a Future', 262–8.
81 AN, AJ-43-60, 'British Zone in Germany – The London Memorandum', Appendix 49.
82 The 260 schools were a mixture of kindergartens, primary, secondary, supplementary, and training/course schools, as well as training colleges; see AN, AJ-43-1162, 'Education of Polish Refugees in West Germany', 47.
83 Jaroszyńska-Kirchmann, *The Exile Mission*, 88.
84 Although many opportunities to Australia were presented, few were ready and willing to take them up as they knew nothing of Australia and feared travelling to the other side of the world. See Balint, *Destination Elsewhere*.

85 RD Collection. Letters from M. Pianowski to Rhoda from Wildflecken, 01 July 1947 and 21 August 1947. Letters concerning M. Pianowski between Rhoda and Royal Opera House, Covent Garden, 09 May 1947 and 30 July 1947; Letter to Rhoda from Sadler's Wells School, 12 May 1947; Letter from J. Pianowski, 24 August 1947.
86 '14 Sworn in as Citizens', *Amarillo Globe Times*, 08 February 1956, 32; 'Dying Man reunited with Son', *Victoria Advocate*, 25 March 1967, 5.
87 RD Collection. Letter from M. Baron [Banon?], 25 July 1947.
88 Salvatici, *A History of Humanitarianism*, 132.
89 AN, AJ-43-209, 'Outgoing Information' – Help the IRO to Help You.
90 AN, AJ-43-209, 'Outgoing Information' – IRO News Digest No. 12, 'Legal and other Protection of Refugees' 14 May 1948.
91 AN, AJ-43-209, 'Outgoing Information' – 'European Movement is Asking Bold DP Action', IRO News Report, Vol. 1, No. 6, 09 August 1950.
92 Pettiss, *After the Shooting Stopped*, 223.
93 McClelland, *Embers of War*, 197.
94 Holborn, *The International Refugee Organization*, 476.
95 Cooper, *The Uprooted*, 136.
96 AN, AJ-43-209, 'Outgoing Information' – 'European Movement is Asking Bold DP Action'.
97 Gatrell, *Making of the Modern Refugee*, 104.
98 Henry B. Murphy, *Flight and Resettlement* (Paris: UNESCO, 1955), photo section III; Shils, 'Social and Psychological Aspects', 9–10.
99 David Nasaw, *The Last Million: Europe's Displaced Persons from World War to Cold War* (New York: Penguin Press, 2020), 358.
100 See Knapton, "UNRRA: 'You Never Really Rehabilitate Anyone'".
101 AN, AJ-43-74, 'Information: Press Communications': See handwritten annotations to *The Legacy of the Wars*, received 11 January 1947, 7.
102 This was the official handover date. See Holborn, *The International Refugee Organization*, 476.

Chapter 7

1 Holian, 'A Missing Narrative', 33.
2 For more on the contested meaning of 'integration' in scholarly debate, see: Tariq Modood, *Multiculturalism: A Civic Idea* (Cambridge: Polity Press, 2007); Sarah Spencer and Katherine Charsley, 'Reframing "Integration": Acknowledging and Addressing Five Core Critiques', *Comparative Migration Studies* 9, no. 18 (2021): 1–22; Karen Schönwalder, 'Assigning the States Its Rightful Place? Migration,

Integration, and the State in Germany', in *Paths of Integration: Migrants in Western Europe (1880–2004),* ed. Leo Lucassen, David Feldman and Jochen Oltmer (Amsterdam: Amsterdam University Press, 2006), 78–97; Floya Anthias and Mojca Pajnik (eds), *Contesting Integration, Engendering Migration: Theory and Practice* (New York: Palgrave Macmillan, 2004).

3 The usage of the term *Flüchtlinge* and *Vertriebene* holds very different connotations today than it did during the early 1950s. The problems of using contemporary terminology in historical writings will be addressed later in this chapter.

4 Holian, 'A Missing Narrative', 33.

5 AN, AJ-43-407/8, 'Repatriation to Poland, 1947–1950' – Conference of IRO and Voluntary Organizations, Geneva, 18–21 January 1949, Summary of Discussions in Section Meetings. Section on Care and Rehabilitation, 30.

6 See Annex 17.a. in Holborn, *The International Refugee Organization,* 202.

7 For more on the 'hard core', see Marrus, *The Unwanted,* 345; Shephard, *The Long Road Home,* 401; Holborn, *International Refugee Organization,* 473.

8 AN, AJ-43-1117, '"Statistics by Nationality of DPs in the British Zone of Germany" – Statistics on Refugees Receiving IRO Care and Maintenance who are Potentially Residual Cases (Non-Institutional), 30 June 1950, pt.1, 1.

9 Ibid., Annex. II.

10 Vernant, *Refugee,* 147, and Shephard, *The Long Road Home,* 401, both give a total of 'around 200,000', whereas Robert Kee, *Refugee World* (Oxford: Oxford University Press, 1961), 7, gives an estimate of 'around 300,000', and Holian, *Between National Socialism and Soviet Communism,* 46, gives a more conservative figure of '100,000 … in mid-1950s'. Alternatively, Institute für Besatzungsfragen, *Das DP-Problem,* gives the estimation of 300,000 with 150,000 who 'for special reasons will be difficult to dispose of', 99.

11 See Annex 17a, Holborn, *The International Refugee Organization,* 202.

12 Proudfoot, *European Refugees,* 401.

13 See Appendix 1, 'Constitution of the International Refugee Organization' in Holborn, *The International Refugee Organization,* 575–91.

14 Ibid., 339.

15 AN, AJ-43-791, 'British zone of Germany' – Minutes of Meeting Between National Advisory Councils and I.R.O. Held at Hamburg, 'Mohlenhof', on 28 February 1951. Point 1, Resettlement Information.

16 See Annex 17 in Holborn, *The International Refugee Organization,* 200–1.

17 A total of 27,482 people were registered under 'Deaths, disappearances, &c.' between 1 July 1947 and 31 December 1951 in the British zone of Occupation, Germany, accounting for nearly 8.5 per cent of the total. See Annex 17 in Holborn, *The International Refugee Organization,* 200–1.

18 AN, AJ-43-175, 'Final Establishment of Refugees in Countries of Temporary Residence (file 21)': Agreed Definitions of Responsibilities Between the Control

Commission for Germany (British Element) and the International Refugee Organization Concerning the I.R.O. Operation in the British Zone of Germany, Annex, Memorandum on Status of Refugees in Germany (21), 37.
19. AN, AJ-43-792, 'British Zone of Germany': IRO. Statement – Outlining the plans made for the transfer of responsibility from the IRO/CCG to the German authorities of all eligible DPs/Refugees not in the processing, staging, embarkation, rehabilitation centres and children's homes in the British zone of Germany on 30 June 1950. Part 1, Point 1.
20. AN, AJ-43-209, 'Outgoing Information: New York, News Reports (not correspondence)' – IRO News Report, March 1950 (IRO/PI/NR/19), 1.
21. For a more thorough discussion of categorizations that led to the refugees being separated and segregated, see Liisa H. Malkki, 'Refugees and Exile: From "Refugee Studies" to the National Order of Things', *Annual Review of Anthropology* 24 (1995): 495–523.
22. AN, AJ-43-1162, '"Education of Polish Refugees in West Germany" – [Booklet] Is it Nothing to You? The Refugee Problem in Europe', January 1949, 11.
23. AN, AJ-43-792, 'British Zone of Germany': IRO. Statement – Outlining the plans made for the transfer of responsibility from the IRO/CCG to the German authorities of all eligible DPs/Refugees not in the processing, staging, embarkation, rehabilitation centres and children's homes in the British zone of Germany on 30 June 1950. Part 1, Point 2, 'Factors Influencing Transfer of Care to German Administration'.
24. See Annex 17a in Holborn, *The International Refugee Organization*, 202.
25. See Vernant, *Refugee*, 144.
26. See Chapter 6. Cooper, *The Uprooted*, 136.
27. Jacobmeyer, *Vom Zwangsarbeiter*, 224.
28. Vernant, *Refugee*, 145. [89,050 Poles, the next largest group were Balts with 28,847].
29. Ibid., 147.
30. AN, AJ-43-792, 'British Zone of Germany' – *Nordrhein-Westfalen: Hinweise für das Einleben*, Section F *'Leid und Freud des Lagerlebens'*, 22.
31. Ibid., 22.
32. Jacobmeyer, *Vom Zwangsarbeiter*, 230.
33. AN, AJ-43-652, 'Final Settlement of Refugees in Countries of Temporary Residence. Germany. Correspondence, June 1950–December 1951', Proposal for IRO Agreement with the German Federal Government, Myer Cohen to Donald Kingsley.
34. AN, AJ-43-652, 'Final Settlement of Refugees in Countries of Temporary Residence. Germany. Correspondence, June 1950–December 1951' – Assimilation of DPs into the German Economy – file viii. Letter 2 November 1950, from Kingsley at CCG to All Three Zones.
35. It's noted in the file that they travelled over 4,000 miles in 3 weeks to conduct the survey.

36 AJ-43-175, 'Final Establishment of Refugees in Countries of Temporary Residence (file 21)' – Mr Grigg's Report (Appendix to Director General's Meeting – no.24). Report on Survey of Conditions of Displaced Persons Transferred to the German Economy, 29 November 1950.
37 AJ-43-175, 'Final Establishment of Refugees, Grigg's Report, 29 November 1950.
38 AN, AJ-43-1268/69, 'The Integration of Refugees in German Life, 21 March 1951', 80–1.
39 AJ-43-175, 'Final Establishment of Refugees, March 1951. Points 65–7.
40 AJ-43-1268/69, 'The Integration of Refugees in German Life, 21 March 1951', 79.
41 Ibid., Conclusion, point 6, 86.
42 Judt, *Postwar*, 235.
43 Dafne C. Reyman, 'The Economic Effects of the Marshall Plan Revisited', in *The Marshall Plan Today: Model and Metaphor*, ed. John Agnew and J. Nicholas Entrikin (London: Routledge, 2004), 82–126, 106, 113.
44 United Nations Department of Economic Affairs, World Economic Report, 1950–1951 (New York, April 1952), 20–1. Accessed 10 October 2021. http://www.un.org/en/development/desa/policy/wess/wess_archive/searchable_archive/1951_WESS_Full.pdf.
45 Schröder, *Displaced Persons*, 349–50.
46 Holian, 'A Missing Narrative', 38.
47 See Stadtarchiv Solingen (StS), 2059 – Fremdarbeiter 1937–38; 1945–48, SG-2456, Blatt 3, 'Polen' cases of 'Diebstahl'; 'Einfacher Diebstahl'; 'Plünderung'; 'Raubüberfall' in Solingen between 19 November 1945 and 12 December 1945.
48 For references to DP criminality, see: Panikos Panayi, 'Exploitation, Criminality, Resistance. The Everyday Life of Foreign Workers and Prisoners of War in the German Town of Osnabrück, 1939–1949', *The Journal of Contemporary History* 4 (July 2005): 483–502; Jacobmeyer, *Vom Zwangsarbeiter*, 208–9.
49 TNA, FO 1052/273 'Polish Displaced Persons (DPs): policy (1945)' – Memorandum on Poles, Allied Liaison Branch, British Army of the Rhine (BAOR) HQ 17 September, 45; Holian, 'A Missing Narrative', 39.
50 United Kingdom, *House of Commons Debate*, 13 November 1952, vol. 507, c84W 'Distressed Relatives Scheme'.
51 The five instances include: United Kingdom, *House of Commons Debate*, 26 May 1952, vol. 501, cc930-1 – 'Displaced Persons (Welfare)'; United Kingdom, *House of Commons Debate*, 28 May 1952, vol. 501, c161W 'Germany (Displaced Persons); United Kingdom, *House of Commons Debate*, 10 November 1952, vol. 507, cc585-7 'Displaced Persons'; United Kingdom, *House of Commons Debate*, 13 November 1952, vol. 507, c84W 'Distressed Relatives Scheme'; and United Kingdom, *House of Commons Debate*, 23 February 1953, vol. 511, c1711 'Refugee Fund (contributions)'.

52 Table created using a combination of the online *Daily Mail* archive (1896–2004), *Telegraph* historical archive (1855–2000) and *Times Digital Archive* (1785–2012). In each instance, the search was limited to the term 'Displaced Persons' between 25 April 1951 and 25 April 1953. Each article was then examined for its content and placed into the category of Germany, UK, or 'Other'. 'Other' largely consists of articles mentioning DPs but not focusing on them in particular or talking about the closure of the IRO.

53 See: Panikos Panayi, *Ethnic Minorities in Nineteenth and Twentieth Century Germany: Jews, Gypsies, Poles, Turks and Others* (New York: Routledge, 2000); Joyce M. Mushaben, *The Changing Faces of Citizenship: Integration and Mobilization among Ethnic Minorities in Germany* (New York: Berghahn, 2008).

54 Laura J. Hilton, 'Cultural Nationalism in Exile: The Case of Polish and Latvian Displaced Persons', *The Historian* 71 (Summer 2009): 317.

55 Łuczak, *Polacy w Okupowanych*, 89–90.

56 AN, AJ-43-652, 'Final Settlement of Refugees – file viii. Letter 2 November 1950 from Kingsley at CCG to All Three Zones.

57 AN, AJ-43-1268/69, 'The Integration of Refugees in German Life, 21 March 1951', Appendix VIA. Social Problems, 2.

58 Although the law's title literally translates as 'homeless foreigners', it refers to stateless peoples.

59 Holian, 'A Missing Narrative', 38.

60 See Knapton, 'Resettling, Repatriating, and 'Rehabilitating'"; Herbert, *A History of Foreign Labour*.

61 Holian, 'A Missing Narrative', 36.

62 Cooper, *The Uprooted*, 135.

63 AN, AJ-43-795, 'British Zone of Germany': Letter to IRO Zonal Offices BAOR, Hamburg (3 August 1951) from the Director of the Refugees and Displaced Persons Branch, BAOR – Subject: Discrimination against DPs/Refugees in Western Germany (3c).

64 Ibid.

65 Jacobmeyer, *Vom Zwangsarbeiter*, 230.

66 Statistisches Jahrbuch für die Bundesrepublik Deutschland (1953), Table 15. Accessed 10 October 2021. http://www.digizeitschriften.de/dms/img/?PID =PPN514402342_1952%7Clog10.

67 Proudfoot, *European Refugees*, 436.

68 United Nations, *A Study of Statelessness* (New York: United Nations, 1949).

69 AJ-43-652, 'Final Settlement of – 'IRO in Liquidation: Position of Displaced Persons', 02 March 1952.

70 Gatrell, *The Making of the Modern Refugee*, 114.

Conclusion

1 Bundesministerium für Vertriebene, Flüchtlinge und Kriegsgeschädigte, *After Ten Years: A European Problem, Still No Solution* (Frankfurt a.M.: Wirtschaftdienst Verlag und Druckerei, 1957).
2 Ibid., 49–64.
3 See Jaroszyńska-Kirchmann, *The Exile Mission*; Hilton, 'Prisoners of Peace'; Bayley, 'Fighting for a Future'.
4 Proudfoot, *European Refugees*, 434.
5 McNeill, *By the Rivers of Babylon*, 37.
6 Danylyszyn, 'Prisoners of Peace', 121, 197–200.
7 For an overview of the social classes in British DP camps, see Sword, Davies and Ciechanowksi, *The Formation of the Polish Community*, 71–3. For an overview of those brought to the Third Reich for labour and an overview of social backgrounds, see Herbert, *A History of Foreign Labour*, 131–8.
8 Gitta Sereny used the term 'goodie-goodie' to describe UNRRA's place among contemporaries at the time and in the historiography since. See Sereny, *The German Trauma*, 25; Knapton, 'UNRRA: "You Never Really Rehabilitate Anyone"', 20–1.
9 UNRRA Washington, DC, *The Story of U.N.R.R.A.* (Office of Public Information, 1948) Ernest Bevin's address to the House of Commons (inside jacket cover).
10 Reinisch, *The Perils of Peace*, 295–6.
11 Lembeck and Wessels, *Befreit aber nicht in Freiheit*; Rydel, *'Polska okupacja'*; Schröder, *Displaced Persons*. To a certain extent the leading historiography also lacks contextualization – Jacobmeyer, *Vom Zwangsarbeiter*; Łuczak, *Polacy w Okupowanych Niemczech*.
12 Kochanski, *The Eagle Unbowed*.
13 RD Collection. Letter from Wanda S. to Rhoda, 25 February 1947 (original spellings).
14 RD Collection. Letter from Wanda S. to Rhoda, 25 February 1947 (original spellings).
15 Although there are no works detailing the specific Anglo-Polish relations between the Warsaw government and organizations in British-occupied Germany, there have been numerous works that look at memoirs and/or governmental archives to understand repatriation and/or the lives of those who returned to Poland under the repatriation transports; see Wróbel, *Na rozdrożu historii*; Lebow, 'The Conscience of the Skin'. Krystyna Kersten's works also merit recognition here, although produced under the control of communist-Poland and, therefore, may have been censored: Krystyna Kersten, 'Repatriacja Polaków z byłej Rzeszy Niemieckiej', *Polska Ludowa* 6 (1967); Krystyna Kersten, *Repatriacja ludności polskiej po II wojnie światowej. Studium historyczne* (Warszawa: ZNO, 1974).
16 Morgan, *Peace and War*, 222–9.

Bibliography

Primary sources

Archives (and collections)

Archives Nationales, Pierrefitte-sur-Seine, Paris, France (AN)
    International Refugee Organization files (AJ-43)
Biblioteka Narodowa, Warsaw, Poland (BN)
    BP 1901-1939 vol. 2 pos. 11465
Höxter Kreisarchiv, Germany (HX)
    B1 – Kreis Höxter mischbestand
Imperial War Museum, London, England (IWM)
    Rhoda Dawson (IWM 95/26/1)
    Lt. Gen. Sir Frederick Morgan (IWM 02/49/01)
    Adam W. Kruczkiewicz (IWM 16528)
    Field-Marshal Montgomery (IWM 1851)
Instytut Józefa Piłsudskiego w Ameryce, New York, United States (PIA)
    Polish Refugees/Displaced Persons in Germany, 1939-1952 (024)
Polish Institute and Sikorski Museum, London (PISM)
    Polish Armed Forces in the Second World War
    Polish General Staff and Ministry of National Defence, 1939-1948
Stadtarchiv Soest, Germany (SoA)
    D1793 – Statistiken über die in Westfalen wohnhaften Flüchtlinge
    D1620 – Besatzungsamt Verfügungen
    D1170 – Druck der Verwaltungsbericht
Stadtarchiv Solingen, Germany (StS)
    2059 – Fremdarbeiter 1937-38; 1945-48
    1621 – Provinzialerziehungsheim
The National Archives, Kew, London, England (TNA)
    Cabinet Papers (CAB)
    Medical Research Council (FD)
    Foreign Office (FO)
    HM Treasury (T)
    War Office (WO)
The Wiener Library, London, England (WL)
    Jewish Relief Units documents (JRU)

Personal archives

Gilles Lapers (Belgium) – Family collection about Maczków (GL)
RS Lawson (London) – Family collection about Wentorf DP camp (RSL)
Rhoda Dawson (London) – Private collection of correspondence (RD)

Internet primary sources

BBC Broadcasts – www.bbc.co.uk/archive
DP camps – www.dpcamps.org
Erinnerung, Verantwortung und Zukunft – www.stiftung-evz.de
Główny Urząd Statystyczny – https://stat.gov.pl
Haithi Trust Digital Library – www.babel.hathitrust.org
Historic Hansard: Sittings in the 20th century – https://api.parliament.uk/historic-hansard/sittings/C20
Katechizm polskiego dziecka by Babcia Józia – www.youtube.com/watch?v=HPmwV1QaXPs
Nato archive – www.nato.int
Ośrodek Karta – www.karta.org.pl
Porta Polonica – www.porta-polonica.de
Przegląd Poznański – www.wbc.poznan.pl
Statistisches Jahrbuch für die Bundesrepublik Deutschland – www.digizeitschriften.de
The UN Documents – www.un.org
United States Census Bureau – www.census.gov/library

Newspapers and journals

Aberdeen Press and Journal
The Berwick Advertiser
The Daily Mail
The Derby Evening Telegraph
The Dundee Courier and Advertiser
The Gloucestershire Echo
The Hull Daily Mail
The Market Harborough Advertiser and Midland Mail
The New York Times
The Times
The Western Morning News

Dziennik Informacynjy (Maczków)
Gazeta Polska
Głos Łudu
Głos Warszawy

Jutro Pracy
Nasze Życie
Orzeł Biały (London)
Polish Daily News/Dziennik Polski
Repatriant (Warsaw)
Robotnik
Tygodnik Przegląd
Życie Warszawy

Published primary sources

Acheson, D., *Present at the Creation: My Years in the State Department*, New York: W. W. Norton, 1969.
Anders, W., *An Army in Exile: The Story of the Second Polish Corps*, Nashville: Battery Press, 1981.
Bundesministerium für Vertriebene, Flüchtlinge und Kriegsgeschädigte, *After Ten Years: A European Problem, Still No Solution*, Frankfurt a.M.: Wirtschaftdienst Verlag und Druckerei, 1957.
Central Office of Information for the Ministry of Labour and National Service, For EVWs: *To Help You Settle in Britain* (Revised, July 1948).
Cooper, K., *The Uprooted: Agony and Triumph Among the Debris of War*, London: Quartet Books, 1979.
Foreign Relations of the United States: Diplomatic Papers, 1945. European Advisory Commission, Austria, Germany. Vol III. – http://images.library.wisc.edu/FRUS/EFacs/1945v03/reference/frus.frus1945v03.i0005.pdf (accessed 10 October 2021).
Harrison, E. G., *The Plight of the Displaced Jews in Europe: A Report to President Truman*, New York: American Jewish Joint Distribution Committee, 1945.
Historical Institute of General Sikorski, *Polskie Siły Zbrojne w drugiej wojnie światowej*, London: Institute of General Sikorski, 1950.
Hulme, K., *The Wild Place*, London: Pan Books, 1959.
Institute für Besatzungsfragen, *Das DP-Problem: Eine Studie über die ausländischen Flüchtlinge in Deutschland*, Tübingen: Verlag J. C. B. Mohr, 1950.
Klemmé, M., *The Inside Story of UNRRA: An Experience in Internationalism; A First-hand Report on the Displaced People of Europe*, New York: Lifetime Editions, 1949.
Królikowski, R., 'Operation Polejump', in *Zeszyty Historyczne*, 150–88, Paris: Instytut Literacki, 1968.
McClelland, G., *Embers of War. Letters from a Quaker Relief Worker in War-Torn Germany*, London: British Academic Press, 1997.
McNeill, M., *By the Rivers of Babylon*, London: Bannisdale Press, 1950.
Niemcewicz, J. U., 'Wygnańcy', 12 May 1841 in *Przegląd Poznański*, 163. http://www.wbc.poznan.pl/dlibra/publication?id=92690&tab=3 (accessed 01 June 2018).

Nowakowski, N., *Camp of All Saints*, translated by Norbert Guterman, New York: St. Martin's Press, 1962.
Pettiss, S. and L. Taylor, *After the Shooting Stopped: The Memoir of an UNRRA Welfare Worker, Germany 1945–1947*, Bloomington: Trafford Publishing, 2004.
Polish Ministry of Information, *German New Order in Poland*, London: 1942.
Renan, E. 'What is a Nation?', Text of a conference delivered at the Sorbonne on March 11th 1882, in E. Renan, *Qu'est-ce qu-une nation?* (Paris: Presses Pocket, 1992 – Trans. E. Rundell), http://ucparis.fr/files/9313/6549/9943/What_is_a_Nation.pdf
Sterner, W., *Gefangeni i dipisi*, Warszawa: Czytelnik, 1979.
The International Refugee Organization, *The Forgotten Elite: The Story of Refugee Specialists*, Geneva, Switzerland: International Refugee Organization, 1950.
The National Planning Association, 'UNRRA: Gateway to Recovery', *Planning Pamphlets* 30–1 (1944).
The Royal Commission on Population, *Report*, London: His Majesty's Stationary Office, 1949.
United Nations, *A Study of Statelessness*, New York: United Nations, 1949.
United Nations Information Organization (Great Britain), *'Helping the People to Help Themselves: UNRRA – The Story of the United Nations Relief and Rehabilitation Administration*, London: His Majesty's Stationary Office, 1944.
UNRRA, *The Story of U.N.R.R.A.*, Washington, DC: Office of Public Information, 1948.
Wilson, F., *Advice to Relief Workers Based on Personal Experience in the Field*, London: John Murray and Relief Service, 1945.
Wilson, F., *Aftermath: France, Germany, Austria, Yugoslavia, 1945 and 1946*, London: Hazell, Watson and Viney, Ltd., 1947.

Secondary sources

Unpublished theses

Bayley, I., 'Fighting for a Future: Postwar Migration Policy and the Displaced of the British Zone, 1945–1951', PhD diss., Central European University, Vienna, Austria, 2020.
Best, S. R. M., 'The British Foreign Office, The United Nations Relief and Rehabilitation Administration (UNRRA), and the Displaced Persons problem in British-occupied Europe, 1944–1947', PhD diss., London School of Economics, London, UK, 1991.
Danylyszyn, J., 'Prisoners of Peace: British Policy towards Displaced Persons and Political Refugees within Occupied Germany, 1945–1951', PhD diss., London School of Economics, London, UK, 2001.

Hilton, L. J., 'Prisoners of Peace: Rebuilding Community, Identity and Nationality in Displaced Persons Camps in Germany, 1945–1952', PhD diss., The Ohio State University, Ohio, US, 2001.

Rossy, K., 'The Plot Against Children: France, Britain, and the United Nations in Postwar Germany, 1945–1949', PhD diss., Queen Mary University of London, London, UK, 2017.

Books

Ahonen, P., C. Corni, J. Kochanowski, R. Schulz, T. Stark and Stelzl-Marx, *People on the Move: Forced Population Movements in Europe in the Second World War and its Aftermath*, Oxford: Berg, 2008.

Anderson, B., *Imagined Communities: Reflection on the Origin and Spread of Nationalism*, London: Verso, 1991.

Balint, R., *Destination Elsewhere: Displaced Persons and their Quest to Leave Postwar Europe*, New York: Cornell University Press, 2021.

Beattie, A. H., *Allied Internment Camps in Occupied Germany: Extrajudicial Detention in the Name of Denazification, 1945–50*, Cambridge: Cambridge University Press, 2020.

Bessel, R., *Germany 1945: From War to Peace*, London: Simon & Schuster, 2009.

Betari, J., 'Witaminy, gulasz i UNRRA', in *Repatriacja na Księżyc*, Słowo Polskie: Dachau-Allach, 1945.

Brand, M., *Verschleppt und Entwurzelt: Zwangsarbeit zwischen Soest, Werl, Wickede und Möhnetal*, Essen: Klartext Verlag, 2010.

Brooks, K. G., 'The Re-establishment of Displaced Peoples', in *When Hostilities Cease: Papers on Relief and Reconstruction Prepared for the Fabian Society*, edited by Julian Huxley H. J. Laski, and W. Arnold-Forster, London: Victor Gollancz, 1943.

Broszat, M., *Nationalsozialistische Polenpolitik, 1939–1945*, Stuttgart: Deutsche Verlags-Anstalt, 1961.

Bullock, A., *Ernest Bevin: A Biography*, London: Politico's Publishing, 2001.

Burrell, K., *Polish Migration to the UK in the 'New' European Union: After 2004*, Surrey: Ashgate Publishing, 2009.

Cheever, D. S. and Jr., H. F. Haviland, *Organizing for Peace: International Organization in World Affairs*, London: Stevens & Sons Limited, 1957.

Cohen, G. D., *In War's Wake: Europe's Displaced Persons in the Postwar Order*, Oxford: Oxford University Press, 2012.

Conradi, P. J., *Iris Murdoch: A Life*, London: Harper Collins, 2002.

Davies, N., *God's Playground: A History of Poland in Two Volumes. Volume I. The Origins to 1795*, Oxford: Oxford University Press, 2005.

Davies, N., *God's Playground: A History of Poland in Two Volumes. Volume II. 1795 to the Present*, Oxford: Oxford University Press, 2005.

Davies, N., *Rising '44: The Battle for Warsaw*, London: Penguin Books, 2004.

Davies, N., *White Eagle, Red Star: The Polish-Soviet War 1919-1920 and 'The Miracle on the Vistula'*, London: Pimlico, 2003.

Dilks, D. (ed.), *The Diaries of Sir Alexander Cadogan, O.M., 1938-1945*, London: Cassell, 1971.

Donnison, F. S. V., *Civil Affairs and Military Government North-West Europe, 1944-1946*, London: Her Majesty's Stationary Office, 1961.

Donnison, F. S. V., *Civil Affairs and Military Government: Central Organization and Planning*, London: Her Majesty's Stationary Office, 1966.

Douglas, R. M., *Orderly and Humane: The Expulsion of Germans after the Second World War*, New York: Yale University Press, 2012.

English, R. and J. Skelly, 'Ideas Matter', in *Ideas Matter: Essays in Honour of Conor Cruise O'Brien*, edited by R. English and J. Skelly, 9-39, London: University Press of America Inc., 2000.

Ezergailis, A., *The Latvian Legion: Heroes, Nazis or Victims*, Riga: The Historical Institute of Latvia, 1997.

Frank, M. and J. Reinisch (eds.), *Refugees in Europe, 1919-1959: A Forty Years' Crisis?*, London: Bloomsbury, 2017.

Friszke, A., *Życie polityczne emigracji*; Paweł Machcewicz, *Emigracja w polityce międzynarodowej*; Rafał Habielski, *Życie społeczne i kulturalne emigracji*, Trilogia. Warsaw: Biblioteka Więzi, 1999.

Fürstenau, J., *Entnazifizierung: Ein Kaptiel deutscher Nachkriegspolitik*, Berlin: Luchterhand, 1969.

Gatrell, P., *The Making of the Modern Refugee*, Oxford: Oxford University Press, 2013.

Gemie, S., F. Reid, L. Humbert and L. Ingram, *Outcast Europe: Refugees and Relief Workers in an Era of Total War 1936-1948*, London: Continuum International Publishing Group, 2012.

Gollancz, V., *In Darkest Germany*, London: Victor Gollancz, 1947.

Graham-Dixon, F., *The Allied Occupation of Germany: The Refugee Crisis, Denazification and the Path to Reconstruction*, London: I. B. Taurus, 2013.

Gransow, V. and K. H. Jarausch (eds.), *Uniting Germany: Documents and Debates, 1944-1993*, Oxford: Berghahn, 1994.

Gross, J. T., *Polish Society under German Occupation: The Generalgouvernement, 1939-1944*, New York: Princeton University Press, 1979.

Grossmann, A., *Jews, Germans, and Allies: Close Encounters in Occupied Germany*, Princeton: Princeton University Press, 2007.

Halicka, B, *Polens Wilder Westen: Erzwungene Migration und die kultrelle Aneignung des Oderraums 1945-1948*, Paderborn: Ferdinand Schöningh, 2016.

Herbert, U., *Fremdarbeiter: Politik und Praxis des "Ausländer-Einsatzes" in der Kriegswirtschaft des Dritten Reiches*, Bonn: J. H. W. Dietz, 1985.

Herbert, U., *Hitler's Foreign Workers: Enforced Foreign Labour in Germany under the Third Reich*, Cambridge: Cambridge University Press, 1997.

Herbert, U., *A History of Foreign Labour in Germany, 1880–1980: Seasonal Workers/Forced Labourers/Guest Workers*, Ann Arbor: The University of Michigan Press, 1990.

Hobsbawm, E., *The Age of Extremes: The Short Twentieth Century, 1914–1991*, London: Abacus, 1995.

Hodorowicz Knab, S., *Wearing the Letter P: Polish Women as Forced Laborers in Nazi Germany, 1939–1945*, New York: Hippocrene, 2016.

Holborn, L., 'The League of Nations and the Refugee Problem', *Annals of the American Academy of Political and Social Science*, 203 (May 1939): 124–35.

Holborn, L., *The International Refugee Organization: A Specialized Agency of the United Nations: Its History and Work, 1946–1952*, Oxford: Oxford University Press, 1956.

Holian, A., *Between National Socialism and Soviet Communism: Displaced Persons in Postwar Germany*, Ann Arbor: University of Michigan Press, 2011.

Holian, A., 'A Missing Narrative: Displaced Persons in the History of Postwar West Germany', in *Migration, Memory, and Diversity: Germany from 1945 to the Present*, edited by C. Wilhelm, 32–55. Oxford: Berghahn, 2017.

Holmes, C., *John Bull's Island: Immigration and British Society, 1871–1971*, New York: Routledge, 2016.

Homze, E., *Foreign Labour in Nazi Germany*, Princeton: Princeton University Press, 1967.

Humbert, L., *Reinventing French Aid: The Politics of Humanitarian Relief in French-Occupied Germany, 1945–1952*, Cambridge: Cambridge University Press, 2021.

Jacobmeyer, W., *Vom Zwangsarbeiter zum Heimatlosen Ausländer. Die Displaced Persons in Westdeutschland, 1945–1951*, Göttingen: Vandenhoeck & Ruprecht, 1985.

Jaroszyńska-Kirchmann, A. D., *The Exile Mission: The Polish Political Diaspora and Polish Americans, 1939–1956*, Athens: Ohio University Press, 2004.

Judt, T., *Postwar: A History of Europe Since 1945*, London: Pimlico, 2007.

Kay, D. and R. Miles, *Refugees or Migrant Workers? European Volunteer Workers in Britain, 1946–1951*, London: Routledge, 1992.

Kee, R., *Refugee World*, Oxford: Oxford University Press, 1961.

Knapton, S. K. and K. Rossy (eds.), *Relief and Rehabilitation for a Postwar World: Humanitarian Intervention and the UNRRA*, Bloomsbury Academic, forthcoming.

Kochanski, H., *The Eagle Unbowed: Poland and the Poles in the Second World War*, Cambridge, MA: Harvard University Press, 2012.

Koehl, R. L., *RKFDV: German Resettlement and Population Policy, 1939–1945*, Cambridge, MA: Harvard University Press, 1957.

Königseder, A. and J. Wetzel (eds.), *Lebensmut im Wartesaal: die jüdischen DPs (Displaced Persons) im Nachkriegsdeutschland*, Frankfurt a. M.: Fischer Taschenbuch Verlag, 1994.

Kowalczyk, W., *Szkolnictwo polskie w Niemczech, 1945–1948*, Warsaw: PZDS, 1961.

Kulischer, E. M., *Europe on the Move, War and Population Changes, 1917–1947*, New York: Columbia University Press, 1948.

Kulischer, E. M., *The Displacement of Population in Europe*, US: International Labour Office, 1943.
Laski, H. J., 'The Machinery of International Relief', in *When Hostilities Cease: Papers on Relief and Reconstruction Prepared for the Fabian Society*, London: Victor Gollancz, 1943.
Lembeck, A. and K. Wessels, *Befreit, aber nicht in Freiheit: Displaced Persons in Emsland, 1945–1950*, Bremen: Temmen, 1997.
Loescher, G. and J. A. Scanlan, *Calculated Kindness: Refugees and America's Half-Open Door, 1945 to Present*, London: Collier MacMillan, 1986.
Lord D'Abernon, *The Eighteenth Decisive Battle of the World: Warsaw, 1920*, London: Hodder & Stoughton Ltd, 1931.
Luciuk, L. Y., *Searching for Place: Ukrainian Displaced Persons, Canada and the Migration of Memory*, Toronto: Toronto University Press, 2000.
Łuczak, C., *Polacy w Okupowanych Niemczech 1945–1949*, Poznań: Pracownia Serwisu Oprogramowania, 1993.
Łuczak, C., (ed.), *Documenta Occupationis Teutonicae IX – Położenie Polskich Robotników Przymusowych w Rzeszy, 1939–1945*, Poznań: Instytut Zachodni, 1975.
Madajczyk, C., *Polityke III Rzeszy w okupowanej Polsce: okupacja Polski, 1939–1945, Vol. I*, Daleszyn: Państwowe Wydawn, Naukowe, 1970.
Mankowitz, Z. W., *Life Between Memory and Hope: The Survivors of the Holocaust in Occupied Germany*, Cambridge: Cambridge University Press, 2002.
Marfleet, P., *Refugees in a Global Era*, London: Palgrave MacMillan, 2006.
Marrus, M. R., *The Unwanted: European Refugees in the Twentieth Century*, Oxford: Oxford University Press, 1985.
Mazower, M., *Dark Continent: Europe's Twentieth Century*, London: Penguin Books, 1999.
Mazower, M., J. Reinisch and D. Feldman (eds.), *Post-War Reconstruction in Europe: International Perspectives, 1945–1949, Past and Present Supplement No. 6*, London: Oxford University Press, 2011.
Modood, T., *Multiculturalism: A Civic Idea*, Cambridge: Polity Press, 2007.
Moorehead, A., *Eclipse*, London: Hamish Hamilton, 1946.
Morgan, G. Sir. F., *Peace and War: A Soldier's Life*, London: Hodder and Stoughton, 1961.
Mushaben, J. M., *The Changing Faces of Citizenship: Integration and Mobilization among Ethnic Minorities in Germany*, New York: Berghahn, 2008.
Niethammer, L., *Entnazifizierung in Bayern: Säuberung und Rehabilitierung unter amerikanischer Besatzung*, Frankfurt am Main: Fischer, 1972.
Nowak, K., *Kingdom of Barracks. Polish Displaced Persons in Allied-occupied Germany and Austria, 1945–1952*, McGill–Queen's University Press, forthcoming.
Orwell, G., '1945: Notes on Nationalism', *Collected Essays*, London: Secker & Warburg, 1961.
Palacz, M. and B. Willems (eds.), *A Transnational History of Refugees in Europe: Forced Migrants in the Age of the Two World Wars*, Bloomsbury Academic, 2022.

Panayi, P., *Ethnic Minorities in Nineteenth and Twentieth Century Germany: Jews, Gypsies, Poles, Turks and Others*, New York: Routledge, 2000.

Paul, K., *Whitewashing Britain: Race and Citizenship in the Postwar Era*, New York: Cornell University Press, 1997.

Phillips, D. 'The Rekindling of Cultural and Intellectual Life in the Universities of Occupied Germany with Particular Reference to the British Zone', in *Kulturpolitik im besetzten Deutschland, 1945–1949*, edited by G. Clemens, 102–16. Stuttgart: Franz Steiner Verlag, 1994.

Phillips, D., *Educating the Germans: People and Policy in the British Zone of Germany, 1945–1949*, London: Bloomsbury Academic, 2018.

Piotrowski, T., *The Polish Deportees of World War II: Recollections of Removal to the Soviet Union and Dispersal Throughout the World*, London: McFarland, 2004.

Piotrowski, T., *Poland's Holocaust: Ethnic Strife, Collaboration with Occupying Forces and Genocide in the Second Republic, 1918–1947*, North Carolina: McFarland, 1998.

Pogonowski, I. C., *Poland, A Historical Atlas*, New York: Hippocrene Books, 1987.

Porter, B., *When Nationalism Began to Hate: Imagining Modern Politics in Nineteenth Century Poland*, Oxford: Oxford University Press, 2000.

Porter-Szűcs, B., *Faith and Fatherland: Catholicism, Modernity, and Poland*, Oxford: Oxford University Press, 2011.

Prażmowska, A., *Britain and Poland 1939–1943: The Betrayed Ally*, Cambridge: Cambridge University Press, 1995.

Prażmowska, A., *Poland: A Modern History*, London: I. B. Taurus, 2010.

Pronay, N. and K. Wilson, *The Political Re-education of Germany and Her Allies after World War II*, Lanham: Rowman & Littlefield, 1985.

Protassewicz, I., edited by Hubert Zawadzki with Meg Knott and translated by Hubert Zawadzki), *A Polish Woman's Experiences in World War II: Conflict, Deportation and Exile*, London: Bloomsbury Academic, 2019.

Proudfoot, M. J., *European Refugees, 1939–52. A Study in Forced Population Movement*, Evanston: Northwest University Press, 1956.

Ramsden, J., *Don't Mention the War: The British and the Germans since 1890*, London: Little, Brown and Company, 2006.

Reinisch, J. and E. White, *The Disentanglement of Populations: Migration, Expulsion and Displacement in postwar Europe, 1944–1949*, London: Palgrave Macmillan, 2011.

Reinisch, J., *The Perils of Peace: The Public Health Crisis in Occupied Germany*, Oxford: Oxford University Press, 2013.

Reyman, D. C., 'The Economic Effects of the Marshall Plan Revisited', in *The Marshall Plan Today: Model and Metaphor*, edited by J. Agnew and J. N. Entrikin, 82–126. London: Routledge, 2004.

Richie, A., *Warsaw 1944: Hitler, Himmler, and the Warsaw Uprising*, New York: Picador, 2019.

Rossino, A. B., *Hitler Strikes Poland: Blitzkrieg, Ideology, and Atrocity*, Kansas: University of Kansas Press, 2003.

Rothstein, R. A., 'The Linguist as Dissenter: Jan Baudouin de Courtenay', in *For Wiktor Weintraub: Essays in Polish Literature, Language and History*, edited by V. Erlich, 391–405, The Hague: Mouton, 1975.

Rydel, J., *"Polska okupacja" w północno-zachodnich Niemczech 1945–1948: Nieznany rozdział stosunków polsko-niemieckich*, Kraków: Fundacja Centrum Dokumentacji Czynu Niepodległościowego Księgarnia Akademicka, 2000.

Salvatici, S., *A History of Humanitarianism, 1755–1989: In the Name of Others*, Manchester: Manchester University Press, 2019.

Schechtman, J. B., *European Population Transfers, 1939–1945*, New York: Oxford University Press, 1946.

Schönwalder, K., 'Assigning the States Its Rightful Place? Migration, Integration, and the State in Germany', in *Paths of Integration: Migrants in Western Europe (1880–2004)*, edited by L. Lucassen, D. Feldman and J. Oltmer, 78–97, Amsterdam: Amsterdam University Press, 2006.

Schröder, S., *Displaced Persons im Landkreis und in der Stadt Münster 1945–1951*, Münster: Aschendorff, 2005.

Seipp, A. R., *Strangers in the Wild Place: Refugees, Americans, and a German Town, 1945–1952*, Bloomington: Indiana University Press, 2013.

Sereny, G., *The German Trauma: Experiences and Reflections, 1938–2001*, London: Penguin Books, 2001.

Service, H., *Germans to Poles: Communism, Nationalism and Ethnic Cleansing after the Second World War*, Cambridge: Cambridge University Press, 2013.

Shephard, B., *The Long Road Home: The Aftermath of the Second World War*, London: Bodley Head, 2010.

Siebel-Achenbach, S., *Lower Silesia from Nazi Germany to Communist Poland, 1942–1949*, London: MacMillan Press, 1994.

Sjöberg, T., *The Powers and the Persecuted: The Refugee Problem and the Intergovernmental Committee on Refugees*, Lund: Lund University Press, 1991.

Snyder, T., *The Reconstruction of Nations: Poland, Ukraine, Lithuania, Belarus, 1569–1999*, New Haven: Yale University Press, 2003.

Snyder, T., *Bloodlands: Europe Between Stalin and Hitler*, London: Vintage, 2010.

Stachura, P. D., *Poland, 1918–1945: An Interpretive and Documentary History of the Second Republic*, London: Routledge, 2004.

Stargardt, N., *Witnesses of War: Children's Lives Under the Nazis*, New York: Alfred A. Knopf, 2006.

Sulimski, J., *Kraków w procesie przemian: Współczesne przeobrazenia zbiorowości wielkomiejskiej*, Kraków: Wydawnictwo Literackie, 1976.

Sword, K., N. Davies and J. Ciechanowski, *The Formation of the Polish Community in Great Britain 1939–1950*, London: The University of London School of Slavonic and East European Studies, 1989.

Szarota, T., 'Poland under German Occupation, 1939–1941', in *From Peace to War: Germany, Soviet Russia, and the World, 1939–1941*, edited by B. Wegner, 47–63, Oxford: Berghahn, 1997.

Tannahill, J. A., *European Volunteer Workers in Britain*, Manchester: Manchester University Press, 1958.

Taylor, B., *Refugees in Twentieth Century Britain: A History*, Cambridge: Cambridge University Press, 2021.

Taylor, F., *Exorcising Hitler: The Occupation and Denazification of Germany*, London: Bloomsbury, 2011.

Teitelbaum, M. S. and J. M. Winter, *Fear of Population Decline*, London: Academic Press Inc., 1985.

Turner, B. S., *The Body and Society: Explorations in Social Theory*, London: SAGE Publishing, 2008.

Turner, I. D. (ed.), *Reconstruction in Post-War Germany: British Occupation Policy and the Western Zones, 1945–1955*, Oxford: Berg, 1989.

Vernant, J., *The Refugee in the Post-War World*, London: George Allen & Unwin Ltd., 1953.

Von Plato, A., A. Leh and C. Thonfeld, *Hitler's Slaves: Life Stories of Forced Labourers in Nazi-Occupied Europe*, Oxford: Berghahn Books, 2010.

Wandycz, P. S., *Soviet-Polish Relations, 1917–1921*, Harvard University Press, reprint: 2014.

Williamson, D. G., *Germany from Defeat to Partition, 1945–1963*, Essex: Pearson, 2001.

Wyman, M., *DPs: Europe's Displaced Persons, 1945–1951*, New York: Cornell University Press, 1989.

Woodbridge, G. (ed.), *U.N.R.R.A. The History of the United Nations Relief and Rehabilitation Administration* (Three Volumes), New York: Columbia University Press, 1950.

Wróbel, J., *Na rozdrożu historii. Repatriacja obywateli polskich z Zachodu w latach 1945–1949*, Łódź: IPN, 2009.

Zagajewski, A., (translation by L. Vallee), *Two Cities: On Exile, History, and the Imagination*, Canada: Harper Collins, 1995.

Zahra, T., *The Lost Children: Reconstructing Europe's Families after World War II*, New York: Harvard University Press, 2011.

Zieliński, H., *Historia Polski, 1914–1939*, Wrocław: Ossonlineum, 1985.

Articles

Anon., 'Farewell to U.N.R.R.A', *Social Service Review*, 21, no. 3 (September 1947): 398–401

Arnold-Forster, A., 'U.N.R.R.A.'s Work for Displaced Persons in Germany', *International Affairs* (Royal Institute for International Affairs 1944–), 22 (January 1946): 1–13.

Bakis, E., 'The So-Called DP-Apathy in Germany's DP Camps', *Transactions of the Kansas Academy of Science (1903–)*, 55 (March 1952): 62–86.

Ballinger, P., 'Impossible Returns, Enduring Legacies: Recent Historiography of Displacement and the Reconstruction of Europe after World War II', *Contemporary European History*, 22 (2013): 127–38.

Banko, L., K. Nowak and P. Gatrell, 'What is Refugee History, Now?', *Journal of Global History*, 17, no. 1 (2021): 1–19.

Beloff, M, 'Europe & 1992', *History Today*, 42 (February 1992).

BMJ, 'Starvation in Germany', *The British Medical Journal*, 2, no. 4482 (30 November 1946): 821.

B, T., 'Relief Work with Displaced Persons in Germany', *The World Today*, 1 (September 1945): 135–44.

Carden, R. W., 'Before Bizonia: Britain's Economic Dilemma in Germany, 1945–46', *The Journal of Contemporary History*, 14 (July 1979): 535–55.

Chamberlain, J. P., 'The Fate of Refugees and Displaced Persons', *Proceedings of the Academy of Political Science*, 22 (January 1947): 84–94.

Cohen, G. D., 'Between Relief and Politics: Refugee Humanitarianism in Occupied Germany 1945–1946', *Journal of Contemporary History*, 43 (July 2008): 437–49.

Cohen, G. D., 'The Politics of Recognition: Jewish Refugees in Relief Policies and Human Rights Debates, 1945–1950', *Immigrants and Minorities*, 24 (2006): 125–43.

Davies, N., 'Lloyd George and Poland, 1919–20', *Journal of Contemporary History*, 6 (1971): 132–54.

Farquharson, J. E., '"Emotional but Influential": Victor Gollancz, Richard Stokes and the British Zone of Germany, 1945–9', *Journal of Contemporary History*, 22 (July 1987): 501–19.

Fox, G., 'The Origins of UNRRA', *Political Science Quarterly*, 65 (December 1950): 561–84.

Fraser, N. and L. Gordon, 'A Genealogy of Dependency: Tracing a Key Word of the US Welfare State', *Signs: Journal of Women in Culture and Society*, 19 (1994): 309–36.

Gatrell, P., 'Refugees – What's Wrong with History?', *Journal of Refugee Studies*, 30 (01 June 2017): 170–89.

Gentile, E., 'The Sacralization of Politics: Definitions, Interpretation and Reflections on the Question of Secular Religion and Totalitarianism', *Totalitarian Movements and Political Religions*, 1 (2007): 18–55.

Grossmann, A., 'Grams, Calories, and Food: Languages of Victimization, Entitlement, and Human Rights in Occupied Germany, 1945–1949', *Central European History*, 44 (2011): 118–48.

Herz, J. H., 'The Fiasco of Denazification in Germany', *Political Science Quarterly*, 63 (December 1948): 569–94.

Hilton, L. J., 'Pawns on a Chessboard? Polish DPs and Repatriation from the US Zone of Occupation of Germany, 1945–1949.' *Beyond Camps and Forced Labour*, (2005): 90–102.

Hilton, L. J., 'Cultural Nationalism in Exile: The Case of Polish and Latvian Displaced Persons', *The Historian*, 71 (Summer 2009): 280–317.

Hilton, L. J., 'Who Was 'Worthy'? How Empathy Drove Policy Decisions about the Uprooted in Occupied Germany, 1945–1948', *Holocaust and Genocide Studies*, 32 (April 2018): 8–28.

Holborn, L., 'The League of Nations and the Refugee Problem', *Annals of the American Academy of Political and Social Science*, 203 (May 1939): 124–35.

Humbert, L., 'French Politics of Relief and International Aid: France, UNRRA and the Rescue of European Displaced Persons in Postwar Germany, 1945–7', *Journal of Contemporary History*, 41 (2016): 606–34.

Knapton, S. K., '"There is no such thing as an Unrepatriable Pole": Polish Displaced Persons in the British Zone of Occupation in Germany', *European History Quarterly*, 50, no. 4 (2020): 689–710.

Kochavi, A., 'British Policy on Non-Repatriable Displaced Persons in Germany and Austria, 1945–47', *European History Quarterly*, 21 (1991): 365–82.

Kulischer, E. M., 'Displaced Persons in the Modern World', *Annals of the American Academy of Political and Social Science*, 262 (March 1949): 166–77.

Lebow, K., 'The Conscience of the Skin: Interwar Polish Autobiography and Social Rights', *Humanity: An International Journal of Human Rights, Humanitarianism, and Development*, 3 (Winter 2012): 297–319.

Malkki, L., 'Refugees and Exile: From 'Refugee Studies' to the National Order of Things', *Annual Review of Anthropology*, 24 (1995): 495–523.

Marshall, B., 'German Attitudes to the British Military Government 1945–47', *Journal of Contemporary History*, 15 (October 1980): 655–84.

Maspero, J., 'Les autorités françaises d'occupation face au problème des personnes déplacées en Allemagne et en Autriche, 1945–1949', *Revue d'Allemagne*, 40 (2008): 485–501.

Maspero, J., 'La question des personnes déplacées polonaises dans les zones françaises d'occupation en Allemagne et en Autriche: un aspect méconnu des relations franco-polonaises (1945–1949)', *Relations internationals*, 138 (2009): 59–74.

McDowell, L., 'Workers, Migrants, Aliens or Citizens? State Constructions and Discourses of Identity among post-war European Labour Migrants in Britain', *Political Geography*, 22 (November 2003): 863–86.

Nowak, K., 'A Gloomy Carnival of Freedom: Sex, Gender, and Emotions among Polish Displaced Persons in the Aftermath of World War II', *Aspasia*, 13 (2019): 113–34.

Nowak, K., '"To Reach the Lands of Freedom': Petitions of Polish Displaced Persons to American Poles, Moral Screening and the Role of Diaspora in Refugee Resettlement', *Cultural and Social History*, 16, no. 5 (2019): 621–42.

Panayi, P., 'Exploitation, Criminality, Resistance. The Everyday Life of Foreign Workers and Prisoners of War in the German Town of Osnabrück, 1939-1949', *The Journal of Contemporary History*, 4 (July 2005): 483-502.

Porter, B, 'The Catholic Nation: Religion, Identity, and the Narratives of Polish History', in *The Slavic and East European Journal*, 45 (Summer 2001): 289-99.

Reinisch, J., '"Auntie UNRRA" at the Crossroads', *Past and Present*, 218, no. Supplement 8 (2013): 70-97.

Reinisch, J., 'Introduction: Relief in the Aftermath of War', *Journal of Contemporary History*, 43 (July 2008): 371-404.

Reinisch, J., '"We Shall Rebuild Anew A Powerful Nation": UNRRA, Internationalism, and National Reconstruction in Poland', *Journal of Contemporary History*, 43 (July 2008): 451-76.

Salvatici, S., '"Help the People to Help Themselves": UNRRA Relief Workers and European Displaced Persons', *Journal of Refugee Studies*, 25 (June 2012): 428-51.

Salvatici, S., '"Fighters without Guns": Humanitarianism and Military Action in the Aftermath of the Second World War', *European Review of History: Revue européenne d'histoire*, 25, no. 6 (2017): 957-76.

Shils, E. A., 'Social and Psychological Aspects of Displacement and Repatriation', *Journal of Social Issues*, 2 (August 1946): 3-18.

Slatt, V. E., 'Nowhere to Go: Displaced Persons in Post-V-E-Day Germany', *The Historian*, 64, no. 2 (Winter 2002): 275-93.

Sollors, W., '"Everybody Gets Fragebogend Sooner or Later": The Denazification Questionnaire as Cultural Text', *German Life and Letters*, 71 (April 2018): 139-53.

Sword, K., '"Their Prospects will not be Bright": British Responses to the Problem of the Polish "Recalcitrants" 1946-49', *Journal of Contemporary History*, 21 (July 1986): 367-90.

Tombs, I., '"Morturi vos salutant": Szmul Zygielbojm's Suicide in May 1943 and the International Socialist Community in London', *Holocaust Genocide Studies*, 14 (Fall 2000): 242-65.

'United States--Great Britain--Soviet Union: Report of Tripartite Conference of Berlin', *The American Journal of International Law*, 39 (1945): 245-57.

Weeks, T., 'Population Politics in Vilnius 1944-1947: A Case Study of Socialist-Sponsored Ethnic Cleansing', *Post-Soviet Affairs*, 23 (2007): 76-95.

Zahra, T., 'Travel Agents on Trial: Policing Mobility in East Central Europe, 1889-1989', *Past & Present*, 223 (May 2014): 161-93.

Index

accommodation   120, 122–3, 137, 163, 167, 170–1
   military   86
   temporary   133–4, 164–6
affidavits   130, 142, 144, 148–50
aid   14–15, 29, 113–14, 151, 155, 168, 173–4
   eligibility for   106, 110, 155
   operations   5, 9, 79, 84, 179, 183
Allied armies   11, 30, 51, 59, 85
Allied Control Council   14, 104
Allied military   4, 82–4, 87, 90, 96, 169
Allied occupation   13–14, 22
Allies   3, 5, 11–12, 17–20, 38, 120, 128–9
   and black market   89
   disagreement with USSR   14
   and displaced persons   75–81, 106, 109, 125, 134, 150–1, 156, 159, 164
   governance of Germany   11, 15, 22, 24, 32
   and Polish/Poland   32, 35–6, 49–51, 53–4, 72, 92, 95, 111–12
Americans   8, 13, 21, 38, 49, 71. *See also* United States; US zone
Anderson, Benedict   35–6, 38, 64, 181. *See also* communities, imagined
Anglo-Polish-German relations   60, 73
Anglo-Polish relations   6–7, 73, 126, 178–80, 183. *See also* Britain, relationship with Poles/Poland
apathy   100, 124–7, 129–53
Armia Krajowa (AK). *See* Home Army
army. *See also* Allied armies; British Army of the Rhine
   British   54, 61, 67, 70–1, 93, 102, 110
   camps   85, 163–4
   officers   3, 47, 67, 85, 87, 89
   Polish   37, 47, 50, 54, 60, 66, 68, 116
   US   59
assembly centres   55, 61, 83, 93, 106, 116, 163. *See also* Displaced Persons Assembly Centres

Atlantic Charter   36, 53
Australia   114, 140
Austria   14, 18–19, 63, 120
autobiographies   7–8, 90–1, 115. *See also* memoirs

Baltic. *See also* Operation Balt Cygnet
   displaced persons   70, 88, 99–100, 114–15, 117–19, 121, 179
   states   12, 16
Balts   16–17, 68, 88, 97, 119, 129
BAOR. *See* British Army of the Rhine
Becker, Liselotte   67–8, 73
Belgium. *See also* Operation Black Diamond
   displaced persons   18
   emigration to   39, 122, 140
   government   121
   mines   121–3, 136
   officers   61
   resettlement scheme   121–3
   returning from   122–3
Berlin   13–14, 83, 104, 165
betrayal, sense of   50, 139
Bi-zone/Bizonia   25, 116, 126–7, 148
black market   27–8, 89, 113, 115, 131, 169
booklets, informational   111, 145–6, 161, 163, 177
Britain. *See also* Anglo-Polish relations; British; British authorities; British zone
   economy   29, 147, 168
   eugenics   88, 114
   European volunteer workers   115–21, 123, 131, 142–4, 169
   global standing   24, 31, 56, 99, 180, 184
   housing shortage   120
   labour shortage   115, 118, 131
   protectionism   115
   rationing   28–9

relationship with Poles/Poland 1–2,
    13, 36, 42–3, 47–54, 61, 66, 99–100,
    104, 122–4, 126–32
  and UNRRA 4, 31, 78, 114–15, 182
British
  denazification policy 20–3
  military 12, 30, 62, 72, 84, 88–90,
    96–7, 102–4, 124, 127, 131, 135,
    160, 169, 171, 181, 183
  military authorities 6, 12, 25, 86,
    159–60
  military government 16, 23, 25, 63,
    82, 143, 147, 160, 182
  officials 69, 71, 103, 113, 117, 148,
    183
  society 115, 118–19
British Army of the Rhine (BAOR) 103,
    130–1, 159
British authorities
  and rehabilitation 23
  and repatriation 124
  treatment of German civilians 25–6,
    29, 129, 173–4
  treatment of Polish DPs 2, 126, 129,
    134, 146–7, 153, 174, 179, 183–4
British zone 12, 14–33, 83, 97, 110, 151,
    157, 166, 168, 170. *See also* Bi-zone/
    Bizonia; Little Poland; zones of
    occupation
  camps in 3, 66, 85
  denazification in 20–3
  discrimination in 173–4
  education in 145–8
  financial strain of 31–2, 79, 82
  food shortages in 25–7, 29–30, 47,
    137, 160
  and Polish displaced persons 6, 8,
    12, 19–20, 22–3, 28, 30, 32–3,
    35, 53, 60–2, 71, 81, 94, 101, 108,
    129, 132–5, 137–9, 157, 171–3,
    179–85
  Polish nationalism in 55, 57, 175
  repatriation from 3, 99, 101, 103–4,
    112, 123–4, 137, 139, 159, 183
  resettlement from 51, 85, 121–3,
    125–6, 142–3, 161, 163, 175
  training in 144–5
  work on 5, 76, 183
bureaucracy 65, 93–4

calories 26, 46, 132, 160. *See also*
    food
camps 2–9, 18–20, 29–30. *See also*
    Little Poland; Maczków;
    Rosenheim; Wentorf; Wildflecken
  apathy in 126, 129, 131, 133, 137,
    148–51, 180
  communities 35–6, 40, 55–7, 67,
    86–7, 100, 110, 133, 161, 170–1,
    178, 181
  concentration 12, 17, 44, 47, 49, 76,
    81, 85, 109
  food in 29, 111, 132–3
  inhabitants of 19, 32, 35, 38, 141,
    144, 160, 180
  labour 47, 85
  life in 59–74, 160
  management of 80–91, 120–1, 160
  recreational activities in 133–5
  rehabilitation in 23, 75–97, 101–5,
    139, 145
  screening process 22, 100, 105–11
Canada 114, 135–6, 140, 148
carers. *See* welfare work
CCDP. *See* Citizens Committee for
    Displaced Persons
CCG. *See* Control Commission for
    Germany
Central Education Committee 146–7
certificates
  birth/marriage 109, 142
  ownership 89
children 16–18, 44, 47, 65, 70, 88, 119,
    143, 159, 172
  education of 65, 145, 161
  illegitimate 81
  missing 17–18, 107
  unaccompanied 17–18
Churchill, Winston 23, 42, 52–4
cigarettes 63, 82, 89
Citizens Committee for Displaced Persons
    (CCDP) 132, 141–3
citizenship 17, 38, 77, 121, 123, 141
classifications 38, 78, 110, 157
cleanliness 88, 90
COBSRA. *See* Council of British Societies
    for Relief Abroad
Cold War 5, 15, 103, 116, 174
collaborators 12, 107, 139

Index

communism 23, 41–2, 44, 54, 99, 124, 181
communities 32, 38, 40, 66–7, 73, 100, 105, 109, 133, 175, 181, 185. *See also* Anderson, Benedict
  camp 86–7, 100, 133, 147, 163
  imagined 36, 38, 53, 60, 63–5, 73, 181
concentration camps 12, 17, 44, 49, 81, 85, 109
Control Commission for Germany (CCG) 23, 116, 159–61, 166
Cooper, Kanty 8, 86–7, 116, 151, 162, 172, 174
cooperation, international 31, 57, 75–6, 113
correspondence 64, 90, 112, 152
Council of British Societies for Relief Abroad (COBSRA) 96, 105–6
criminality 131, 169, 176

Dawson, Rhoda 8, 59, 68–70, 73–4, 84, 92–6, 99, 101–2, 107, 109, 135–6, 148–9, 184. *See also Stagnant Pool, The*
democracy 4, 23–6, 28, 146, 166, 178
denazification 13, 20–2, 106
dependants 15, 72, 100, 119–21, 123–4, 143, 181
diaries 8, 43, 68, 70, 88, 111
diaspora 41, 62, 64, 66, 130
displaced persons (DPs) 2–6, 11–13, 16–20, 23–7, 29–30, 59, 67–78, 80–102, 105–27, 130–53, 155–79, 182–5
  apathy of 126, 133, 135, 137, 151, 180
  former 117, 122, 134, 137, 175
  groups of 9, 19–20, 30, 76, 88, 99, 134, 142, 151, 165, 183
  individual 7, 96, 110, 135–6, 183
  refugees 83, 164
  Soviet 5, 12, 18–19, 32, 54, 81, 92, 103
Displaced Persons Assembly Centres (DPACs) 116
displacement 2, 4, 7, 9, 11–12, 121, 127, 133, 174, 176–8, 183
Distressed Relatives Scheme 116, 169
distrust 15, 57, 95, 139

DPACs. *See* Displaced Persons Assembly Centres
DPs. *See* displaced persons

Eastern Europe 41–2, 44, 76, 82, 113, 163
education 21–2, 63, 65, 67, 145–7. *See also* schools; training
elites 22, 38, 40–1, 44, 143–4
embodiment 32, 60, 165, 180
Emerson, Sir Herbert 119–20, 123, 127
emigration 123, 131, 144, 146, 150
employment 106, 114, 131, 144, 149, 159, 163, 167
enclaves 20, 50, 56, 60–1, 64, 86, 170
ethnic
  cleansing 40, 44
  Germans 15, 44, 89, 155–6, 165, 172–3, 176–7
  homogeneity 9, 51–2, 55–6, 100
  identity 1, 32
  minorities 32, 51, 172
ethnicity 5, 41, 45, 59–60, 96, 112, 132, 136, 179, 181
eugenics 48, 114
European Volunteer Worker (EVW) 100, 113–21, 124, 142–3, 169
EVW. *See* European Volunteer Worker
exile 6, 36, 39–40, 56–7, 66, 68, 116, 174, 183
expellees 16, 25, 32, 156, 163, 170, 177–8
ex-POWs 18, 23, 63, 65, 67, 78, 109

Federal Republic of Germany (FRG) 151, 155–6, 162, 164, 168, 171–2, 174, 177
First World War 11, 24, 36–7, 51, 77, 101, 105, 116
FO. *See* Foreign Office
food 23, 25–8, 30, 45–7, 63, 70, 84–5, 90, 111, 113, 130, 137, 139. *See also* calories; starvation
  imports 25–6, 29
  shortages 25–6, 28–9, 137
Foreign Office (FO) 16, 18, 24, 28, 43, 68, 104

France   8, 13–14, 39, 43–4, 47, 50, 61–2, 92, 94, 116, 122
freedom   35, 37, 39, 50, 57, 129–30, 132, 138–9, 147, 152, 160
French zone   3, 5, 13, 26, 95, 147, 157. *See also* zones of occupation
FRG. *See* Federal Republic of Germany

Gatrell, Peter   151, 176
German
  aggression   24, 172
  authorities   27–8, 153, 155–6, 159–61, 163, 165–6, 168, 170–1, 173–6, 178, 184
  citizens   12, 14, 17, 20, 23, 25–6, 129, 164
  communities   163, 171–2
  economy   115, 130, 165, 168, 173, 175
  education system   21–2
  expellees   18, 156, 165, 177
  industry   15, 166
  people   11, 13–17, 21–9, 45, 48, 62, 64, 66, 73, 86–7, 105–6, 129–31, 163–4, 169–70, 172–8
  refugees   155–6, 172–4, 176
  society   22, 150–1, 153, 163–4, 167, 171, 174, 176
Germanization   17, 45, 107–8
Germany   1–8, 11–34, 48–9, 59–73, 89–93, 101–4, 110–16, 120–3, 127–8, 130–4, 137–60, 162–78

Haren   3, 60–1, 63–4, 66, 73, 147. *See also* Maczków
'Help Poles in Germany' Polish Social Committee   49, 127, 131, 143
Herbert, Ulrich   18–19
hierarchy   48, 67, 71, 100, 110
Hilton, Laura J.   99, 141, 171
Hodorowicz, Józefa Zalewska   47, 50–1, 60
Holian, Anna   95, 156, 169
home   1, 15–17, 36, 55, 57, 59, 78, 80, 102, 104–5, 129, 131, 136–7, 139, 163–4
Home Army (*Armia Krajowa*)   19, 49, 55, 67
homeland   6, 9, 35, 57, 95, 111, 179, 184
homeless   11, 30, 139, 164, 172

Homeless Foreigners Law   6, 151, 155–6, 162, 164, 169, 172, 174–5
House of Commons   146, 169–70, 176, 182
housing   63, 82, 156, 159, 163–5, 167–71
Hulme, Kathryn   73, 111
humanitarianism   5, 9, 30–1, 57, 121, 176, 179, 185
  international   2, 5, 30, 75, 93, 182
humanitarian organizations   4, 6, 11, 18, 79, 149, 155
humiliation   34, 49, 57, 128, 161

ICRC. *See* International Committee of the Red Cross
identities   1, 5, 32, 37, 105, 107, 171
idleness   106, 123, 125–53
IGCR. *See* Intergovernmental Committee on Refugees
independence   35, 37, 39–42, 53, 64, 146, 181
industry   12, 14, 16, 21, 52, 79, 105, 131, 167
integration   115, 150–1, 153, 156, 164–5, 167, 169, 171, 176, 178–9
intellectuals   143–5
intelligentsia   38–9, 44, 47, 51
Intergovernmental Committee on Refugees (IGCR)   77, 113–14, 119, 127, 130, 150, 178
International Committee of the Red Cross (ICRC)   4. *See also* Red Cross
International Refugee Organization (IRO)   4, 113, 116, 120–1, 123, 125, 132–3, 135–41, 143–4, 147–53, 155–62, 164–6, 171–2, 176, 178
IRO. *See* International Refugee Organization
Italy   47, 53–4, 120

Jackson, Commander Robert   31, 79, 87, 113, 120, 140
Jacobmeyer, Wolfgang   27, 162, 164, 169, 174
Jaroszyńska-Kirchmann, Anna D.   28, 133
Jews   32, 34, 40, 48, 51, 90–1, 95, 106, 129, 134

Jullouville   61–2, 71, 92, 94, 102

Kerr, Sir A. Clark   62
kindergartens   147–8
Klemmé, Marvin   8, 71, 96–7, 129, 131, 135–6

labour   107, 115, 117–19, 129–31, 144–5
  agricultural   19, 39
  camps   47, 85
  division of   182
  forced   2, 12, 16, 18–19, 44–8, 51, 67, 73, 81, 97, 109, 131, 134, 179–80
  foreign   18, 85, 97, 131
  shortages   117–18
  slave   85, 138–9
language   37, 68, 73, 108, 130, 143, 158
  English   68, 72, 119
  Polish   33–5, 40, 56, 72, 105, 138, 140
  training   61–2, 105–6, 144
Lawson, Major R. S.   67–9, 86
lawyers   143–4, 174
Lehman, Herbert H.   30, 76, 78, 90
letters   15, 34, 61, 94, 112, 120, 130, 136–7, 147–9, 184
liberation   34, 50, 81, 85–6, 110, 134, 160, 183
limbo   114, 124, 126, 132, 152
Lithuania   12, 16, 38, 46, 56
Little Poland   3, 59–73
Lloyd George, David   36–7
London Document   150
London Memorandum   127–30, 143
loyalty   20–1, 62, 105
Łuczak, Czesław   32, 65, 171

McNeill, Margaret   5, 8, 69–70, 105, 117–18, 135
Maczków   3, 60–7, 72, 74, 86, 95, 109–10, 123, 146–7, 171. *See also* Haren
magazines   137, 140, 142
Marshall Plan   29, 168
memoirs   7–8, 41, 54, 67–70, 79, 99, 110, 128, 136, 149, 151. *See also* autobiographies
migration   1, 9, 19, 35, 39, 41, 175
military   30, 32, 71, 74, 76, 80, 82–8, 91–3, 95–6, 101, 104, 106–7, 129. *See also* soldiers

authorities   1, 3, 5, 7–9, 29–31, 74, 76, 82–4, 86–7, 95–6, 105–6, 109–10, 144–5, 179, 182
personnel   4, 70, 76, 82, 85–6, 91, 106–8, 129
Military Government Detachment   60–1, 86
miners   19, 121–2, 144
Morgan, Lieutenant General Sir Frederick   4, 24, 28, 57, 87–8, 90–1, 101–2, 105, 107, 111, 123, 136

nationalism   33, 36, 38, 55, 57, 60, 63–5, 74, 181
Nazism   5, 21–2, 26, 33–4, 40, 43–5, 48, 51, 55, 106–7, 160, 180–1
newspapers   63, 90, 92, 108, 113, 118–19, 128, 140, 155, 169–70, 176
NGOs. *See* non-governmental organizations
Niepodległość (independence)   35–41, 43, 51, 55–6
non-governmental organizations (NGOs)   4, 71–2, 86–7, 95–6, 116, 129, 132, 142
Nordrhein-Westfalen   85, 162–3, 167
normality   134–5, 145
Nowakowski, Tadeusz   109, 125, 134

Operation Balt Cygnet   117
Operation Barbarossa   44
Operation Black Diamond   100, 116, 121–3
Operation Carrot   8, 99, 103–4, 111–12, 128, 133, 184
Operation Pole Jump   100, 116, 123, 169
Operation Swallow   16, 25, 89
Operation Westward Ho!   100, 117–18, 121, 124, 169

pamphlets   78, 141, 149, 163–4
partitions   36–7, 40–2, 50
PCIRO. *See* Preparatory Commission of the International Refugee Organization
peace   1, 11, 32, 42, 56, 83, 113, 146, 182
peasants   38–41, 57, 67, 180
Pettiss, Susan   8, 70, 73, 135, 150
Pianowski, Mieczysław   148–9

Poland 1–3, 12–19, 32–47, 50–60, 66, 68, 71–3, 78, 95–7, 123–4, 127–8, 136–8, 145–6, 183–4
  pre-war 32, 44, 181
  repatriation to 111, 114, 183
Polish 1–5, 18–20, 32–41, 45–57, 60–8, 70–3, 80–2, 85–95, 99–111, 114–34, 137–8, 141–6, 179–81
  camps 35, 60–8, 72–4, 82, 86–8, 111, 129, 137, 145
  communities 35, 64, 86, 100, 105, 110, 133, 140, 147, 171, 175, 181
  displaced persons 5–13, 22–8, 32, 59–60, 63–8, 71–6, 88–92, 96–103, 110–12, 123–36, 142–8, 160, 171–85
  European volunteer workers 118–19
  in exile 6, 33, 36, 56, 122–3, 128, 143, 157, 178, 180–1
  government-in-exile 49, 52, 180
  identity 6, 35, 42, 62, 181
  liaison officers 38, 61, 103, 108
  nationalism 33, 37, 53
  repatriation of 5, 54, 81, 88, 102, 112, 157
  schools 145–7
Polish First Armoured Division 20, 60–3, 66, 72
Polishness 33–48, 54–7, 60–2, 73, 100, 106, 110, 175, 178, 180
Polish Provisional Government of National Unity 5, 8, 50, 54, 59–60, 127
Polish Resettlement Act 66, 100, 116, 123
Polish Resettlement Corps (PRC) 66, 100, 116
Polish Second Corps 50, 53–4
Polish-Soviet War 41–2
Polish Union (PU) 63, 127
political prisoners 47, 65, 67, 110
post-war
  Germany 16, 32, 57, 68, 92, 178, 185
  humanitarianism 2, 148–9, 180
  world 1, 5–6, 9, 36, 40, 43, 53–5, 64, 75–6, 82, 103, 180, 185
Potsdam Conference 5, 12–15, 36, 59, 72, 81, 174
POWs. *See* prisoners of war
Poznań 46, 63, 184
PRC. *See* Polish Resettlement Corps

Preparatory Commission of the International Refugee Organization (PCIRO) 120, 122–3, 141, 145, 158
prisoners of war (POWs/PWXs) 2, 12, 18–19, 23, 30, 47, 69
professions 121–2, 144
protectors 4–5, 74–7, 79–97, 100, 178
Proudfoot, Malcolm J. 3, 17, 19, 82, 84, 87, 101, 157–8, 175, 178
PU. *See* Polish Union
PWXs. *See* prisoners of war

Quakers 4, 69, 86, 105, 112, 116–17, 129, 150, 172

rationing 28–9, 31, 104, 113, 137, 168
reconstruction 2, 4, 7, 13, 21, 78, 101
Red Army 12, 47
Red Cross 82, 84, 101, 105, 147. *See also* International Committee of the Red Cross
  Polish 64, 82, 95, 145–6
  Societies 120
refugees 75–84, 113, 117–23, 132, 156–8, 160–78
  and displaced persons 151, 158
  in Germany 17, 162, 168
  Polish 44, 128, 148
rehabilitation 23, 71, 76–9, 83–5, 91–3, 96, 101–5, 127, 131–2
Reinisch, Jessica 29, 31, 182
rejection 35–6, 100, 123, 158, 181
relief 78–9, 83, 86, 91–3, 96, 101, 147, 149, 153, 176, 179
  and rehabilitation 4, 79, 92–3
  work 2, 69, 71, 87, 96, 105, 179
repatriation 12, 17–18, 30–2, 54, 77, 81–3, 86, 95, 99–108, 111–20, 123–33, 137–40, 146–8, 150–2, 157–9, 183
  to Poland 3, 16, 54, 66, 99, 103–4, 111, 116, 127, 137, 146
  and resettlement 99–100, 112, 116, 120, 124–5, 133, 143, 161
resettlement 4, 6, 99–100, 112–26, 132–3, 135, 138–40, 142–4, 148–52, 155–9, 161, 163, 175, 179–80
  in Britain 117, 119, 121
  countries 70, 124–7, 133, 144–5, 152

opportunities   100, 113, 121, 125, 127, 130, 134, 140, 148
propaganda   126, 140–3, 149
schemes   3, 117, 121–2, 136
Resettlement of Polish Displaced Persons   130, 142–3
Rosenheim   70, 94
Rousseau, Paul   65–6, 72
Russia   36, 43, 56, 177. *See also* Soviet Union

Save Europe Now (SEN)   25
Scheuner, Professor Dr Ulrich   174
schools   21, 33, 65–6, 109, 143, 145, 147–8. *See also* education
Schröder, Stefan   169, 176
screening   80, 86, 100, 104, 106–11, 183
Second Polish Republic   35–8
Second World War   2–3, 40, 42, 50, 52–3, 56, 75, 78–9, 176, 179, 183
SEN. *See* Save Europe Now
SHAEF. *See* Supreme Headquarters Allied Expeditionary Forces
Shephard, Ben   107
slaves   48, 86, 109, 122
social work   94, 96. *See also* welfare work
soldiers   72, 78, 84–5, 171. *See also* military
Soviets   5, 12, 14, 16–19, 42, 44, 51–2, 102, 111, 124
Soviet Ukrainians   117–18
Soviet Union   7, 12–15, 25, 34–5, 43–4, 47, 49, 51–3, 55, 62, 78, 102–3, 115, 127. *See also* Russia
Soviet zone   3, 5, 13, 18, 26, 29, 32, 56, 165, 173. *See also* zones of occupation
Stagnant Pool, The   74, 84, 94, 149. *See also* Dawson, Rhoda
starvation   15, 26, 46. *See also* food, shortages
statelessness   72, 77, 162–3, 175
status, legal   123, 159
students   1, 65, 119, 144, 148
Supreme Headquarters Allied Expeditionary Forces (SHAEF)   18, 23, 25, 80, 82–4, 92, 96
surveys   164–5, 171

teachers   65, 143, 146, 148
theatre   63, 83, 135
Third Reich   20, 48, 50, 92, 131, 180
training   67, 144–5, 147. *See also* education
transit centres   29, 54–5, 69
transports   61, 69, 84, 87, 173

Ukrainians   12, 17–18, 32, 34, 37, 51, 68, 70, 100, 115, 117–19
UNHCR. *See* United Nations High Commissioner for Refugees
United Nations   25, 76, 158
United Nations High Commissioner for Refugees (UNHCR)   170, 177
United Nations Relief and Rehabilitation Administration (UNRRA)   3–4, 11–12, 17–18, 27–31, 60, 63–8, 71, 74–88, 90–7, 99–103, 105–16, 120–1, 124–5, 128–9, 136–7, 139, 145–6, 152, 178–80, 182–5
   Intergovernmental Committee   112
   teams   59, 61, 66, 70, 72, 83–4, 90, 92–3, 147
   welfare workers   27, 40, 69–72, 76, 79–88, 91–7, 102–10, 117, 123–4, 135
United States   13, 29, 31, 33, 53, 70–1, 73, 78, 113–14, 116, 130, 132, 140, 142, 148–50, 179–82
UNRRA. *See* United Nations Relief and Rehabilitation Administration
USSR. *See* Soviet Union
US zone   3–6, 13, 19–21, 25–9, 59, 64, 69, 74–6, 90–4, 99, 107, 110, 121, 126–7, 136, 140–2, 147–8, 157, 179–81. *See also* zones of occupation

venereal diseases   81
Versailles
   Little Treaty of   37
   Treaty of   37, 42
Vilnius   37–8, 45, 106
Vocational Training Section   144–5
Volksliste   45, 51, 106, 108–9, 175

Warsaw   5, 42–4, 46, 49, 62–3, 100, 103, 109, 112, 128, 147
   government   124, 146
   uprising   19, 49–50, 67, 86, 109

welfare   69, 71, 82, 88, 99, 128–30, 135, 145, 165
welfare work   1–8, 12, 68–76, 92–5, 100–1, 105–6, 125–6, 135–6, 149–51, 155–6, 179–82. *See also* social work
Wentorf   60, 66–9, 74, 86
Western Allies   14, 49, 53, 150–1
West Germany   14, 45, 65, 145–50, 156, 162–8, 174
Wildflecken   20, 59, 64, 136–7
women   44, 67, 80, 84, 86–8, 96
work   3–8, 59, 71–4, 85, 90–7, 103–4, 114, 117–23, 126–38, 149–50, 157, 167–8, 178–85. *See also* labour
   opportunities   129, 136
   schemes   6, 114, 119
workers   16, 38, 93, 97, 117–24, 172
   agricultural   118
   foreign   49, 97

Yalta agreement   12, 14, 16, 18, 36, 52–4, 81, 174

Zimmer, Dr Szczepan   146–7
zones of occupation   3, 5, 13–22, 32, 54, 59–60, 65, 79, 94, 101–7, 140, 145–52, 157, 162–6, 185. *See also* Bi-zone/Bizonia; British zone; French zone; Little Poland; Soviet zone; US zone

www.ingramcontent.com/pod-product-compliance
Lightning Source LLC
Chambersburg PA
CBHW062133300426
44115CB00012BA/1909